COPS, DRUGS, LAWYER X AND ME

COPS, DRUGS, LAWYER X AND ME

PAUL DALE & VIKKI PETRAITIS

hachette
AUSTRALIA

Authors' note: In some instances, pseudonyms have been used. At other times, names have been withheld. We have records of transcripts, statements and court documents that support everything discussed in this book.

Publisher's note: Paul Dale's story was originally published in 2013 by Five Mile Press in the book *Disgraced?*. This new book updates Paul's story and includes new material and important information from the ongoing Victorian Royal Commission into the Management of Police Informants (RCMPI) and revelations that Nicola Gobbo was police informant Lawyer X.

hachette
AUSTRALIA

Published in Australia and New Zealand in 2020
by Hachette Australia
(an imprint of Hachette Australia Pty Limited)
Level 17, 207 Kent Street, Sydney NSW 2000
www.hachette.com.au

10 9 8 7 6 5 4 3 2

A catalogue record for this book is available from the National Library of Australia

ISBN: 978 0 7336 4380 4 (paperback)

Cover design by Luke Causby, Blue Cork
Cover images courtesy of Andrew Tauber/Newspix (bottom); Angela Wylie/Fairfax Media (top)
Thank you to Pia Akerman and Adam Shand for permission to reproduce their words.
Typeset in Sabon LT Std by Kirby Jones
Printed and bound in Great Britain by Clays Ltd, Elcograf S.p.A

'*I will tell you what happened long story short re; statement,*
I made one statement, and that was against Dale and
Rod, Dale is a copper, and like you said fuck him – and Rod
is 63–64 years old, and he looks like being in jail for ever.
So long story short is at the end of the day my statement
won't affect him ...'

Carl Williams, prison letter to Horty Mokbel
15 October 2009

CONTENTS

2018 – The story 'breaks'

In 2013, my book *Disgraced?* detailing the Victoria Police's use of Nicola Gobbo as a police informer – a decision later described in the High Court as 'reprehensible conduct' – was at the time one of few stories questioning her behaviour or the actions of the Victoria Police in using a lawyer against her own clients.

Before the book's release, journalists Pia Akerman and Adam Shand, both writing for *The Australian*, questioned the dubious practices of the police. Most other articles at the time repeated the same old stories about me with facts so contorted they were the envy of gymnasts.

A year after *Disgraced?* opened Pandora's box, journalists began looking into Nicola Gobbo – Lawyer X, informer number 3838 – and uncovered a much broader history of her work with the Victoria Police as a police informer while acting as a defence barrister. Ruling on the lifting of a suppression order governing the release of her name, the High Court described this as 'fundamental and appalling breaches of [her] obligations as counsel to her clients and of her duties to the court'. No mincing words there.

On 3 December 2018, Police Commissioner Graham Ashton gave a press conference. In it, he said: 'I acknowledge the decision of the High Court which has determined that our use of a lawyer as an informer between 2005 and 2009 was not appropriate.'

No shit, Sherlock.

•

When my book came out in 2013, I finally got the chance to tell my story. With author Vikki Petraitis, I documented the journey from where it all began. What came before I was the 'disgraced former detective' splashed regularly across the front page of the *Herald Sun*, made to look like a gangster courtesy of weird photo angles?

There was a time, long ago, when I was a cop. I did my job well; I was a team player, and I fought on the side of good. Or so I thought. How did a kid from the country who dreamed of joining the Victoria Police end up on the wrong side of the bars? There are a lot of reasons, and I hope this story will help clarify some of them, for you and me, because a lot of the time I am left shaking my head, wondering how things went so wrong.

I didn't speak out at the height of this whole thing because my words would more than likely have been twisted and turned to suit whatever image of me the Victoria Police and the media wanted to create. I tried once, and gave an interview to the *Herald Sun*. The headline screamed, 'I didn't kill Carl Williams', which was not what the interview was about at all.

To a lad from the country, this has all been a steep learning curve. My parents urged me to speak out. I think it hurt them most to read stories that called their son a killer. But my story was too complicated to be told in soundbites or interviews, and I couldn't trust the lenses of journalists who played judge and jury.

Now the Lawyer X scandal has broken, it is time to revisit what happened to me in the broader context. Now I know that this didn't just happen to me; the world of crazy was visited on many others, all with the knowledge, support, and financial backing of the Victoria Police – once my place of work.

•

To fully understand my story, here, in a nutshell, is what I have been accused of:

1. Conspiring with fellow cop Dave Miechel and with Terry Hodson, a known drug dealer and informer, to rob a drug house that my own team from the Major Drug Investigation Division (MDID) had under surveillance and was preparing to raid.

2. Organising that Dave and Terry rob the house and split the proceeds evenly with me, while I stayed safely at home with a bunch of alibis.

3. Driving to the St Kilda Road MDID headquarters as soon as I heard that Dave and Terry had been arrested at the scene, to spirit away a copy of Terry Hodson's informer folder – otherwise known as the 'blue folder' – despite the fact that my superintendent was on duty at the office at the time, as well as a number of other cops, none of whom reported seeing me stealing folders.

4. Spreading the information in the blue folder around the underworld to let them know that Terry Hodson was a police informer – even though the minute Hodson was arrested with a drug cop everyone knew anyway.

5. Arranging for a hit man to kill Terry Hodson despite the fact that his evidence against me was uncorroborated.

6. Getting well-known crime figure Carl Williams to organise a second hit man to kill Terry and his wife just to be on the safe side because I did not have faith in the first hit man, and paying a $150 000 fee.

7. Lying to and misleading the Australian Crime Commission (ACC) when I said I couldn't remember what I was doing on particular days three and four years earlier – without being allowed to refer to my confiscated diaries.

8. Organising to have Carl Williams murdered in prison so he couldn't testify against me at my trial for the murders of Terry and Christine Hodson, despite the fact that his word, again with no corroboration, would not have been believed.

9. Being so dangerous that I had to be shackled and held either in complete isolation or with Muslim terrorists for eight months in Barwon Prison's notorious Acacia Unit, even though I had worked every day at my service station and raised my family in Wangaratta for five years before that without being dangerous at all.

10. Being so dangerous that Garry Livermore, a lawyer for the Australian Crime Commission, said at a hearing that, 'People who assist authorities in endeavouring to prosecute Paul Dale have got a pretty poor life expectancy. Two of them have been murdered.' This quote is now used regularly in articles that mention my name.

And because all these things are regularly reported in the media, most of the public think I'm guilty of something when I have never actually been convicted of anything.

What has happened to me has been a witch hunt. I never believed the police could operate like this. If I was so guilty, why didn't they just present their evidence and convict me?

But the story is bigger than just me. The wider political and social implications of what happened to me need to be recognised in order to prevent this happening to someone else, or at least serve as a warning that it could.

I was summoned before the Australian Crime Commission, legally compelled to give up my right to remain silent, and promised indemnity and secrecy to answer all their questions – questions like: *If you didn't kill the Hodsons, who do you think was responsible?* Before I knew it, transcripts of my 'secret' testimony were circulating in the prisons and I was being contacted by dangerous killers who weren't happy. My family and I received death threats; one dangerous thug regularly rang my work and threatened to cut my wife's throat. When asked to justify how this breach occurred, the ACC wrote to me basically saying, *Um, we changed our mind about the secrecy bit.*

This is dangerous stuff.

What is also dangerous is the growing tendency for the Victoria Police to pay for testimony from convicted criminals who have zero credibility, and then to try their case in the media if they don't get the result they want.

The wider implication is that if it happened to me, it *can* happen to anyone.

And then there is Lawyer X, my lawyer and onetime friend. When I first went public with my claim that I consulted her on many occasions as a lawyer and, as such, it was unconscionable for her to wear a wire during one of our meetings, I was pretty much a lone voice. As the recent Royal Commission in Victoria reveals the extent of Nicola's involvement in so many cases, it turns out I wasn't the only one affected by this.

Bit by bit, I have pieced together this investigation by obtaining documents – both official and ones that were never meant for my eyes. The following story is not only drawn from my recollection but it comes from official police statements, and also from those documents the police and the government didn't want anyone to know about. Any reconstructions of events are based on the words of the people themselves from their sworn police statements.

As you read how this story unfolds, you can decide for yourself if it is a house of cards or a line of dominoes – bump out one and the rest fall down. I realise that during my trial by media, a lot of people have already judged me guilty; all I can do is humbly ask for you to consider both sides of the story before making up your mind.

Paul Dale

PROLOGUE

Picture this. You are a detective sergeant working at the Victoria Police Major Drug Investigation Division, enjoying a day at home watching the AFL Grand Final with a bunch of mates. You've been working nonstop on a big drug bust, and a couple of hours in front of the TV is just what you need to recharge the batteries.

The phone rings and you listen, perplexed. A member of your crew, Dave Miechel, is ringing you from the back of an ambulance. He tells you that something has happened at the Oakleigh drug house in Dublin Street – the house your crew has had under surveillance for months.

What? you ask, worried.

He tells you he has been attacked by a police dog and bashed by the dog handler.

Again – *what?*

You ring your bosses and tell them that something has gone down at Dublin Street and you are on your way to see Dave in the hospital. More cops ring you and you find out something unbelievable: Dave has been caught at the scene of the break-in and arrested! But it gets worse, because he wasn't alone. Your chief informer, Terry Hodson, has been arrested at the scene as well. The implication is that they were arrested for doing something *together*.

It is unfathomable. Unbelievable. You try to curse, but there just aren't words bad enough for how you feel at that very moment. You put your foot down a little harder on the accelerator and get to the hospital as quickly as you can.

Dave has some nasty injuries. He looks black and blue. And bitten. You don't say much when you see him – just ask about his health, coz you know he's up shit creek without a paddle.

On the way to meet your bosses at the drug squad, you wonder what the hell has happened. Terry Hodson, sure, he's an old-time crook and drug dealer; he's even done hard jail time. You'd kind of expect it from him – but *Dave* ...

Afterwards, at the drug squad headquarters, you meet the bosses who are on duty, and you are all pretty much shaking your heads, going into damage control. As you watch the bosses clear out Dave's desk and take all his stuff to lock up as evidence, you search your mind for any inkling of how this happened. How did Dave get close enough to Terry to get involved in something like this? But, then again, Terry is that kind of guy. He bombards you. He rings you every day with a new lead, a new mark. And his information is usually good.

In fact, you know if you allowed yourself to, you could investigate only his leads and keep yourself in solid work forever. But you try to keep some professional distance. You remember the phone calls: *No, Terry, we can't talk right now; we're sitting off a drug crop*, only to be told, *Drug crop! That's nothing! I can give you cocaine! Kilos of it!* It's tempting to be drawn into it, but you know you also have to protect Terry from himself.

Before your time, the drug squad had let him dob in most of his mates; they even arrested some of them leaving Terry's house. As an informer, Terry has police indemnity to sell small quantities of drugs, but if the drug squad kept arresting everyone who bought from him and never arrested *him*, how long would it take for dealers to notice? When you joined the squad you tried to change that, because if you let him Terry will keep dobbing people in until one day someone will make the connection. Questions have already been asked. People who move in that world don't forgive and forget. So you try to protect Terry from himself because he really is a likeable guy.

And while you can hardly believe what has occurred at the Dublin Street house, you can imagine how it must have happened. Senior Constable Dave Miechel, a quiet loner, must have been taken in by the warmth and hospitality of the Hodson family. It wouldn't be the first time something like this has happened.

But aside from coming to terms with a fox in the henhouse – or in this case a detective in a drug house – you need to try to salvage what you can out of the operation. You've had the house under surveillance for months, the warrants are ready to go, and you just have to move.

•

The rest of the week is taken up, in equal measure, with rounding up the bad guys and doing damage control. In among that, you accept that Ethical Standards police are going to drag the rest of the drug squad in – but you don't expect members of your team to come back snorting fire. *Leading questions*, they tell you. *Trying to make you say stuff that didn't happen. Twisting the bloody truth.*

Bloody toecutters. Like everybody else, you dislike them; but, even so, you can't believe what happens next. You hear a whisper that they got Terry in a room, told him he was up shit creek and offered him a deal if he could finger any other cops. *Terry, you're done for. Terry, you'll probably die in prison. Terry, you're fucked.* You can almost picture Terry, his mind ticking over, whirring with possibilities, the cornered rat coming out fighting.

And you can picture Terry Hodson's eyes narrowing, brow furrowed mid deal. 'It's Dale,' he says. 'Dale was in on it too.' But while you can picture him saying it, saving his skin, wheeling and dealing, what you *can't* picture is your colleagues leaning forward, eager for another cop's scalp. Believing him when he says you were in on the deal to rob the drug house. Believing that two guys would agree to rob a drug house and take all the risk while you stayed safely at home.

Believing that a deal like that could be struck.

Because this is what they would have had to believe:

– Hey Dave and Terry! You go rob the drug house and give me a share of the takings while I stay at home with my alibis.
– Sure, Dale. We'll take all the risk and give you a third of the takings. You might end up with a couple of hundred grand for sitting on your bum. Hope you and your alibis enjoy the footy. Don't worry about the risk to us. It will be worth it just to give you the money for doing nothing.

Believing him.

Believing something that just didn't make sense. Would never make sense.

Believing the madness.

That's what you can't picture.

Not in your wildest dreams.

You can't accept that cops would believe a crook, a drug dealer, an arms dealer, someone who has served serious jail time, someone who was trying to weasel his way out of a jail sentence – believe him over you, a decorated police officer with an unblemished record.

You can't believe it because it defies belief.

But that's not the end of the story. You will soon find out the Ethical Standards Department's faith in Terry Hodson is only the beginning of your nightmare.

For the next eight years you are going to be dangerously duped by the Australian Crime Commission, and the Victoria Police will offer *millions* of dollars in incentives to a couple of convicted killers in return for statements against you. They will pay hundreds of thousands of dollars to protect your lawyer Nicola Gobbo for ten months in order to get her to testify against you, only to have her pull out and sue them for $2.88 million. You will be jailed for eight months in one of the state's most notorious prisons without being found guilty of anything. You will be held in solitary confinement until you nearly go mad, and then – when your new lawyer likens your conditions to those of Guantanamo Bay – you will be put in a cell with Muslim terrorists for company. The charges against you will be dropped, and more reinstated, only to be dropped. Reinstated. Dropped. Again and again, in a cycle of madness. The media will take creepy-looking pictures of you and splash them across the front page of their newspapers. Your parents will weep for you, and the public will judge you guilty, believing everything they read in the press because the media don't lie.

Only, by then, you will know that they do.

CHAPTER 1

The killings

On Sunday, 16 May 2004, Andrew Hodson didn't visit his parents like he usually did. On the way to their son's footy game in Canterbury, in Melbourne's eastern suburbs, Andrew and his partner, Linette, drove past Terry and Christine Hodson's house in Harp Road, Kew. The house sat at the end of a long driveway; it was one of two on the block, with another house at the front.

As Andrew and Linette drove past they noticed Christine Hodson's BMW in the driveway, which normally meant the Hodsons were up and about. Terry and Christine were night owls and the cars were a sign to visitors. Cars in the garage meant they were still in bed. Cars in the driveway meant they were up and Terry was using the garage space to work.

When the junior footy game was over, around 1.30 p.m., Linette asked Andrew if he wanted to call in to see his parents, but he told her that he didn't think they would be out of bed. Having seen Christine's car parked in the driveway earlier, Linette disagreed. Nonetheless, Andrew didn't stop and continued to their home in East Brunswick.

All day, Andrew Hodson seemed unsettled. He told Linette that something was wrong, but she said he couldn't quite put his finger on it and he didn't explain any further.

Linette did some chores in the afternoon then lay down on the couch and fell asleep. When she woke around 5.45 p.m. her husband was gone. According to their young son, Andrew had left a quarter of an hour before to get cigarettes. When he'd been gone nearly an hour, Linette tried calling his mobile. He didn't answer.

She figured that he had probably changed his mind about seeing his parents and made the half-hour drive back to their house.

Which was exactly what he had done.

Andrew later told police that as he pulled up to the Harp Road house he noticed his dad hadn't taken out the bins. Without going inside to ask his parents if they had any more rubbish, Andrew dragged the bins down the driveway to the front nature strip. He was standing there when his sister Mandy pulled up in her BMW.

While Mandy, her boyfriend, and her daughter had been invited for dinner, Mandy arrived alone at the appointed time, she said, to check on her parents because she'd tried to ring them earlier and they hadn't answered the phone.

Mandy used her remote control to open the garage door. Her parents' two German shepherd guard dogs were locked in the garage. The poodle was nowhere in sight. The door Mandy usually used to get from the garage into the house was locked, so she went around and through the backyard while Andrew finished with the bins.

A scream pierced the air.

'They're dead! They're dead! They've murdered them!'

Andrew ran up the driveway in the direction of the screaming and around to the TV room at the back of the house. Coming to a stop beside his sister, he saw his parents lying face down on the floor. Terry and Christine Hodson had both been shot in the back of the head. Andrew noticed a spent .22 calibre shell placed deliberately on the back of his father's head. It looked like an execution-style hit – like they'd been made to lie down then shot in cold blood.

Andrew later said he rang 000 straightaway and asked to be put through to the Ethical Standards Department detectives who were handling his father's case. At least that was what he told police in his first statement, hours after finding his parents' bodies.

He actually rang his lawyer, Nicola Gobbo, who rang Inspector Peter De Santo from Ethical Standards to see if she could pass his number on to Andrew. She called Andrew back and gave him the number. Andrew rang De Santo and told him that his parents had been murdered and that he reckoned Dale had done it. Later, when the police arrived, Andrew refused to speak to anyone but De Santo.

But Andrew Hodson didn't make these calls straightaway.

•

None of us know what we would do if we found our parents murdered, but here's what 34-year-old Andrew and 36-year-old Mandy Hodson did.

In a second statement to the police, Andrew later expanded on his actions following the discovery of his murdered parents. After he found them on the floor, shot in the head, he decided to look around for the handgun that his father usually kept beside him as he watched TV in the back room at night. Paying homage to gangster slang from the 1930s, the gun was apparently nicknamed Roscoe. After finding his parents dead, Andrew noticed that Roscoe wasn't in the TV room and asked his sister where the gun might be. She disappeared for a while, returned with the gun and gave it to her brother.

'Shouldn't you hand it over?' Mandy asked him.

Andrew checked the gun and found it loaded. 'No, I'll take it because Dad wanted me to have this.' He put it down the front of his pants.

Andrew rang his partner, Linette, at 6.20 p.m. 'Lin, Mum and Dad have been knocked,' he told her.

Linette made immediate plans to join Andrew at the house.

•

The first police on the scene were greeted by an agitated Andrew Hodson, who 'smelt strongly of intoxicating liquor' – which meant that unless he had driven drunk to his parents' house, he had used some of the time before calling the police to drink enough alcohol to reek of it.

'My parents have been fucking killed,' he told the police officers. 'Call ESD. This is an ESD matter.' Andrew refused to speak to any cops unless they were from the Ethical Standards Department, or to be separated from his sister. 'It's me mum and dad,' he said. 'I'm not speakin' to you until I speak to De Santo. They're shot in the back of the head with a .22. Point blank range.'

The police officers saw the German shepherds roaming around the yard and didn't want to go anywhere near them. One of the cops asked Andrew to secure the dogs. He took them to his car and locked them inside. At that point, it was too chaotic to wonder how any hit man could have gotten past the vicious Hodson guard dogs.

There was no sign of Christine Hodson's nine-year-old poodle, Ty.

•

By the time Linette got to Harp Road there were police cars everywhere. At Andrew's suggestion, she had dropped off their son at Mandy's house. As senior police and forensic experts combed through the house, the family stood around in the limbo that surrounded the crime scene.

Linette later told police how her husband described finding his dead parents. 'He told me that he was the one that found them,' she said in her statement. 'He said he sat near them. He kissed both his parents. He said he held his mum's hand and kissed her on the head. He said he talked with them. I don't know what he said to them; he didn't tell me.'

Linette didn't mention whether or not Andrew had told her that his parents had both been shot in the back of the head. It certainly might have made her shudder at the mental picture of Andrew kissing his mother on the head.

She also didn't say whether he talked to them and kissed them before or after he went searching through his parents' things for items he was sure they would have wanted him to have.

•

In Mandy's first statement to police she too spoke of getting to the house, finding her parents, then calling the police. Just like her brother, she left a couple of things out. After she called for Andrew when she found her parents' bodies on the floor of the TV room, she stepped around her dead mum and dad, and made her way over to a small coffee table next to the couch, down the end where her father always sat. On the table was a silver butter tray with a small pile of cocaine on it. Next to the pile was a line of cocaine and a 22-carat gold-plated straw that her father had had specially made. On her mother's side table was a plastic Tupperware container filled with another stash of cocaine. Mandy later told police that she 'panicked' and picked up the tray, took it into the kitchen and snorted a line of cocaine. She offered her brother a line, but he was on the phone. She said she washed the evidence off the tray, but kept the straw and the container for herself – again, because she 'panicked'.

Her story about finding the gun called Roscoe differed from her brother's. She said that she and Andrew both went looking through drawers in their parents' bedroom and they found the gun together.

She also didn't mention telephoning her teenage daughter during this time, but she must have because by the time Linette dropped off her son at Mandy's house, the girl already knew that her grandparents had been murdered.

•

After receiving the phone call from Andrew, Inspector Peter De Santo made his way to the house in Harp Road, Kew, arriving around an hour later. After a briefing from police at the scene, he approached Andrew Hodson.

'Fucking Dale's done it!' Andrew said. 'They've been executed, both shot in the back of their heads face down in the back room. He's left his fucking calling card: a spent shell was on the back of Dad's head. It's been placed there.'

In his official statement, Inspector De Santo doesn't mention whether Andrew told him about kissing his mother on the head as she lay dead on the floor, or shoving a gun called Roscoe down his underpants. Nor does he mention the importance of the date of the Hodsons' double murder – it was two years *to the very day* since Andrew had been arrested on drug-related matters. Back then Linette had to arrange bail because, for some reason, Terry had refused to fund the bail application for his son. Because of Terry's refusal to dip into the wads of tens of thousands of dollars that he had hidden around the house, Andrew had served ten months on remand. Terry had, however, funded Mandy's bail; she had been charged at the same time as her brother. Mandy was released shortly after her arrest. Andrew had, according to Linette, been 'shattered' at his father's actions. It was rumoured that Andrew and Mandy had in fact been charged after Terry had informed on them in the first place. Another rumour had Terry becoming an informer *because* they had been charged. If that version was true, he hadn't used his informer status to bargain for his son's freedom.

But that, apparently, was water under this particular family's bridge.

And what a family they were. For one thing, both Andrew and Terry had served jail time. The Hodson family disputes were larger than life. Terry Hodson had been a police informer for a couple of years, and it didn't sit well with his kids. Mandy had been shocked when she found out, because her father had always taught her not to lag on people. Andrew knew about Terry and his informing but they had tried to keep it from their other sister, Nikki, for as long as they could because of Nikki's husband, Peter Reed, who had been charged over the infamous Russell Street police bombing and been convicted of the attempted murder of a cop.

Indeed, Nikki had met her husband through her father, who had been in jail with Reed. Terry Hodson urged his daughter to visit Reed because no one else ever did. Romance bloomed. One of the reasons that the family might not have wanted Reed to know about Terry's informing was that Terry had informed on Reed, which had also led to Nikki's arrest. But, despite the secrecy, rumour had it that Reed knew about it and wasn't happy.

The two crims had a big falling out.

About a year and a half before the Hodsons were murdered, Terry told his daughter, Mandy, that Peter Reed had spoken to another man and asked him to not only rob Mandy's house but to rob Terry and Christine's house while they were at home and terrorise them into the bargain. When the man refused, the story went that Reed asked him to organise some guns, but the man couldn't. Everyone was a little on edge.

Andrew Hodson responded to the threat by getting his parents some sensor lights.

Nikki had tried to patch things up with her parents and had been visiting them since January 2003. Behind her husband's back.

And with all the Machiavellian twists and turns of the Hodson family, they said *I* looked guilty.

Maybe it was the moment the police got there and Andrew Hodson jumped up, a stolen gun down his jocks, crying, 'Fucking Dale's done it!'

Who knows? All I know is that a family steeped in crime – drug dealing and selling stolen guns, with connections to some of the most dangerous criminals in the Melbourne gangland wars, including Tony Mokbel and Carl Williams, not to mention a son-in-law accused of the Russell Street bombing and convicted of the attempted murder of a cop – pointed the finger at me.

And the detectives looked in my direction.

CHAPTER 2

Back at the beginning

I was born in the safe cocoon of a small town called Yackandandah. It's about twenty minutes away from Wangaratta in country Victoria. We lived on a farm; my dad was a justice of the peace and owned the local butcher shop, and my mum was a nurse and, later, the town mayor.

I was the youngest in a family of four siblings. One brother and two sisters. My big brother left home for an apprenticeship when I was ten, and one of my older sisters got married and moved out, leaving just me and my other sister to be teenagers together. My childhood was idyllic. We never went without anything. Our folks were busy with civic duties, the shop and the farm, and we were left to our own devices a bit. Not that there was a lot of opportunity for mischief – the only waywardness available to us farm kids was the mischievous and illegal use of our trail bikes.

We had a close family relationship with the local policeman, Senior Constable Kevin Smith, who had clipped me behind the ear a couple of times for trail-bike tomfoolery. If he saw me and my mates out on our bikes he never bothered chasing us, because he knew who we were. The way he dealt with it was to give Dad a ring and then I'd cop it from both of them. Nonetheless, Smithy was a good bloke and I liked him. He was even the barman at my sister's eighteenth birthday. Mine too.

The fact that Smithy could clip us all across the ears then turn up at our family's social functions, holding a six-pack rather than a grudge, was something that all the kids really admired.

So I guess, if I think about it, Smithy was the role model for who I wanted to be.

On rare trips to Melbourne with my family, I always watched for policemen directing city traffic. I was mesmerised by what they did. My dad and my uncles were all butchers, and my brother and lots of cousins had followed in their footsteps. But me, I really wanted to break the mould. As a teenager I did work experience at Wodonga Hospital, and knew that it was going to be a toss-up between ambulance officer, fire brigade or cop.

I did exams for police forces all around Australia, and got accepted to all of the ones I applied for. In the end, I chose the Victoria Police. I imagined I would see lots of action in the city, even though I had no idea what it would really be like. As much as I admired Smithy, I didn't want to be the one man in a one-man country police station.

My early years in the job formed the foundation for my later years as an officer in the Victoria Police. Right from the start, I wanted to be the best cop I could be. I was keen to get ahead, and equally keen to do the hard yards to get there. I was never a shortcut kind of person.

I joined Victoria Police in 1988 when I was just nineteen years of age. Growing up in Yackandandah, I didn't realise how sheltered my life was until I did night shift in the western suburbs. As a young constable my eyes were opened in ways I never imagined.

My first cot death.

Prostitution.

A junkie collapsed in an alleyway.

Druggies doing unspeakable things for drug money.

Suicide.

Death.

You never forget your first death notification. My first death knock was to the family of a fireman who had died in a car accident on Christmas Eve. From the doorway where I stood, hat in hand, I could tell the guy came from a nice family. Mum and Dad opened the door and saw us in uniform. I think for a moment they thought we were there to ask for their son in a professional capacity.

For a moment.

Then their eyes opened wide with the realisation that we were about to change their lives forever.

•

It wasn't as much a learning curve as a learning cliff dive with a thin bungy cord. I saw so much before I even turned twenty. And I coped the same way most cops did back then.

We went to the pub.

Debriefing down the pub after work became not only a popular pastime but a necessary one. My work buddies were as quick to listen to my horror stories as I was to theirs. It helped to talk about things that made an impact – not that we talked about events in an emotional way, because we didn't. Rather, just the retelling of an experience seemed to demystify it. And if that didn't help there was always the sliding scale of horror to provide perspective. If I was feeling crappy about delivering a death message, the bloke on the barstool next to me might have gone to a triple fatal collision and delivered three death messages to the same family. What you saw might have been bad, but your mates had stories that were a constant reminder that things could always be worse.

In the bizarre alternate police universe, we didn't talk about how we *felt* about delivering the death message or about the cot-death baby, but in a way just saying it meant that nothing really built up inside. At least, nothing we'd ever admit to.

I can't even imagine what our drinking conversations might have sounded like to civilians listening in.

My second death message was the polar opposite of the first, and it illustrated the diverse nature of the people cops dealt with. I had to do a death knock to tell a woman that her son had been killed. As soon as she opened the door and saw two police officers on her doorstep, her face twisted with loathing.

'Fuck off,' she sneered, 'I hate coppers.'

'Ma'am, I need to deliver some news ...' I persisted.

'Fuck off,' she said, almost spitting at us.

'Ma'am, your son has been killed,' I said, hat in hand.

'Fuck off,' she said, slamming the door in our faces.

And that was that.

•

In Yackandandah, no one locked their front door. You trusted your neighbours. You thought that all people told the truth. When you join the police force, you imagine everyone is like you – decent people who respect the order of things. But within a couple of years my thinking about the world changed. It didn't take me long to lose that trust, and it was a struggle to get it back.

In one early experience I picked up a weedy drug dealer who'd been caught shoplifting. At the police station, he swore black and blue that he would give me information on lots of local crime if I agreed to bail. My superiors encouraged me to go with it, so I helped him organise bail and arranged to meet the guy the next day. Of course, he didn't show up and I was left feeling like an idiot. Learning a hard-won lesson.

Another time, I pulled over a guy in the western suburbs. He was driving a hotted-up car, and we got him on an .05 charge. We took him back to the station and put him in an interview room to ask him some questions. It would turn out that the car was stolen and the guy's ID was false. But until this information came through on the computer check, the guy spun us all sorts of yarns.

In a break in the interview, a more senior officer asked who we had in the interview room. He recognised the name and asked if we'd searched the man.

'No,' I said, my stomach sinking.

He walked into the interview room and demanded that the guy strip.

Obligingly, the guy peeled off layers of clothes. Each layer revealed a new and highly dangerous weapon, including a gun strapped under his armpit, a scabbard with a lethal-looking knife, and a garrotte in one of his pockets. Until that moment I didn't even know what a garrotte was. I quickly found out that the odd-looking weapon with two handles strung together with a piece of wire was for strangling – and, possibly, slicing into your victim's throat.

I felt sick to think that at any time during the interview he could have pulled out one of those weapons and killed us.

You can't live life without trusting people – you just have to get better at picking the ones you can trust and the ones you can't. What I learnt from that experience was that I needed to be better able to tell the difference.

•

While a lot of cops spend time in quiet suburban police stations, I went from Yackandandah to the western suburbs of Melbourne without much space in between. My way of learning on the job was to identify the detectives and senior officers whose qualities I admired, then watch how they operated. I made mental notes of the traits of the good detectives. The detective who read the newspapers every morning, over four cups of coffee, before he hit the streets wasn't the detective I wanted to be. The detectives who took over the corner of the office, surrounded by piles of recovered stolen goods they were processing – they were the ones I aspired to be like.

There was a huge difference between reactive and proactive policing. If you were interested, you could catch crooks every day of the week. And you didn't do it sitting at your desk reading the newspapers. Stationed at Brunswick, in Melbourne's inner north, we would make daily visits to one of the plethora of Sydney Road second-hand dealers and go through their books. We would randomly pick names and addresses from their registers and go round and see people who'd sold stuff to the dealer. Of course, many of them were crooks and we charged them.

But it wasn't all catching crooks.

One time, I saved a guy on the Moreland Road bridge. He was on the other side of the rails threatening to jump, and a bunch of cops had spent ages trying to talk him down. Finally, I got close enough to lurch forward and grab him. I got a commendation for saving him, but my mates ribbed me about it, because the guy ended up being a crook and they all joked that I should have let him jump.

After Brunswick I did a stint at D24, the Police Communications Centre, which taught me a lot about Melbourne geography. Being from the country, I had little idea of the outer suburbs – but I soon learnt. The six months I spent there gave me a good understanding of how that area worked and how to utilise available resources.

While D24 wasn't seen as the pinnacle of policing, the division offered promotions to attract officers to go there. I met a lot of people who were there purely for promotion – a quick stepping stone to something better. I understood that: I too had entered the police force with a huge drive to better myself and get promoted. My goal was to be a detective sergeant – a rank senior enough to still catch crooks. The perception was that any rank higher than a sergeant meant you spent a lot of time buried under piles of paperwork, polishing a seat with your bum.

While the police force has its share of personality clashes, I think that I was well respected among my colleagues. I made sure I put in as many working hours as the best of them, and I was right there alongside others working as hard as me.

As soon as promotion opportunities came my way I did everything I could to earn them. After five years there used to be an automatic promotion from constable to senior constable. They changed that and shortened the non-promotion period to four years. I transferred to Wangaratta, both to get a wider range of experience and because I longed for home, country air, footy and folks I knew. Wang was about twenty minutes from my mum and dad's place.

The police at Wangaratta had created a group to target drug crops, dealers, and any criminal activity that arose from drugs. I joined them and went into plain clothes. Even so, the situation in Wangaratta was nothing like what I had seen on the streets of Brunswick. The people in Wangaratta were nice, and it was refreshing to get a dose of humanity. No one lied to you; no needle-addled junkies offered sexual favours in interviews in exchange for leniency. No one carried a concealed garrotte. In fact, even the people growing the drug crops were often farmers fallen on hard times.

I felt refreshed and rekindled by the time my year there was up.

On the very day I qualified to apply for promotion I typed up my application. I soon got shortlisted for a couple of positions and was offered a senior constable position at the Protective Services Group (PSG) based at the old Russell Street police station. Like the name suggests, the PSG protected witnesses.

One of the first people I protected at a safe house was Wendy Peirce, wife of notorious criminal Victor Peirce. Wendy had been placed in witness protection after she gave evidence to police implicating her husband in the Walsh Street police shootings. On 12 October 1988, constables Steven Tynan, twenty-two, and Damian Eyre, twenty, were gunned down after a routine call to check an abandoned car in Walsh Street, South Yarra. As a result of Wendy Peirce's statement, four men – including her husband – were committed for trial.

While I was one of the many police protecting her, most of us weren't allowed to speak to her, so I gained little insight into her nature or the upcoming trial. I did, however, learn a huge lesson when, during the pre-trial hearing, she denied ever seeing her husband with a gun. Without her testimony there was nothing to link Victor Peirce to the murder weapon, and he and the others were found not guilty.

I tucked that knowledge away in the back of my mind: don't rely on people who have something to gain. Their statements often aren't worth the paper they're written on. This understanding was later reinforced when I worked on the task force of yet another double police shooting.

A typical day at the PSG would begin with a couple of hours of physical training. We might then be called in to do a line search for one of the detective squads. Or if there was a bikie event in a country town, a bunch of us would go and mingle with the bikies in an attempt to keep some kind of order. We had a ball: plain clothes, overnight expenses paid, use of a work car, fun times.

Despite the adventures, it was hard to get crook-catching out of my system – and the PSG was more focused on protection than arrests. When I was away on trips I couldn't help myself: I kept arresting law breakers – which, paradoxically, was frowned upon because it meant laying charges and then being called back to the country areas for days at a time to give evidence in the court cases.

•

Looking after protected witnesses taught me about the kind of people who ended up in that situation. In many cases, we were protecting people who had turned on their families or close friends for personal gain. While most of us would never do that, these people were raised differently.

Being so keen to understand these things, I regarded every experience as something I could learn from. Human nature in my childhood in Yackandandah was a pretty simple study. Honest, kind, well-meaning people were easy to understand. It was the ones with the hidden agendas, always out for themselves, ones who would sell their own grandmothers – they were the ones I didn't understand, but I knew I had to try in order to do my job.

Protecting people like that was a thankless job. We protected them and they resented us. When we provided nice meals and clean accommodation, they resented us because they wanted

McDonald's and freedom – and, often, drugs. The ones we dealt with were after something and trying to manipulate us. And we wanted their testimony, so we manipulated them in return.

As an interested sidelines observer, I pondered this paradox. I think it boiled down to survival. They were often people dealing their way out of their own criminal charges. Once everything else was stripped away, the people we dealt with were trying to survive in any way possible, whatever it took.

After a while, all good cops get a hard-won sixth sense when it comes to crooks. Arresting them, protecting them, studying them – I learnt to spot them a mile off.

•

In my early days in the police force, I was heavily into playing football in the VFA in Brunswick. I was also focused on my fitness and trained hard. I competed in triathlons and was very health conscious – which luckily didn't stop me being there till the end at most of the post-game drinking sessions.

The unofficial cop motto – work hard, play hard – might have been written with me in mind.

Every Wednesday during the footy season, police teams would play each other and also teams from the fire brigade, the navy and the army. Senior members of the Victoria Police ran the draw and it was taken very seriously. I was seconded into the Western police footy team when I worked out that way. It was a fantastic opportunity to get cops fit and introduce a bit of competition, but it was also an invaluable time to network. Everyone who had any spare time would go to the games. During footy time I met a lot of contacts, and I reckon that my career flourished as a result of my enthusiastic participation.

So enthusiastic was my participation that along with a tuxedo I wore twelve stitches under my left eye to my wedding, courtesy of a semifinal the week before I walked down the aisle.

Hanging out with detectives was different from hanging out with uniform cops. Talk to the uniforms and they told you about the mundane jobs they'd attended and complained about their crowded rosters, but it was propping up the bar with the local CIB detectives that ignited in me a burning desire to be a part of the cases they talked about. One guy at Brunswick called Ray Dole had been promoted to uniform, but had come from the legendary squads like the Armed Robbery Squad and the now disbanded Major Crime Squad. Guys like Ray – and there were a lot of them at Brunswick – were quick to identify the spark in the young cops coming through who might have the initiative to become a good detective. They saw that spark in me and included me in their group.

Between the uniforms and the detectives there was a real us-and-them attitude – and I wanted to be with *them*. Footy was the entrée into the group before I earned the title of detective. That was why I jumped at the job of special duties around 1992. Special duties would put me in plain clothes and I would be doing small-scale drug investigation and targeting local issues like theft from motor vehicles.

This was where I first met fellow police officer Dave Miechel.

•

At that time there weren't a lot of witnesses in protection, so I was sent as a senior constable out to Moonee Ponds special duties. Dave Miechel was a constable back then and we both worked plain clothes. By chucking off the uniform and getting into plain clothes, we were in fact stepping up to the first level towards being a detective.

Our motto was simple – catch crooks. And Dave Miechel was a very good crook-catcher. Without getting paid overtime, Dave and I never left work if there were leads to follow and crooks to catch.

There was a look that undercover officers needed to adopt. While I would always be spotted as a cop just because I seemed to have that clean-cut look about me, Dave could blend in with the best of them; with his ponytail and unshaved appearance, he didn't look like a cop at all. When we needed someone to walk through a pub or someplace where we didn't want to spook anyone, Dave was our man.

While Dave and I had a lot of similarities, there were also differences. Unlike most cops, Dave didn't give much away about his life outside the police force. Spend eight hours on surveillance with another human being and you chat about all kinds of stuff, but with Dave it was different. Most of his talk was about his motorbike, and a hotted-up car that he was doing up from scratch. Even so, most of our conversations involved talking about the job.

So while we worked together, and spent a lot of time together, I'm not sure that I knew Dave Miechel much better by the time we parted company. The next time we worked together would be at the drug squad.

•

After Moonee Ponds I went back to Brunswick as a senior constable. I did well on the Criminal Investigation Branch exam, and applied for a position at the Brunswick CIB. I knew a lot of the detectives there, and was thrilled when I got the job; there was an elite feeling to joining the ranks of the CIB.

My welcome to the squad was held at the local pub. We celebrated by drinking a beer or twenty, and at the end of the night I was a fully fledged, if rather drunk, detective.

In one of my early jobs as a detective I got called to a block of units in Brunswick. People in one of the lower units had complained of water overflowing from an apartment above. When the uniformed members knocked on the door of the upstairs flat an Asian man answered, dazed and covered in blood. The uniforms arrested him and put him in the van, then called the CIB to the scene. Uniformed police guarded the entrance to the flat but didn't go inside.

That was our job.

Policing is like a gory version of Forrest Gump's box of chocolates – you never know what you're going to get. There's a bit of an adrenaline rush as you step into the unknown.

We saw the source of the overflowing water as soon as we entered the bathroom: there was a headless body in the bath. The dead woman's unrecognisable head was found pulped in the toilet. Her throat had been cut out and stuffed into her handbag.

The scene was clearly a homicide case, so we called in the Homicide Squad. When the Homicide Squad detectives arrived they were all wearing their trademark sweeping coats, and there was an atmosphere to their arrival – an electricity.

With great professional interest, I watched them do their job. Homicide Squad detectives were the elite investigators. Observing them, I acknowledged a dawning realisation – I wanted to be one of them.

•

My first Christmas season as the most junior CIB detective I was rostered to work all the shifts that the other blokes wanted to spend with their families. I also copped the 1997 New Year's Eve shift and we got called to a murder.

At a local nursing home called Brunswick Lodge, the body of a 95-year-old resident called Kathleen Downes had been discovered by staff. At the scene we found Mrs Downes half lying on the bed. There was a small amount of blood from a wound in her throat. She was wearing a nightie, which was pulled up, and her underwear was around her ankles. Medical opinion was that the woman would have died quickly.

The Homicide crew called to investigate the Downes murder case wanted to tap into local knowledge, and I was seconded into the Homicide Squad for the investigation.

Years later, notorious serial killer Peter Norris Dupas would be the only suspect in the unsolved killing. But when Kathleen Downes was murdered Dupas hadn't yet come onto the police radar. When he did, detectives found two unexplained phone calls from his house to the nursing home five weeks before the murder, and the killing fell on the anniversary of Dupas's ex-wife leaving him. While Dupas never admitted to the Downes murder, he allegedly mentioned 'the old sheila down the road' in a jailhouse discussion about another murder close by.

But in early 1998, despite not finding the killer in the Downes case, I stayed on at the Homicide Squad. There was one main difference between the CIB and Homicide: as a CIB detective every case was different and there was a huge variety to the work. At the Homicide Squad, every case we were called to was a dead body. There are only around fifty murders in Victoria each year, so a lot of our cases hit the news, which helped cement Homicide as the elite squad.

One murder took us to a little house in the country. The victim was about the age of my mum, and she had been killed with a huge kitchen knife. The husband was in custody by the time we got there, but the blood splatter around the house told us the story. As his wife had tried to flee the husband had stabbed her over and over again, spraying the walls with her blood. Of course, it didn't tell the *whole* story – just the death part. A family of teenagers had just lost their mum to murder and their father to jail.

The guy in the interview room was sane. He had no explanation; reckoned he'd just 'snapped' during an argument. The realisation of what he had done had hit home. By the time we questioned him, he was a broken man.

But that didn't change what he'd done.

Cases like this one really made me wonder. Sure, there were psychopaths out there – Dupas being typical of this type of offender – but what made someone 'snap'?

While these were the kinds of questions I asked myself, they weren't widely discussed among the squad. We liked to find a motive – a lack of motive was why the Kathleen Downes murder remained unsolved for so long – but aside from questioning the sanity of the offender for legal reasons, we didn't really spend much time with the *why*. Mostly, we needed hard evidence;

reasons why weren't necessary for an arrest or a conviction. The Homicide Squad was a reactionary squad – they killed, we caught.

And we didn't have time to question the whys before someone else took a knife or a gun to a loved one or a stranger, and our phones rang in the middle of the night.

CHAPTER 3

The Lorimer task force

On Sunday 16 August 1998, the phone call in the middle of the night was the one that every cops dreads.

A colleague: 'Mate, there's been a couple of members shot in Moorabbin. There's a car on the way to pick you up.'

Fuck! I rolled out of bed, knowing that any event involving police was massive. Not that we didn't go all-out on every investigation, but it was different when it was one of our own. Or two of our own in this case.

The crime scene at Cochranes Road, Moorabbin, was full of flashing lights and police activity on a huge scale.

Two cops gunned down in cold blood.

We were quickly brought up to speed. Gary Silk and Rod Miller were part of an extensive undercover operation to catch two bandits who had been terrorising restaurants for years. The crims' MO was to wear masks and burst into out-of-the-way restaurants near closing time. Waving weapons around and screaming and shouting, the bandits would rob the restaurant owners of the night's takings, and restaurant patrons of their jewellery and wallets. Silk and Miller had been sitting off the Silky Emperor Chinese restaurant on Warrigal Road when they saw a suspicious-looking car entering the underground car park. Other surveillance detectives nearby had seen Silk and Miller follow the small blue car out of the car park and pull it over for questioning just before the shooting.

By the time the call went out, Rod Miller was missing and Gary Silk was dead. After a frantic search, Miller was found in bushes around the corner from where the shooting had taken place. He had staggered towards the main road, trying to get help. He was rushed to hospital in critical condition.

The body of Gary Silk lay a couple of metres away from the unmarked police car. He was curled up in the foetal position on the nature strip. The single blue light from his unmarked car still flashed.

Along with other detectives, I examined the crime scene. People always asked how we felt at such moments, and while they might want to hear that we felt sad or upset, there's little room for that reaction. Our job was to read the scene, find the clues and catch the bastards who did this.

Investigating came first. Reflecting would come later.

While the bosses circled the periphery, dealing with media, the core group of Homicide detectives went straight to the evidence. Theories were tossed about as we walked the scene, trying to figure out what had happened. Straightaway we noticed the broken glass in front of the parked police car. It looked fresh and it didn't come from the police vehicle. Right from the start, there was the possibility that either Silk or Miller had fired a return shot at the offender's vehicle.

We watched crime scene and ballistics experts examining the scene and listened to their conclusions. They suspected we were looking for a car with its back window shot out. If the blue car Silk and Miller had been seen following was indeed connected with the restaurant robberies, there was the possibility we were looking for two offenders, because there were always two offenders in masks who robbed the restaurants.

When we received word from the hospital that Rod Miller didn't make it, the investigation became a double murder.

As dawn broke we started door-knocking nearby factories. Special Operations Group (SOG) members were called in to help. These highly trained and heavily armed police operatives were necessary because we were dealing with killers who would shoot coppers down like dogs. For all we knew, the killer or killers might have come from one of the factories.

Later that day I was asked to attend the autopsies. A colleague and I went to the city morgue at Kavanagh Street. The new morgue had a glass viewing room, which removed us a bit from the examination but we could still talk to and hear the forensic pathologist through a speaker system.

Up until this moment, in the flurry of the new investigation, I hadn't really let it sink in that these two slain men were colleagues. But as the morgue attendant removed the clothing from their bodies, I saw that both officers had a pancake holster – a flat holster used by plain-clothes detectives – strapped to them. I had used one all the time when I was in plain clothes.

As the pathologist emptied the pockets of the dead cops, it struck me that the contents were practically the same as mine. He pulled out a drink card from the Prince of Wales Hotel.

'Used last night,' said the pathologist.

I pictured Gary Silk having a quiet beer at the pub before he went on night shift.

Our reality check came when the pathologist removed police badges from their pockets. The shield; the ties that bind. It brought the murders very close to home. These men were ours. And we were responsible for catching their killers.

•

Right from the start, the investigation into the Silk Miller shootings was approached differently from the way the Walsh Street police shootings had been conducted a decade earlier. The failure of the Walsh Street prosecution had been a massive blow to the Victoria Police. But for those who cared to learn from it, it was also an important lesson.

Inspector Paul Sheridan from the Homicide Squad was chosen to head up the Lorimer task force into the Silk Miller murders. Paul Sheridan wasn't your typical detective. He wasn't big and burly, and he wasn't someone who you might get to know on the police social scene. He was a small-framed man with glasses, articulate and educated, and, most importantly, he had a history at the Homicide Squad.

Because I was part of the on-call crew on the night of the murders, I was automatically included in the task force. Other detectives from the Homicide Squad were called to volunteer. Some declined because of a negative experience with the Walsh Street investigation – and who could blame them? Others were champing at the bit to be a part of the team. Gary Silk had been around for a long time and was well known socially in the police force. Rod Miller was less well known at the detective level, but the fact he was a cop who'd left behind a wife and baby son was motivation enough.

The Silk Miller case was the ultimate integrated investigation. Because the driver of the small blue car was linked with the restaurant armed robberies, detectives from the Armed Robbery Squad joined us, as well as covert operations. Career wise, it was an incredible investigative opportunity. We would be dealing with everyone from the police hierarchy to crooks to detectives from all over the place.

Inspector Paul Sheridan was the kind of boss who let us get on with the investigation. He dealt with the red tape but shielded us from it, so that we could be most effective on the ground. He guided us in a methodical way that was all about building a case that wouldn't fail in court. As far as Sheridan was concerned, every part of the investigation was as important as the next. The guy checking the car records on computer was just as important as the guy out banging on doors. Sheridan ran a tight ship.

Thousands of information reports came in, and every one of them had to be investigated. Because of the identikit photo of a shifty-looking guy with a skinny face and long dark hair that came from the other surveillance crew at the Silky Emperor, people reported every skinny-faced shifty-looking guy with long dark hair they knew. All had to be checked out.

Along the way we locked up some major drug dealers and gun runners, and disrupted a lot of criminal activity in the hope of rattling cages. We looked very closely at drug dealer and standover man Nik 'the Bulgarian' Radev, and another underworld figure, who just happened to be in the area at the time of the Silk Miller murders. They had been meeting in a takeaway place when Gary Silk and Rod Miller came in to buy their dinner.

We started poking the wasps' nest.

Radev and the other man were active criminals. We got Radev on a violent armed robbery charge – during the course of the offence he had shoved a gun in the mouth of an eighteen-year-old youth and tied a five-year-old child to a bedpost.

After Nik Radev was in the lock-up, he called us with a proposition. Fellow Homicide detective Sol Solomon and I drove out to the prison to meet with him. We listened as Radev promised to tell us who killed Silk and Miller if we got him and a bunch of other crooks out of jail, took them all to a motel, and provided a menu of crayfish, cocaine and call girls.

Sol Solomon and I couldn't believe our ears. Here was Radev wanting to hand us the Silk Miller shooters in exchange for a night out on the town. Seven months into the investigation, we were all worn out, stressed and frustrated. This could be the break we were looking for.

Could it be that simple to crack this thing wide open?

Driving away from Port Phillip Prison, Sol and I were excited. We hurried into Paul Sheridan's office and told him about Radev's offer.

'You've got to be joking,' Sheridan said, looking at us as if we were idiots.

'Well ... we don't have to give them the cocaine and the prostitutes,' I said, knowing I sounded lame. 'Maybe seafood and a hotel?'

'These guys are career criminals,' Sheridan said in his quiet voice. '*Nothing* they say is worth anything and *will never* stand up in court. Whatever they said would have to be corroborated tenfold.'

While I had walked into Sheridan's office feeling elated and hopeful, I walked out feeling stupid. I knew the boss was right. And, worse, *I knew this already.* These guys were scumbags and couldn't be trusted. They were violent, vile people who would put a gun in the mouth of a teenager and terrorise a five-year-old. And because of their vague promises of information I'd been so excited, bursting to do *them* a favour. It was crazy but – for a blind, euphoric, grasping-at-straws moment – utterly feasible and believable … until Paul Sheridan pointed out the error of our ways.

I vowed again never to be taken in by what crooks offered in exchange for incentives. Police must never be willing to do a deal with the devil, no matter how much we wanted to find the Silk Miller shooters.

The simple message from Sheridan was worth its weight in gold: *you can't buy information.* And with that, suddenly, the real message of the failure of the Walsh Street prosecution became obvious. This was exactly what the detectives had done – dangled the golden carrot in exchange for information in order to close a tough case.

But the golden carrot only gave them fool's gold in return.

There is little credibility in paid-for information, and there's no guarantee that the informer will ever keep his or her end of the bargain. Hence the Walsh Street acquittal when Wendy Peirce ended up denying seeing her husband with a gun.

Standing alongside me for the dressing-down from Sheridan was my mate Sol Solomon. Years later he would sit opposite some of the state's most violent killers and offer them million-dollar incentives to make statements.

Against me.

And years later notorious drug dealer and killer Carl Williams would be taken from prison, fed and allowed visits with his girlfriend. All, according to Carl, under the auspices of the police.

But more about that later.

•

We could have arrested Bandali Debs and Jason Roberts a year before we did. But here's why we didn't. When we met Bandali

Debs for the first time, there was little to suggest that he was the ruthless killer he turned out to be.

After close forensic examination of the broken glass at the crime scene, the scientists concluded it had come from the rear window of a blue Hyundai. Accordingly, we had a sweep on any such car that had had its rear windows replaced around the time of the Silk Miller shooting. One of the more senior detectives at the Lorimer task force asked me to go along with him to speak to a bloke about his daughter's Hyundai that had had a back window replaced.

The ordinary-looking father of five told us how he had broken the window of his daughter's car. He said he had put some tiling strips in a bucket in the back, then accidentally smashed the window when he closed the hatch. The other detective and I listened, twiddling our thumbs, lamenting the fact that we had been taken away from investigating Nik Radev and associates to listen to this guy.

Debs told us how he had put a new window in himself to save money, but when his daughter had driven it the window had popped out. That was why he had taken it to the window repairer and that was how he had come onto our radar.

Bandali Debs was one of hundreds of citizens with a similar story. While his daughter's car was an exact match to the blue Hyundai we were looking for, Debs didn't seem a likely candidate for the vicious police shooting.

Nonetheless, his name went into the huge pool of possibilities. It would have stayed there if it hadn't come up in another investigation. Linked into our task force, the Armed Robbery Squad was running the parallel Hamada investigation, going over old ground, looking at all their suspects from the original restaurant robberies.

A detective called Steve Beanland came up with the pivotal link. He had been going over phone records from the restaurant robberies task force. In one of the robberies in the early years, the crooks had been chased by a security guard who had taken down their car registration number. The car had been found burnt out a short time later. When Steve Beanland was going through all the old records, he identified that the owner of the car, a young man called Jason Ghiller, had made phone calls to Bandali Debs, who was his uncle. At the time, Ghiller had denied being a part of the restaurant robberies. He said his car had been stolen.

From that moment on, it all clicked into place and Bandali Debs moved right into our crosshairs. Here was a suspect with the exact make and model car in his possession, and now we had a connection with the earlier restaurant robberies via Jason Ghiller.

We found out that Jason Ghiller was a car fanatic and loved a particular make and model of car. We provided an undercover officer with the exact car and got him to park it near where Jason worked. Sure enough, it wasn't long before Ghiller approached our undercover and asked him to go for a beer to talk about cars. Our undercover came across as a tough guy and established his street cred, spinning yarns to make his new buddy believe he was a violent criminal. Soon, Jason began swapping stories with the undercover and told him all about the armed robberies that he did with Bandali Debs. When he nearly got caught, he explained to the undercover, he stopped doing the robberies.

Bingo!

We immediately got a warrant to put listening devices into the Debs household. People are products of their upbringing, and we listened in amazement as much of the Debs family conversations revolved around stealing. If one of them was going shopping, another would warn them about the position of security cameras in the supermarket. Debs's daughter's boyfriend, Jason Roberts, would talk about a shipment of air conditioners that came in to his work, and Debs and Roberts would make immediate arrangements to go and steal them that night. The thieving was constant.

While we were getting a lot of good intel, Inspector Paul Sheridan was reluctant to make the ultimate arrests because he wanted to gather as much evidence as possible to ensure a watertight case and conviction. Things started to heat up when the listening devices picked up Bandali Debs making threats against Rod Miller's widow, Carmel, and their baby. In Debs's warped way of thinking, if he killed Carmel it would make it look like the Millers were the targets and push the investigation in a different direction, away from him. We put immediate protection on Carmel Miller.

Debs also talked about going over to the other side of town to kill cops, to make it look like the killers lived in the western suburbs. His bizarre plans kept us on a bit of a knife edge.

To arrest or not to arrest? But that decision fell on Sheridan, not us.

We were happy to keep on with the intelligence gathering. Jason Ghiller was still talking to our undercover, and we were doing things to make the Debs family talk. We had listening devices in the car and the house, and had recorded many covert conversations that were very incriminating.

Finally, the bosses put all of our evidence to Jeremy Rapke of the Public Prosecutions Division and he agreed that we had enough for a successful prosecution.

In a sting operation, we got Bandali Debs to come and quote for a tiling job, and arrested him without incident.

I have photos of the party at the Lorimer task force taken after the arrest. It was a drinking and cigar-smoking carnival that seemed to go on for weeks.

The St Kilda cops – mates of Gary Silk's – took us all out for dinner. The feeling was like winning a footy grand final. We knew without a shadow of a doubt that we had the right guys. There was no second guessing. We had covert tapes of them talking about the murders and talking about planning to kill more cops. We had the glass from the windscreen that matched the glass found at the scene of the shooting. We also found one of Rod Miller's bullets embedded into the footwell of the Hyundai. The physical evidence matched the crime scene. We had the links via Jason Ghiller with the original restaurant robberies. A search of Bandali Debs's mother's house turned up guns hidden in a wall cavity. The guns were matched with the Silk Miller crime scene as well as other crime scenes. There was definitely a feeling of a job well done.

All up, it took two years to arrest Debs after one of the most thorough and successful task force investigations. Debs was given two life sentences with no minimum and Roberts was jailed for life with a minimum term of thirty-five years.

With his arrest, Bandali Debs's DNA was added to the national database of offenders and there were two matches to unsolved murders. In separate incidents, two women had been shot in the head after unprotected sex and dumped on the side of the road – mother of three Donna Anne Hicks in 1995, and eighteen-year-old Kristy Harty in 1997. DNA samples taken from both women matched Debs and he has since been convicted of their murders.

After a successful Silk Miller conviction, detectives from Lorimer were invited to Government House to receive commendations.

•

As I packed up boxes at the Lorimer task force, I knew that what I had learnt from my time there was like gold. The methods we had used were the right ones. We were right to knock back Radev's offer of information. Of course, the irony didn't escape any of us that Radev couldn't have known Bandali Debs killed Silk and Miller because Debs was pretty much a cleanskin who didn't associate in criminal circles. The only thing Radev could have done was to pick someone he had a grudge against and put him in the crosshairs or used the opportunity to get rid of a competitor. We could have wasted months or even years chasing shadows.

It was an important lesson, but the fact that some didn't learn from it would have echoes for me for many years to come.

CHAPTER 4

The streets of Brunswick

After the Lorimer task force I took promotion to sergeant, which involved going back into uniform. While a lot of cops were critical of having to go back into uniform to get promoted, I loved it. With a detective's background, I was able to be an effective working uniform sergeant. An example of what an experienced detective can bring to the uniform branch is that if my young cops brought in a shoplifter, they would have to come and brief me before they interviewed him. I'd go and have a look, and recognise a crook from fifty paces.

'Has he got a car?' I'd ask the young constables.

'Don't know,' they'd say.

'Go ask him.'

So they would ask the guy where his car was, search the car, find it full of stolen goods and get a bigger fish for their troubles.

A less suspicious sergeant might not have taken it any further.

I had worked Brunswick both in uniform and as a detective and was happy to come back as a sergeant. Brunswick had been a rough-and-ready northern suburb before a real-estate boom in the early 1990s made it trendy, pushing the rougher crowd a little further afield. When I was first there it was still a little wild and a great place for a young policeman to earn his stripes.

The northern and western suburbs of Melbourne were considered the harder places to work, because, of course, this was where the crooks were. The bright lights of Sydney Road burned twenty-four hours a day, and in there somewhere lived the likes of Tony Mokbel, Mick Gatto, and a weedy drug dealer called Carl Williams.

Because of my experience as a detective at Brunswick, I was asked to lead a group of young constables in a special duties team. Since I didn't aim to stay in uniform anyway, I got back into plain clothes and did what I did best – catch crooks.

A successful method I taught my small team of juniors was to talk to anyone we caught with drugs and see if we could coax out of them who was dealing. We were mostly talking with street-level junkies who would tell us anything we wanted in order to get bail so they could go score their next hit. The only thing we offered in return was bail on their own undertaking; since this was something we would do anyway, it was a win-win situation.

Emanating from these junkies was the kind of intel that would allow us to catch low-level dealers or recover stolen goods. These situations gave me the chance to teach the young cops the skills of watching a suspect's house, and how to obtain information then verify and utilise the intel.

During this time we received information about a young crook called Little Tommy Ivanovic, who was rumoured to be growing marijuana at his parents' house in Brunswick. With further investigation, we found out that he was the suspect in a shooting and had prior convictions for drug-related crimes. He also associated with well-known criminals from the so-called Carlton crew. Given his background, I told my team that we weren't dealing with a typical commission-flat crim – we had found someone with much broader connections.

We pursued Little Tommy enthusiastically, if cautiously – he was red-flagged on our system as someone with a propensity to carry firearms. On the strength of our intel we got a warrant to search his house but, disappointingly, we didn't find the marijuana he was rumoured to be growing there. The only thing we found was a single ecstasy tablet in the pocket of a coat hanging in a wardrobe in a spare bedroom that used to belong to Tommy's brother, who was studying in the US. We had been hoping for drugs or guns, but – on this occasion – Little Tommy was clean.

On the brief of evidence I recommended that no charges be laid on the one tablet found in the brother's bedroom, since there was no way of proving who it belonged to. My senior sergeant agreed with my assessment and signed off on it.

Nonetheless, the crew and I took Tommy in for questioning and released him soon after. Once we all knew what he looked like, we were able to spot him in local watering holes. I had learnt this tactic as a detective and passed it on to the crew. We would do our Friday night drinks at certain pubs, and if we happened to overhear certain things, all the better for us.

The Union Hotel in Union Street, West Brunswick, was notorious for the folk it attracted. On Thursday and Friday nights it was well known for its topless barmaids and stripper nights. For any cop who worked at Brunswick in the late 80s and early 90s, the Union Hotel was always a place where we would find someone we were looking for – and if they weren't there, someone would tell us where to find them. In the olden days, we also made it clear to the licensee of the hotel that it would be in the best interests of their licence that we find the people we were looking for. Within twenty-four hours we would normally get the information we were after.

The Brunswick CIB had a corner at the Union Hotel on a Thursday or Friday night, and we kept an eye on the crooks while they watched the motley strippers who mostly looked like they were dancing to support their drug habits. Most of the time I stood with my back to the performers, keeping an eye on what was perhaps the cream of Brunswick's crop of criminals. The lifeblood of detective work is information, and you can't get that at a computer. While we have received a lot of criticism in hindsight about watching crooks there, we had to be where the crooks were, find out who they were associating with, and find out what they were up to.

You drank for a couple of hours in your CIB corner then went to the men's room, where you might stand next to a bloke that you'd arrested or had dealings with. Sometimes these side-by-side urinal meetings were deathly uncomfortable, and at other times a conversation would start up.

It was in this pub that I bumped into Little Tommy again. He knew the owner.

The way things worked was that the owner of the pub was a conduit between the cops and the crooks. He'd come over and chat with the cops, but he usually perched in his spot at the end of the bar and most people would pay their respects to him, then split off into their own separate groups: bikies, burglars, thieves and drug dealers. And cops.

When I spotted Little Tommy, I waited for him to greet the owner then went over to him to play cat and mouse.

'How ya going, Tommy?' I asked, taking a sip of beer. 'What brings you to this pub?' I hadn't seen him there before and I had certainly spent enough time scanning the faces.

Little Tommy was cautious but friendly enough in his response. He knew the lie of the land – no hard feelings.

After that, I saw him occasionally at the pub and always made a point to say hello. One time I spent a few minutes chatting to Tommy and the owner of the pub, and after Tommy had left us a drunk guy came over and asked what we were doing talking to Little Tommy.

'He's a fuckin' dead man walking,' slurred the man.

Given that you'd hear that kind of talk a hundred times a night in that pub, I told him to bugger off. The only difference was that the guy said it so early in the evening. Most death threats came later, when everybody was pissed. But I didn't think anything of it at the time, nor did I make a note of it, or put it in an information report, because there was nothing to indicate that the guy was serious.

The more I learnt about Little Tommy, the more I saw how connected he was. After a couple of months in Brunswick I was moved to Broadmeadows Regional Response Unit, based in a covert location in Essendon. There were about thirty plain-clothes police supported by a surveillance unit of around a dozen members.

For me, this was a step closer to getting back to detective work. I was put in charge of a small crew. We did mostly drug operations because that work dominated in our area.

I had a knack for talking to crooks and getting information, and decided to target Tommy Ivanovic because he had entered my radar. All along, I was looking for promotion. I wanted to work my way up past the small fries of junkies and topless bars of Brunswick. A detective is only as good as his information, and I knew that I had to be innovative in my approach. I wanted to court Little Tommy as a possible human source. This was a delicate process.

In those days, registering an informer meant that you needed to let your bosses know, and then the informer's name would be written on a sheet of paper kept in the safe of the local detective superintendent. This was how I registered Little Tommy as an informer without his knowledge. That way, if he did let anything slip that I could later use he would have a registered number that would protect his identity.

I didn't know if he ever would provide any information, but it was worth listing his name anyway. Registering informers was a detective's job. When you went for promotion, the board would always ask about the informers you'd registered. The fact that I could tell a future promotions board that I had listed Tommy Ivanovic would be good for my career. When I read off his list of associates – which consisted of some big names – it would sound even better.

Only a day or two after I officially listed him as an informer, I got a phone call telling me that Tommy Ivanovic had been arrested for murder. He'd been involved in a shooting outside his parents' place. Apparently, a motorbike rider had followed him home after a road-rage incident. Fearful and suspicious, Tommy had shot the guy he thought was after him. The security cameras Ivanovic had installed at his house had captured the shooting on film.

After his arrest Little Tommy asked to speak to me, but the arresting officers refused his request. I was glad. While I had developed a bit of a rapport with him the couple of times we'd met, there was nothing I could do for him, and I would have had nothing to say except: *Bad luck, mate, they got you on video. Better fess up to your sins.*

After Little Tommy had been locked up for a while, facing a trial and long jail sentence, I changed my mind about seeing him. I discussed this with my bosses and they agreed it was worth going to see if he wanted to do any deals. He was connected to all the good crooks and there was no telling what a desperate man might give up. Nothing ventured, nothing gained.

The first time I saw him in jail, we had a general chat about the Union Hotel and the owner. I told him who I'd been locking up and we discussed people we knew.

Tommy Ivanovic didn't give much away, but rapport must be built slowly and carefully. At no time did I ever tell Little Tommy that I had registered him as an informer. He would never have agreed to take the risk. Being an informer from prison was the same as painting a big red target on your forehead. Murder might have carried a stiff penalty, but being an informer carried a death sentence.

CHAPTER 5

The drug squad

After training my small crew in the ways of tracking druggies to find their dealers, I was seconded into a crew working exclusively on suburban-level drug dealers, which operated from a secret location in Essendon.

While you enter the fight against drugs fists raised, wanting to make a difference, it soon becomes apparent that there is no chance of stamping out the scourge at a grassroots level. We were dealing with a multi-million-dollar industry and the police powers-that-be wouldn't even give us a mobile phone while the guys we were chasing were changing mobile phones as often as they did their underpants. We were under-resourced, and there didn't seem to be much support for this type of criminal investigation.

After my experience as a detective and my time at task force Lorimer, my CV was looking pretty healthy. I could manage a team and lead people, and – after working on drug cases at a local level – the drug squad seemed the next logical step. I imagined a well-oiled machine with much bigger budgets, giving us the ability to hook much bigger fish. I went for a couple of interviews and was offered a position as a detective sergeant.

After a spotted history in the 1990s the drug squad had been renamed the Major Drug Investigation Division – or MDID if you're in a hurry. It is worth exploring the troubles *before* my time, because what happened *during* my time certainly echoed what had come before.

In 1996 drug squad detective Senior Sergeant Wayne Strawhorn had done a study tour overseas and returned home with an innovative plan. Undercover operatives would sell police-supplied pseudoephedrine to illegal drug manufacturers, then detectives would follow the trail and nab those further up the chain. The difficulty for illicit drug manufacturers was always in the supply. If the Victoria Police kept the supplies flowing then the meth cooks, the dealers and the bigwigs were there for the catching.

So the theory went.

While there were some great busts from the so-called Clandestine Laboratories program, there was the niggling view that Victoria Police was sort of in the drug business too. Members of the drug squad were selling chemicals that the police purchased from chemical companies for a few hundred dollars for forty times that amount.

By the time I got to the Major Drug Investigation Division in 2002, the Clandestine Laboratories program had been shut down and some of the key officers involved were facing charges. Strawhorn himself had been transferred to another division and would later be charged with supplying Mark Moran with two kilos of pure pseudoephedrine without the approval of his commander. It cost $340 and was sold to Moran for $12000 through an intermediary. After the shake-up came the horsetrading; a couple of officers, caught up in the scandal, agreed to give evidence against Strawhorn in return for reduced charges, which of course meant reduced jail sentences.

Any squad that requires its officers to mingle with crims and befriend them to get information is always open to failures in the system. Nonetheless, procedures had been put in place to address this. There was a new commander, Anthony Biggin, who was highly regarded for his work during Operation Bart – the 1990s Victoria Police window shutters scandal. His fight against corruption and his ethical standards were well known; he would run a tight ship.

While my arrival came after the upheaval in the drug squad, there was a palpable reverberation. When I moved to the Major Drug Investigation Division in June 2002, the scandal had died down and the people responsible for it had gone. New name, new era. Or so the thinking went.

At the MDID I ran into David Miechel again after several years. Miechel had been a detective senior constable at the drug squad since 1997; he had weathered the recent changes and witnessed the fallout from Clandestine Laboratories.

Within the St Kilda Road police complex, the MDID occupied the twelfth floor. While parts of the Victoria Police complex had impressive views of the city, Albert Park Lake or the green oval of Melbourne Grammar School, our section looked inwards to the clutter of the office. We were surrounded by safes and filing cabinets, chock-a-block full of blue folders from past and current cases.

As the fresh-faced new guy I noticed a whiff of suspicion as soon as I arrived, which I guessed was the result of the place having suffered a recent siege. I half wondered if they thought I was a mole in the squad. I could understand it, because they had been through such an upheaval. The only friendly face was one of the sergeants called Graham Sayce. And while Dave Miechel was a familiar face, his wasn't exactly a friendly one at the beginning of this second time we were to work together.

My first impressions of the Major Drug Investigation Division were a little disappointing. The environment was not friendly, and I suspected it might be tough to stamp my authority as a detective sergeant – the guy with fresh ideas meets the brick wall of an established squad. Nonetheless, I was keen and raring to go. I pictured myself targeting the Mr Bigs of the drug world and making a difference.

The truth was a long way from that.

•

Experience had taught me that to run a good investigation you needed a good budget and generous resources. I soon found out that resources were little better than they had been anywhere else I'd worked. While we were officially called the Major

Drug Investigation Division, before long I began calling us the *Medium* Drug Investigation Division, because even though we could run a good investigation and hunt down a chain of suppliers, budgetary constraints meant that we would often be called to end an investigation before getting to the big fish.

An example of this was if we needed, say, $20 000 to do a big drug buy to facilitate an arrest – we would be told we couldn't have it. While these figures were small change in the drug world, to the tight purse strings of the Victoria Police, they were insurmountable. It was impossible to play in the big league without the big bucks. (It is galling to note that while we couldn't afford to do our job properly, the purse strings would be very much loosened when it came to the *many millions of dollars* later spent to pursue me.)

After the recent troubles, a tightening of the rules had occurred. The MDID could no longer supply pseudoephedrine to drug dealers, although Strawhorn's technique of supplying some of the elements required in drug manufacture was still used. We could supply things like a pill press and then arrest the dealers who used it. If we knew of crooks who had a pill press, we might point an informer who could supply key ingredients of ecstasy in their direction and hook them up. Then we would come in at the end of the operation and arrest all the key players. This meant the Victoria Police was no longer supplying drug chemicals: we were simply introducing crooks who needed each other.

When Dave Miechel was allocated to be on my crew, I was happy to have an experienced investigator. The fact that we had worked together years earlier was good and I thought Dave would be a great asset.

Dave was still as private a person as he had ever been; he'd be happy to sit for an eight-hour shift and say nothing at all. But that had a downside: while his head was full of intel, Dave would share very little of it.

One pattern that quickly established itself was that I would run a meeting as the sergeant and invite input. Dave, as a senior constable, would say nothing. Then I would make a decision about something we were going to do, and I could sense that Dave was fuming. It became really frustrating – he was happy to sit there and add nothing to the decision-making process, but when others made decisions he would feel resentful.

Dave had been at the MDID for years and had a good arrest record. I wondered if he resented me as a newcomer. A small part of me also wondered if Dave Miechel saw me as a plant, since he had been part of Wayne Strawhorn's team, who had been targeted and charged. Or maybe Dave thought, *Who is Dale to come in here and tell me how to work drugs when I've been doing this for five years and he's been doing it for five minutes?*

Something had changed in the intervening years that had closed him off. It was almost like our days of catching crooks together at Moonee Ponds had never happened.

•

When I got to the MDID I spoke to the bosses about Little Tommy Ivanovic. He was still waiting for his case to go to trial, and I discussed the possibility of continuing to court him for information. They agreed and I went to see him in prison.

On that first visit I got a sense of some potential. On the second visit Little Tommy mentioned a very good friend of his called Carl Williams.

'You wanna know what's going on out on the streets, go meet Carl,' Little Tommy said. He gave me Carl's phone number.

I'd never heard of Carl Williams, but was happy to meet him to see what he had to say. In a historical context, before *Underbelly* hit the TV screens, the crooks who are now household names had never been heard of.

I took this information back to the MDID bosses. A couple of people knew about Williams, but because I didn't I typed his name into the police LEAP computer system and found out that he was on bail for a large drug-trafficking arrest. He'd been caught with a couple of hundred thousand dollars in cash and the corresponding crooks had been caught with drugs.

I could see from Carl Williams's record that he was the type of crook we could possibly use.

'What do you reckon?' I said to the bosses. 'I've got his phone number.'

'Go meet him,' they said.

When I rang Carl Williams he was expecting my call and agreed to meet at a shopping centre out Airport West way. He sounded friendly. Before the meeting I was briefed by some other detectives who also wanted intel from Carl, but at this early stage the fewer the people who knew about our meeting, the better.

I asked Dave Miechel to go with me because we were a crew of two. Dave filled me in on Carl Williams and his history. Carl had an ongoing feud with the Moran brothers; one of them had even shot Carl in the guts during a confrontation in a park. At that stage, the big question was whether the shooter was Jason or Mark Moran, so that was on our list of conversation topics.

We met in the food court of the shopping centre. Carl Williams was alone, although we wondered if he had support nearby but out of sight. Carl would later be portrayed on TV as the dumbarse from Broady, but he wasn't as silly as he looked. As much as we had a game plan, so did he.

We sought information from him, but he wanted it from us too. The police had a strategy of providing misinformation in return. At the first meeting we talked about historical stuff. I think, in hindsight, that first meeting was a bit of a credibility test. Fortunately, Dave was a wealth of knowledge on the past stuff, and he was able to keep the conversation going.

We talked about Tommy Ivanovic, since Tommy was our introduction. Soon, I led the discussion around to the intel that I was asked to get about the Morans and asked the big question.

'We know one of them shot you,' I said. 'So which one?'

'Jason,' he said.

In that one word we got what no other cops had been able to.

Once we had established a rapport, we told him that we'd like to chat with him further if he was happy to.

'Yeah, no worries. Any friend of Tommy's is a friend of mine,' he said.

And that was that.

Back at the office, we met with the bosses for a full debrief and gave them everything Williams had given us. We wrote up our notes from the meeting into statements, which were handed to the bosses.

And pretty much after that it was business as usual. Dave and I were lucky. We had an informer called Terry Hodson who was providing us with enough information to keep us busy, and our other investigations also kept us on the hop.

There was a spillover of paranoia that I inherited. Since the squad had been targeted ruthlessly by the Ethical Standards Department, the MDID began doing things a little differently to protect itself. One thing they did was to bypass the ISIS computer system used by the Victoria Police. What you were supposed to do was type in information about jobs you did or information you received, and that could be accessed by other people in other squads. Because the MDID was paranoid about ESD second guessing their investigations, detectives decided not to make it easy for the toecutters. A lot of information was not, therefore, added into the system.

Information about Terry Hodson was a prime example.

CHAPTER 6

Terry Hodson

Terence Bernard Hodson was born in 1947 in Wombourne in England. With two brothers and two sisters, he was the youngest of five children. Christine Hodson was born two years after him in the same town. She too came from a family of five kids. Terry and Christine married in 1967 and had three children of their own: Mandy in 1967, Andrew in 1969 and Nicola in 1971. Three years after Nicola was born, the Hodson family immigrated to Australia in 1974. They lived in Western Australia before finally moving to Melbourne in 1986. Six years later, Terry and Christine began renting the house in Harp Road, Kew, and lived there until someone murdered them in the TV room on 16 May 2004.

Terry Hodson had prior convictions for trafficking in drugs, armed robbery, dishonesty and firearms offences. Add to this a strong desire to be in the thick of things and it meant that he made a really good police informer.

•

As soon as I had set up my desk at the MDID, Sergeant Graeme Sayce did the official handover. Sayce was an incredible worker – first one at work, last one to leave – and a fair cop to boot. Sayce told me that Dave Miechel had an informer who would keep us both busy.

And that was when I first met Terry Hodson.

Dave and Sayce and his entire crew and I met at a pub. There were about eight or ten of us in a private room. Right from the start I was a little worried, wondering why Graeme and Dave weren't keeping Terry more secret. Gossip and the police force go together like steak and chips. Some of the people at the pub dinner were only at the MDID on short secondments and would leave the squad knowing about Terry and his undercover informing.

Over dinner, I got the impression that Terry Hodson was someone who could hold court. He was an amiable guy and I could see how everyone had become friends with him.

This was a first for me, and I wondered if this was how the MDID operated – by becoming dinner buddies with their informers. A part of me found this really weird, but then another part of me thought, *You're in the big squad now; this is how things are done.* But I admit it felt odd because, ordinarily, the only time we got intel from crooks was when they were sitting on the bad side of the interview table and were using knowledge as a bargaining chip.

While Terry held court I studied him. He certainly didn't look like any drug dealer I'd met before. For starters, he was much older. At fifty-six, Terry had clearly survived the treacherous waters of dealing and consuming drugs, and he was obviously high on something during the dinner. He also seemed to have a bottomless glass of scotch.

Christine Hodson was at the dinner too. She was a small woman who seemed happy to sit quietly by her husband's side. When Terry introduced his wife, he told me that she came everywhere with him. His flamboyance was balanced by her quietness. Both of the Hodsons had pronounced English accents. Christine was small and pretty, and Terry looked like a tradie in going-out clothes.

I walked away from the dinner and went back to the office to find out more about Terry Hodson and the information he provided which had warranted such a friendly relationship. And that was when I found out that what Graeme Sayce had said was true: Terry Hodson would keep our squad of two very busy. Very busy indeed.

But when I looked through the files to find out how Terry was assisting us, alarm bells went off in my head. Some of what I read was bumbling Keystone Cops stuff. Terry would dob in drug dealers and then they would be arrested on the way to his house or just after they'd been there to buy drugs. I could very clearly see that all roads were leading to Terry.

I didn't know whether it was the thrill of the catch or the easy pinch, but the people who were working with Hodson seemed blind to the fact that his life was in danger. Coming from the Homicide Squad, I was well aware of the propensity for people in the drug industry to kill each other. I'd also seen it at Lorimer when we looked at Radev. I wondered if anyone before me had had serious concerns about Terry Hodson's safety.

In the files, there were so many similar stories that I knew it was only a matter of time before the dealers started to see the very exposed common denominator. And even if the crooks were too dumb to see it, their barristers would ask the right questions to identify Hodson sooner or later.

Who knew you were doing a buy?
Terry Hodson.
Whose house had you just left?
Terry Hodson's.
Who did you buy the drugs from?
Terry Hodson.

Over several months I watched the situation carefully. I got to know Terry and Christine, and could see the patterns that I had read about in the files. I approached my senior sergeant, Jim O'Brien, and told him of my concerns. Part of what I was worried about were the daily phone calls from Terry to Dave Miechel. Terry was treating us like his own private detectives. We would be up in the bush staking out a clandestine lab and Miechel's phone would ring – it would be Terry telling us that he was trying to source bigger and better deals. We would sit there and shake our heads. Here we were in the country waiting for some drug dealer to show up and we could be back in Melbourne catching the sitting ducks that Terry was all too willing to line up for us.

While I realised the attractiveness of this for our arrest rate, I knew that the people he was giving us weren't going to take this lying down. The more Terry craved the action, the bigger the fish he offered us. Our hauls were huge and his information was putting some big names behind bars.

But, for all this, Terry and Christine Hodson seemed like nice people and I worried for them. In my meeting with Jim O'Brien, I told him that even though Terry was an incredible resource for our office, he would soon be a dead resource because of the way he was being managed. We agreed that if he was handled correctly, Hodson could continue to provide us with good intel.

O'Brien asked for my take on what the situation was. I told him about dealers being arrested going to and from Hodson's house. Terry's informer number was cropping up on court documents. I told him about my recent court visit, when barrister Nicola Gobbo was asking who informer 4/390 might be. Many of her clients were arrested on drugs charges, and informer 4/390 – Terry Hodson – was the common factor. Gobbo was the predominant lawyer working for clients charged with major drug-related offences, so of course she was bound to make the connections.

In those early days in court, Nicola Gobbo was an Amazonian figure. Her short skirts, exposed cleavage, and long, blonde hair stood out in courtrooms dominated by men in dark suits. She was confident and professional and easy to talk to. She certainly told you how things were; she laid her cards on the table. Nicola Gobbo came to our Major Drug Investigation Division offices a lot, speaking to her clients and horsetrading with us. She seemed to love the limelight that came with dealing with both the major criminals and the detectives who caught them.

At one of our pub nights in South Melbourne, Nicola Gobbo turned up. We all got well and truly wasted. Nicola drove us to the casino in her tiny Mercedes coupé piled high with drunken detectives. We hit the Heat nightclub and kept drinking beer.

The next thing I knew, it was morning. I woke up in her bed feeling very ordinary. Beer and guilt is a bad combination. I was a married man. Nicola was lying naked next to me. I had no recollection of anything between the nightclub and the twenty pots of beer I probably drank, and waking up. I didn't know how I got to her place. I had no memory of what we'd done, but I assumed we'd had sex. Both of us were feeling very seedy and probably still half drunk. After that our contact changed from being adversarial and a rapport developed, even though we never repeated our one drunken mistake.

When Nicola came into the St Kilda Road MDID offices, she would seek out me or any of the sergeants because she needed to talk to people of rank. My dealings with her grew in frequency, because by using Terry Hodson's prolific information we were making frequent arrests.

Nicola also had contact with detectives at Ethical Standards because some of her clients had given information against corrupt police. When the detectives from the old drug squad had corruption allegations levelled against them, Nicola would march her clients off to bail hearings and tell the court that because of allegations of police corruption her clients might not come to trial for years and should, therefore, be granted bail. The courts agreed and the crooks were often let out on bail. Carl Williams, Lewis Moran and Tony Mokbel were some of the infamous underworld figures who benefited from this glitch.

Mokbel's bail applications were a masterstroke of legal work. Nicola Gobbo and her colleagues – in a great legal twist – used Inspector Peter De Santo from Ethical Standards to assist in her case to get Mokbel *out of jail*. De Santo was subpoenaed by Mokbel's lawyers because he had charged two drug squad cops before my time, in 2001. Mokbel's lawyers used De Santo to show that the arrests might cause unacceptable delays in their client's court case.

Gobbo and other lawyers acting for Mokbel had made a number of applications to get him released on bail. Finally, in September 2002, because of the delays caused by the drug squad upheaval, the judge finally came to this conclusion:

'The community will not tolerate the indefinite detention of its citizens with no prospect of charges being tried within a reasonable period. Accordingly, despite the nature of the offences with which the applicant is charged, and despite the serious reservations that I have expressed about the granting of bail, the situation facing the applicant cannot be allowed to exist indefinitely. For those reasons I propose to grant bail subject to strict conditions.'

So it was that in the pursuit of cops, big-time crooks were released.

Of course, Mokbel would use his freedom to scarper to the greener pastures and sunny climes of Greece, but that would come later.

•

At first, crooks and their lawyers merely took advantage of the problems in the drug squad, but it quickly morphed into something more sinister – captured crooks would allege police corruption in order to try to get bail. It seemed to us that every couple of weeks another one would be released on allegations of police corruption.

Terry Hodson was aware of our frustration; it upset him as well. He felt just as let down because he had helped put some of these crooks away. One crook who Terry helped us arrest was let out, then went round to Terry's place and threw a bottle at his house. I think he'd realised that he'd been caught twice after doing a deal with Terry, and the older man's denials of any involvement were beginning to sound hollow.

Once Nicola Gobbo started asking if Terry Hodson was informer 4/390, Jim O'Brien and I talked.

'They're gonna find out who he is and he's going to be killed,' I told O'Brien.

He agreed.

We both arranged a meeting with Hodson to discuss our concerns. We didn't want to do it in the office or at any of his favourite restaurants where I had seen crooks walk past all us cops dining with him. One crook had even stopped and given us the evil eye. These kinds of connections were the most dangerous. Despite the plain clothes, most crooks could spot a cop a mile off. Just like we could spot them.

For the meeting we hired a conference room at a nondescript suburban motel. Jim, Terry and I met at the motel – Dave Miechel had been invited to attend but he had been disgruntled at what he saw as our interference.

'Mate, there was an original agreement with him,' he snapped.

'I want you to be a part of this,' I told him. 'His safety is the whole issue here. I'm not saying that we're going to stop working with him, but if we keep going the way we're going, he's in danger.'

'Then I'm not having anything to do with it,' Dave said abruptly.

I mentally rolled my eyes. I couldn't understand why he didn't want to be part of the bigger picture. It wasn't just about him and Terry. To me, Terry's safety needed to be the first consideration and nobody seemed to feel the same way. I was grateful that at least Jim O'Brien had acknowledged my concerns straightaway.

Not only did Dave not attend the meeting, he went on immediate leave. He certainly seemed to resent the fact that I was stepping in and changing the way things were run. But I think it went deeper than that: it was like he felt a certain ownership of Terry.

Inside the conference room, we used a whiteboard to create a comprehensive picture of what Terry was doing for us. The big picture was no surprise to me – but I think the complex web of names and connections opened Jim O'Brien's eyes to the enormity of Terry Hodson's involvement in our jobs.

I had briefed Jim on the way to the meeting about how much Terry *wanted* to help us, but it was a catch-22 situation: you want the arrests and you want to stop the big drug deals, and in front of you sits this likeable guy, champing at the bit to help, but he is ultimately in grave danger *because* he's helping us.

We told Terry that while we appreciated his help, we didn't want to put him in any more jeopardy than was absolutely necessary. We also told him that we wanted to keep him a couple of steps away from the action; the buy–bust method was just plain dangerous. We would do one job at a time and take it through to the end.

By the close of the meeting, we told Terry we would change his informer number to give him a break from appearing in too many briefs. We assured him that his safety was paramount. I think Terry was relieved to be pulled back a bit too.

Contrary to popular belief, Terry wasn't paid for what he was doing – except for when I lobbied to get him a small payment after a number of successful busts had sent a few good crooks to jail. Terry was one out of the box: he informed on everyone – his family, friends, colleagues. No one was off limits, except maybe his wife.

Some suggested he was in it to get rid of his opposition. Maybe. But one thing that should be remembered: Terry Hodson was operating his own drug-dealing business with a complete green light from the Victoria Police. While he was helping us, dining out with detectives, and hobnobbing with the police hierarchy, he was also in possession of his own get-out-of-jail-free card. He was given the green light and the protection to carry out his business with the police on his side. To a guy who'd been dodging police most of his adult life, and who had done jail time, this had to be an attractive proposition.

When Dave went on leave I had to handle brief after brief where Terry was the informer. It was to protect Terry that we kept his paperwork out of the system by typing our information reports into a computer that was not connected to the network. Every time we spoke to Terry or met with him, we duly typed out an IR. Every time we printed the report, the computer automatically printed three copies. We gave one to Jim O'Brien, we put one in a blue folder and we shredded the third copy.

Once, I asked why we were doing it this way and was told that the squad didn't want Ethical Standards knowing all our business. Some of my bosses had come from ESD and endorsed using this standalone system, so I figured that it was okay.

Graeme Sayce would later explain this in his statement. 'At some stage, I believe in early 2002, I was advised by Detective Senior Sergeant O'Brien, that an analysis of the Intel Manage database was insecure and able to be accessed by many outside persons. Miechel and I were instructed to compile the information reports directly as a Word document and file the information report with Detective Senior Sergeant O'Brien for the inclusion in the informer management file. The informer management file was retained secured within the detective senior sergeant's office.'

•

When the proverbial later hit the fan, higher-ranking cops documented their concerns about the relationship between Dave Miechel and Terry Hodson, but these concerns were never as big as the concerns for Terry's safety. Jim O'Brien would say that he had warned Miechel about the formation of any inappropriate relationships and reminded him of the need for professionalism, but if this happened I wasn't aware of it. Once I became his handler too, Terry Hodson didn't ring Miechel more than he rang me, and O'Brien wouldn't have known how often Hodson rang anyone.

One thing that I also insisted on was that Terry should be paid for his informing. I asked for $25000 – which was about $5000 for each of the large-scale jobs that had resulted in big hauls and big arrests. The minute I put the paperwork in, things got more official and Victoria Police agreed to pay him a smaller amount.

On 23 July 2003, Inspector Adrian White and I drove to Albert Park Lake and met Terry in a car park. He jumped into the back seat of our car and White handed Terry a thick envelope containing $10000.

'Thanks!' said Terry, clearly chuffed – not at the amount of cash, which would probably seem like small change to him, but at the official recognition of what he was likely increasingly seeing as an adrenaline-fuelled vocation. In fact, having barely put the envelope down the front of his overalls, he began talking about another job. He was impressed that Adrian White was an inspector and off he went.

'I know you all are really busy and I've been trying to get Dave and Paul involved – I know a guy who's bringing in blocks of cocaine —'

'Come on, Terry, remember what we agreed,' I said.

Terry ignored me and talked straight to the inspector. 'If you can just get the boys organised, we can —'

Adrian White raised his hand. 'One job at a time, Terry. One job at a time.'

•

Prior to my arrival at the MDID, one of the jobs ran into a snag when the brass wouldn't authorise payment for a big purchase of ecstasy tablets. The squad had asked for around $25 000 to make a buy of 1000 tablets with a street value of $50 000, but the money wasn't available.

Unwilling to let the deal slide, Terry offered to pay for the drugs himself. This had been okayed. I think Terry paid around $22 000 of his own money to buy the tablets. He then ordered another 3000. The crook he bought them from, Jayson Rodda, had been pinched as a result when the MDID arrested him in possession of the second lot of drugs.

A part of Terry Hodson's longevity had something to do with his people skills. He had the charm to convince everyone that he was their best friend. Terry was able to convince Jayson Rodda that he had nothing to do with dobbing him in.

When I was reviewing the Hodson folders of information, I wondered at the whereabouts of the 1000 tablets – an amount that legally constituted a commercial quantity and carried a life sentence in jail. Also an amount that far overstepped Terry's police indemnity. Under Section 51 of the *Drugs, Poisons and*

Controlled Substances Act, he was authorised to buy no more than a 'small' amount of illegal drugs for the sole purpose of a dedicated investigation.

Here we were, managing Hodson, and the drug squad had let him buy a commercial quantity of drugs – *and he still had them.* I wanted to handle this delicately because I was aware that Terry had used his own money to help the squad, and we didn't want to jeopardise our ongoing relationship.

At our next meeting with Terry, I asked him if he still had the 1000 ecstasy tablets.

'Yeah, sure,' he said. 'I've got them at home.'

'Hold onto them,' I told him.

'I've got a bloke that I can set up with them —'

'No,' I said, shaking my head. 'Just hold onto them. It's a commercial quantity, Terry. Your immunity only gives you the right to buy small amounts. A thousand tablets would put you in jail forever.'

Terry always knew when he was offering something we didn't want, and shrugged. I told him I would find out what we could do about his tablets.

Back at the offices at MDID, Dave and I went in to see a more senior officer. I briefed him about our current operations then flagged the issue of Hodson's 1000 ecstasy tablets.

'Go get them off him,' he said.

'Er … but the problem is that he paid for them with his own money.'

The officer was fully aware of the value of Terry's information and none of us wanted to lose him as an informer. He hesitated.

'Can't we just pay him what he paid for them and destroy the drugs?' I asked.

'Hmm,' said officer.

We discussed some scenarios where the Victoria Police could benefit without having to pay for the drugs. The officer suggested Terry onsell them and we could arrest the people who bought them from him. I strongly disagreed. This had happened too often and if we arrested everyone who bought drugs from

Terry, but Terry remained free and unarrested, surely the crooks themselves would put two and two together.

Finally, the officer told us to tell Terry to onsell the drugs and just get rid of them. We were also instructed to forget this conversation ever took place and not record the meeting in our diaries.

But it's hard to forget a conversation like that.

As the senior officer later told the Royal Commission, he did agree for Terry to onsell the drugs on the understanding that he made no profit on the sale and the decision was formally documented by another senior officer. He also denied telling us to forget the conversation.

So there you go.

Terry took it all in his stride. He was happy to onsell the drugs, but he was a little disappointed that they wouldn't be used to make more arrests. Silly bugger. He never showed any concerns for the consequences of what he was doing. This might have had something to do with his frequent snorting of cocaine and drinking of scotch.

To Terry, it was the thrill of the involvement; it was never about the money. You only had to meet him a couple of times to know that. To this day, I don't really understand what his motivation was. He certainly didn't fit the criteria of a normal informer – to have someone so willing to provide information so that he could feel like part of the team. He was an extraordinary man, using his own money and his own drugs to ensure that we got arrests. When we weren't working with him on a job he would constantly call us, and he knew how to press the right buttons. If we weren't interested in a small ecstasy bust, he'd immediately offer us a bigger bust. It was certainly a gift for the MDID – one that Victoria Police is unlikely to see again.

I get that Terry wanted to be part of the action – most cops join the force for the same reason. But the bit that I don't get was that he was willing to give up anyone, including his own kids and his best friends and his favourite associates. He didn't care. Anyone was fair game.

And I had to wonder if Christine knew and was okay with her husband dobbing in their kids. She seemed like a really caring woman. Did she know and approve? Or did Terry keep her in the dark?

So it was more than just being a frustrated would-be cop.

•

One day, Dave Miechel and I met with Jim O'Brien and discussed the possibility of getting Terry to introduce an undercover police officer into some of the operations we were running. The purpose of this was to move Terry a further step behind the action. If there was an undercover operative, the officer could do the deals and get named in the subpoenas rather than Terry. Or one undercover could introduce another so that if links were made, one cop would be pointing at another, rather than at Terry.

While O'Brien agreed, Dave was against the idea because he said that Terry's identity would be disclosed if he had to appear in court. This was an overreaction on Dave's part. We never would have allowed Terry to be named in court – that was the purpose of the undercover operatives. But Dave, who had nurtured Terry as a police informer, was upset to think that O'Brien and I would introduce a new element into what he and Terry had previously agreed on.

We decided to ask Terry; he agreed with Dave – he did not want to disclose his identity and did not want to give evidence in court, even though we told him this would never happen.

Dave was incredibly protective of Terry. It was bred into cops that if you had a good informer, you looked after them. While it was a little bit frustrating, Dave was only acting on policy. You had an informer, you kept them secret, and you guarded them. And they were yours.

•

Such was his desire to be in the thick of things, Terry Hodson was happy to talk to any cops. Most informers would only talk to one or two cops because they didn't want it to be widely known that they were informers. Terry wasn't like that. When Dave Miechel went on leave I would take, as per protocol, another member with me to meet Terry and he would be as open and friendly with the new cop as he was with Dave and me.

At times, I wondered about him. It was like he felt part of the MDID family. He hated being ignored, and would always offer us bigger, better and brighter to get our attention. One thing we did realise was that while there was mostly truth in what he told us, things were never quite as grand as he made them out to be. A classic example of this was his frequent promise of a big cocaine bust. Because large seizures of cocaine were rare at a state police level, we always followed his information, but it would take me a year of working with Terry to realise that for as many times as he commanded our full attention with the promise of a big bust, not one lead ever panned out and we never made one cocaine arrest.

After a while, I began to wonder if he was actually protecting his sources because he was such a prolific cocaine user, and that he promised us cocaine because he wanted to keep our attention firmly and squarely on him.

And he always knew exactly what to offer to get that result.

We rarely met at Terry's house. It was a no-go zone because he had drug dealers and buyers calling by. We didn't want to bump into any nefarious characters. That's not to say we never went to his house in Kew. We occasionally went there – two or three times that I can think of – to debrief after an operation. We usually met at Romeo's on Toorak Road, or in little coffee shops we tried to vary so as not to put him in danger. I always tried to keep the meetings to twenty minutes because the longer we were together the more dangerous it was for him. Some meetings lasted ten minutes if he was only handing over drug samples he'd bought. After we were spotted in Toorak Road by a crook, we began going further afield. A location that I suggested was a café called the Boathouse, because it was kind of hidden. It was also convenient to both the St Kilda Road police complex and Terry's place in Kew.

At all times, there were supposed to be two cops when we met with Terry. Despite this, Dave Miechel began to break the rules.

CHAPTER 7

Little Tommy goes to trial

It took about a year for Tommy Ivanovic's murder case to come to trial. Tommy's barrister, Robert Richter, one of the top criminal lawyers, flagged a claim of self-defence. After the road-rage incident, the L-plater motorcyclist had followed Tommy to his home and a scuffle had broken out. Tommy later said that he shot the unarmed man in self-defence. He said that he lived in fear of his life.

One day, a detective from the Homicide Squad approached me and asked if Tommy had ever told me of any threats made against him.

No, I told the detective, Little Tommy never said anything to me about being in danger – but the conversation reminded me of the incident in the pub where the guy had called Tommy a dead man walking. I told the detective but explained that I didn't take the threat seriously at the time, and nothing had changed in the meantime to make me think any differently. Nonetheless, I was asked to make a formal statement and include the threat. The pub owner, who had been standing with me at the time of the dead-man-walking comment, corroborated my story.

The Homicide detectives weren't happy: here was a cop who could potentially provide the defence with some corroboration that there *were* threats against Tommy Ivanovic.

To counterbalance this, the detectives wanted me to name Tommy as a police informer in my statement. They knew that if I did this, Tommy and his lawyers would never use my statement in court. If it came out that Tommy was an informer – a 'dog', in prison parlance – it would be dangerous for him.

I flatly refused to add it to my statement for two reasons.

First, Tommy had never *agreed* to become an informer – I had put him down as one in the hope of getting intel out of him, and he never even knew. Second, if Tommy was outed as an informer it could get him killed.

I wrote my statement and made it very clear I didn't consider the threat at the pub a serious one, then or now. I was called into the Office of Public Prosecutions and questioned by a senior detective and senior prosecutor over that bit of my statement.

'But that basically gives him an out!' the prosecutor said.

I shrugged. 'It's the truth,' I replied, in the mistaken belief that the truth was the right thing.

'But why are you only saying this now?' he asked.

'Hey mate, no one's asked until now,' I said. 'Homicide came to me. I never knew anything about this.'

When the murder happened I had rung a mate at Homicide and told him that I had registered Tommy as an informer. At the time the detective told me that because the whole thing was caught on film, they wouldn't need a statement from me. No worries, I said.

I explained all of this to the OPP guy but I sensed that all was not well. I had left a senior prosecutor and a senior detective behind, looking very upset. Next thing I knew, Ethical Standards detectives were down in the Homicide Squad copying all my records. Gossip being what it is in the police force, I heard almost immediately, but I shrugged it off. I knew I had done nothing wrong, and knew they wouldn't find anything. Even so, I knew I'd shot myself in the foot career-wise by refusing to do what was asked where Little Tommy was concerned. But there was an integrity line I would never cross. I sat down with Superintendent Tony Biggin and told him what was happening. He told me not to put in the statement that Tommy was an informer.

'And if the guy threatened him in the pub, that's what happened,' said Biggin.

'It's not going to make them happy,' I told him.

'Well,' the superintendent shrugged.

While Little Tommy's barrister, Robert Richter, wanted to meet with me, I didn't feel comfortable meeting with the defence, and in the end I wasn't called as a witness on either side. But this whole incident was later spun in the media in an article in *The Age* on 29 May 2010 by Andrew Rule, Chris Johnston and Nick McKenzie. In it they wrote: 'Dale's statement raised doubts and for the first time his reputation was publicly called into question. He was deemed an "unreliable witness".'

They also said that my 'secret was unravelling'.

This article was so typical of what the media did with my story. What is really difficult for me and my family is that the public have no context and no background to read it in any other way.

But I race ahead of myself.

It's probably worth adding something here that came up at the 2019 Royal Commission in a statement by Assistant Commissioner Neil Paterson. While this wasn't on my radar at the time, it is worth a mention.

Paterson detailed the long years of participation Nicola Gobbo had in operations run by the Victoria Police. He wrote that in mid 2003, Nicola was briefed to appear at a bail application for Lewis Moran but told police that Tony Mokbel and Carl Williams had told her she was not to act for him. Despite their warning, she did, and Moran got bail. The next week, Nicola was threatened by Carl's mate Benji Veniamin. Undeterred, a week later she was back in court for Lewis Moran.

If Mokbel and Williams thought their lawyer was there to do their bidding, they were sorely mistaken.

CHAPTER 8

Operation Galop

One job that we began at the MDID that had nothing to do with Terry Hodson was codenamed Operation Galop. It began in June 2003. The purpose of the operation was to investigate the manufacture and trafficking of ecstasy tablets on a large scale. The prime target of Operation Galop was a crook called Azzam Ahmed. He and some others were buying large quantities of ecstasy from a New South Wales–based Israeli group and they were cutting down the tablets and selling them in Victoria. Later, we found out that Tony Mokbel was also involved in this operation.

The primary investigator for Operation Galop was a new recruit to our squad, Senior Constable Samantha Jennings. Sam Jennings had just begun her very first detective position with me at the MDID. I think she came from a policing background, and right from the start she was clearly an efficient operator. I recognised in her all the attributes of a good detective. She had a great work ethic and took to every task with vigour and enthusiasm.

We all went away on one of those team-building rope-climbing trips somewhere near the Grampians. Dave Miechel didn't go. He rarely socialised with the squad. Sam really held her own and was a great asset to the team.

It was for this reason that I gave her control of Operation Galop. Sam's job was to monitor the phone intercepts and keep us updated on what our targets were doing. My faith in Sam was justified: she put her heart and soul into the operation.

In July, we became aware of a pill press that had been collected by our targets and taken to an address in Clayton South. We had executed a covert warrant on the address and found that the pill press was being kept on a trailer on the property. We didn't have the resources to monitor the house all the time, and a day after we'd located it, covert surveillance found that the pill press had been moved. Luckily, our surveillance on other targets involved in the operation helped us find it again.

Bit by bit, Operation Galop chipped away at the supply chain. On 15 August, detectives in New South Wales arrested an Israeli national who had met with Azzam Ahmed in Clayton. The Israeli was carrying $218 500 in cash after the meeting. It was in order to distance the arrest geographically from Operation Galop that it occurred in New South Wales. That meant we could continue following Ahmed around Melbourne and keep our leg of the investigation going.

By 25 August we had identified a likely safe house in Dublin Street, East Oakleigh, that was 'babysat' by a young woman we'll call Tayluh Jones. The old-fashioned red clinker-brick house looked like it might contain a set of grandparents rather than a drug stash. Drug houses often had babysitters so that they were never empty. Surveillance told us that Tayluh Jones took her responsibilities seriously and stayed at the house all the time; this meant that we couldn't make a covert entry to plant listening devices.

Instead, we monitored the phones of those involved, and installed a camera at a nearby house which gave us a view of who was coming and going from the address. In a house around the corner we set up another recording device. A civic-minded resident let us have a key to his house and once a day one of our members would go in and change the tape.

While Terry Hodson didn't have anything do with the Dublin Street house, there was one connection that came out later: Tayluh Jones had supplied ecstasy tablets to a crook known as Lucky Pantelopoulos and Terry had bought some of the tabs from Lucky. Aside from this, Terry should have known nothing about our surveillance of the Dublin Street house.

Over time, we found out that large amounts of ecstasy tablets were being moved from Sydney to Melbourne and around $600000 or more had changed hands. Azzam Ahmed usually chartered light aircraft from Moorabbin Airport to make his transactions. On 11 September 2003 Ahmed's girlfriend drove to Sydney with a large sum of money, to buy 20000 ecstasy tablets. We were monitoring her the whole way.

On Friday, 26 September, things came to a head in the investigation of Azzam Ahmed. Even though we were not ready to raid, we were preparing the warrants because we knew that his girlfriend was planning to fly to Sydney on either Sunday or Monday to collect the ecstasy tablets.

At 1.30 p.m. on the Friday, I spoke to Acting Superintendent John Shawyer and told him that we had received word of a telephone intercept which suggested that Azzam Ahmed himself was going to travel to New South Wales on either Sunday or Monday. But by then I'd lost count of the amount of times Ahmed had talked of going to Sydney then hadn't gone, so nothing was cast in stone.

Intelligence said that he would carry between $600000 and $700000 to buy 50000 to 60000 ecstasy tablets. It was only an educated guess, since we did not know exactly how much he was paying per tablet with such large quantities. And we always had to take into account the code that drug dealers used when they talked to each other. A conversation about horse racing with a particular horse in race 5 might actually mean 5000 ecstasy tablets.

There had been a bit of interstate disagreement between our squad and the NSW Drug Squad. We wanted them to conduct surveillance on the deal just like they had the week before, then let our targets return to Melbourne, where we could arrest them ourselves.

Our investigation, our arrests.

But the NSW Drug Squad had other plans: they told us they would make the arrests in New South Wales. Our squad was devastated after working three solid months on this one case.

Ideally, we wanted to conclude the operation catching Azzam Ahmed red-handed in the Dublin Street house punching out pills.

The NSW decision didn't go down well with our force command, either. I got approval for me and Sam Jennings to go to Sydney to participate in the arrest when the time came. At least we would get to play a small part in the end of our operation and fly the flag for the Victoria Police.

•

Around 4 p.m. on Friday, 26 September 2003, Dave Miechel dropped me home in the work car. I had to pick up my baby son from crèche and was off for the rest of the evening on bottle-and-bath duty. Unless I was away on a police trip, I was on baby duty most nights. My wife had returned to work not long after our son was born. She put her name down with an on-call nursing bank for evenings, since I worked during the day. My wife and I had the same work ethic, and we were both keen to pay off our mortgage as soon as we could.

Dave returned to work to finish the briefs with the rest of the squad. We all knew that the next couple of days would be important.

Little did we know that they would change the lives of some of us forever.

•

On the morning of Saturday, 27 September, I spoke to Superintendent Shawyer and told him that the telephone intercepts had contained no new information about Azzam Ahmed's trip to Sydney, so we were all a bit in limbo.

Even though I wasn't rostered on, I kept abreast of the situation. I was taking a well-earned break to host my annual AFL Grand Final BBQ. I set up my backyard with a TV and a keg, and had the BBQ fired up and ready to sizzle snags and steak. Salads at the ready, eskies full of ice cradling stubbies and cans. My wife and I had invited around thirty people, a mixture of police and non-police friends along with their wives and kids. The only difference between this Grand Final barbie and those I'd held previously was that this time I limited myself to one beer every couple of hours, just in case I was called into work. But I was hopeful that the day would be quiet, because there had been no updates.

If I got to the end of the night sober and nothing happened with the job, I figured the worst that could happen was that I'd be a little annoyed to miss a big drinking day.

•

Around 11 a.m. on the Saturday morning I sent Sam Jennings a text to ask who was changing the tapes at the surveillance house. She texted a reply: 'Miech is mate'. Sam normally did it, but it was fine that she had allocated Dave Miechel to do it. I thought nothing of it.

Around midday, after some of our guests had arrived, Dave Miechel unexpectedly knocked on my door. He told me what I already knew – that he would be changing the surveillance tapes – and asked if I needed the work car, or did I just want him to come over in the morning – Sunday morning – to pick me up.

I invited him in for a drink, but he said that his girlfriend was in the car and he didn't want to stop. I could see the white Holden Jackaroo from work parked in my driveway, but I couldn't see who was sitting inside it. Normally, I would have craned my neck to get a look at the mystery girlfriend, but with a houseful of guests I had other things on my mind.

Dave and I made plans for him to pick me up the following morning at 9.30 a.m. Our crew was scheduled to work the next day, and I had to be ready to fly to Sydney at a moment's notice for the arrests.

My footy team wasn't playing in the Grand Final but I picked Brisbane over Collingwood for a win – mostly because it was fun to stir my mates who were silly enough to barrack for Collingwood. Of course, being the typical Aussie barbie, the guys were outside while the women largely ignored the game on TV and sat around chatting inside.

I stayed sober while all my mates were downing beer after beer and getting louder and louder. As much as I enjoyed my day off, I occasionally checked my phone for updates on the operation. At this crucial stage of an investigation, it was hard to totally switch off from work.

When a phone call came, it was one that would change everything. It dropped like a big fat stone in a pond, sending out ripples far and wide.

CHAPTER 9

The Oakleigh robbery

Just after 8 p.m. on Saturday, 27 September 2003, I got a phone call from Dave Miechel. By this stage, the footy was over and some of the BBQ crowd had thinned out, but the stalwarts were still at my house.

'There's been an incident out here,' Dave said.

'Out where?' I asked, not understanding.

'Near our target address.'

'What's happened?' As far as I knew, the only thing he had to do was change the surveillance tapes around the corner from Dublin Street, and I thought he was doing that much earlier in the day.

That was when he told me he was in an ambulance and being taken to hospital.

'Are you okay?'

'Yeah,' he said in a voice not far from his normal voice. 'I've been attacked by the police dog and hit by the handler.'

What? I couldn't take in what he was saying. 'How did it happen?'

'I had changed the tapes earlier and I was checking things out on my way past. I saw a div van and offenders running. I gave chase and was attacked by the dog.'

Because Dave sounded okay, my next concern was whether whatever had happened at the house had compromised our operation. I told him I would head straight to the hospital to see him.

I immediately rang the Glen Waverley police. They would be the ones dealing with whatever had gone down at the Dublin Street house. The senior sergeant I spoke to told me that Dave Miechel was being taken to Epworth Hospital. I told him about the MDID interest in the Dublin Street house. The senior sergeant couldn't really clarify what had happened there.

The Brisbane Lions' fifty-point victory over Collingwood quickly forgotten, I phoned the special projects unit who had been keeping an eye on the intercepts, to see if there was any update in the movement of our targets. I then rang my immediate boss, Senior Sergeant Garry Barker, to tell him that something had gone down at the Dublin Street house. I told him that I would head off to Epworth Hospital to check on Dave.

On my way to the hospital I got another call from the senior sergeant from Glen Waverley I had spoken to earlier. He told me something that took a moment to sink in.

Two males had been arrested at the Dublin Street house who were believed to have been involved in a burglary there.

One was Terry Hodson. The other was Dave Miechel.

Holy shit.

What the hell was going on?

After that call was over, I barely had time to process it before calls flooded in from the special projects unit. Their telephone intercepts confirmed that there had been a break-in at the Dublin Street house. I couldn't believe that our three-month operation had been compromised.

Could there have been some kind of mistake? Had Dave just stuffed up and gone out there with Terry? Or had Dave's story been true – that he had seen people being chased away from the Dublin Street house and had joined the chase? But if that was true, what the hell was Terry doing there? And what was Dave doing there at this time of the night?

Around 9 p.m., I got to the hospital but wasn't allowed to see Dave straightaway. It took a couple of phone calls and liaison between my office and Glen Waverley before I finally saw a battered and bloody Dave Miechel. He looked like he had been severely beaten. One side of his face was black and blue and swollen. One eye was puffy and closed. He was covered in dried blood.

'Are you okay?' Dumb question – he looked shocking.

'Been better,' he said in a voice thick with painkilling medication.

'What happened?' I asked him. 'Were you changing the tapes?'

'No, I changed them earlier. I dropped in on the way past to check things out.'

Dave seemed barely conscious, and no doubt because he was clearly medicated to the eyeballs he didn't seem to be feeling the pain of the injuries, the looks of which made me wince. I couldn't believe that a member of my own crew could do what the Glen Waverley cops were accusing him of; nonetheless, I knew he was in a world of shit and that he was going to be grilled by people much higher up the pay scale than me. And in his condition, I wasn't going to add to that. My job as his immediate boss was to check on his welfare. Anything else I couldn't help with.

I didn't want to keep him talking any longer. He obviously needed to sleep, but I couldn't help myself. 'I have to go back to the office to see what's going on. How did you get all those injuries?'

'Dog Squad,' he muttered.

'Take it easy. I'll see you later.'

On the way out, I passed the nurses' station to get an update on Dave's physical condition. A nurse told me that his injuries were severe and that he would need surgery. From what I had seen, I wasn't surprised. Apparently, when the police dog caught him Dave had struggled and the handler had brought him down with a blow to the head using the police-issue Maglite torch.

As soon as I was finished at the hospital I rang Superintendent Shawyer and updated him on Dave's condition. He was at the office already, since he was working the afternoon shift. I told him that we needed to get my crew together to head straight to Dublin Street.

Then I telephoned every member of my crew I could get a hold of, telling them to meet me at the office as soon as possible to coordinate things from there. I met Superintendent Shawyer as well. We agreed we needed to execute the warrants straightaway. The next step was to ring the guy whose house we had the surveillance equipment in. The guy told me that the tape was running and that a cop called Dave had changed the tape around 1 p.m. that afternoon. I figured that Dave must have driven there straight after he called into my place around midday.

Some of us stayed at the office coordinating the search warrants while other officers led by Graeme Sayce went to the Dublin Street house to execute the search warrant.

As soon as a bunch of us had arrived at the MDID office, we held a briefing. The upshot was that we knew the Ethical Standards Department would handle Dave, but that wasn't something we could think about at length. The first thing we had to do was coordinate the warrants for a number of different people.

But still.

Had Dave Miechel committed the ultimate betrayal?

While Dave had said that he was simply checking on the drug house, the officer from the Victoria Police Dog Squad who arrested him clearly thought otherwise. According to the officer, he and some other cops were responding to a neighbour's report of a break-in. At the scene they saw a guy dressed in dark clothes and a beanie, and called for him to stop. While the arresting officer admitted that Dave had cried out that he was in the job several times, the officer said that as soon as he called off the dog, Dave tried to flee the scene.

It wasn't just Dave I was worried about, though – I was more worried about Terry. As soon as it got out that he had been arrested robbing a drug house with the MDID detective who had arrested all his mates, *everyone* would make the connection.

Once the likes of Tony Mokbel and company understood that Terry's involvement had lost them hundreds of thousands – if not millions – of dollars, he was going to be in great danger. I had done everything I could to protect him and keep his identity a secret. Now his picture would be in the paper doing the perp walk, flanked by his arresting officers.

One of the people arrested in the ensuing sweep on the night of the robbery was Tayluh Jones the drug-house babysitter. On the understanding that her statement could only be used by the Ethical Standards Department to prosecute the people charged with the Oakleigh robbery – and therefore not used against her – she described her part in the drug operations. Her lawyer was Nicola Gobbo.

She said she had lived at the Dublin Street house for about six weeks. She had leased the house from a real estate agent and moved in a couple of days later. A friend – who she refused to name – provided furnishings, and she moved her few meagre possessions and her two dogs, a Rottweiler and a Rottweiler cross, into the house.

Despite rarely leaving the house, thus thwarting our covert surveillance team, she told the detectives that she did leave the house on the Saturday night of the robbery to visit a friend in Prahran. The friend – who she also refused to name – had phoned her earlier in the day to invite her over. Around 6.30 p.m. she had left the house locked, the verandah light on and the dogs inside.

In her statement, she gave the police a long and precise list of drugs that were in the house, including 'a large quantity of ecstasy tablets ... many thousands of tablets with various colours ...', 'a large quantity of MDMA [ecstasy] powder', and elsewhere in the house, 'one kilo of Ice amphetamine and a large amount of ecstasy tablets ... white in colour and a small amount may have been green splits ... packaged in various quantities ranging from 100 to 1000 bag lots'.

●

While Dave Miechel was in hospital with a pummelled face and dog-bitten legs, Terry Hodson was taken to a holding cell at the Oakleigh police station. A little after midnight, Detective Senior Sergeant Murray Gregor from the Victoria Police Ethical Standards Department met with Terry and told him to remove his clothing, which was then collected as evidence. Terry was given the standard disposable overalls to dress himself in.

Around 2 a.m., Terry had another visitor to his cell along with Detective Senior Sergeant Murray Gregor – Detective Acting Superintendent Dick Daly. Daly informed Terry that they would talk to him after they had conducted more enquiries. They asked Terry if he wanted to contact anyone and he said that he wanted to talk to his wife but couldn't remember the phone number.

Leaving Terry in the cell, detectives Gregor and Daly spent the next three hours combing the streets around the Dublin Street drug house, getting the lie of the land before they spoke to their suspect. At the same time, Gregor used Terry's key remote to try to locate his car. Finally, they heard a blip and saw the accompanying flash of tail-lights: Terry Hodson's black BMW had been parked a few streets away, near a primary school. Inside the boot were gloves, a black balaclava, a loaded .45 calibre pistol, a holster, and a piece of cardboard that looked like a fake registration plate.

•

Just before 5 a.m. Terry Hodson was taken into the interview room at the Oakleigh police station and spoke to Senior Sergeant Murray Gregor and Acting Superintendent Dick Daly for an hour. Their interview technique was simple: Gregor and Daly would give Terry the chance to explain himself, then knock down his story piece by piece using the information they had found out from the arresting officers at the crime scene, and from the search of Terry's car.

After reading him his rights, Gregor began by asking Hodson to state his movements the previous evening. Terry peppered his story with references to police – clearly wanting Gregor and Daly to see him as one of them.

'I left at 7 o'clock … I am a registered police informer,' he began, 'paid registered police informer. And I've been working on a guy from St Kilda who called in … say roughly, 6.30.'

'Called in? What do you mean by called in?' asked Gregor.

'He called at my home there … Yeah, I've been chasing some coke for the drug squad and he came and picked me up. He said he was going out towards Chadstone there.'

'What's the name of this person?' Gregor asked.

'His name is – I call him Lucky … and Paul Dale and Dave Miechel know all about him. Also does Jim O'Brien.'

'Are these persons you're referring to now, are they members —'

'Of the drug squad,' finished Hodson.

'Okay, and the person you referred to, Lucky, do you know his correct name?'

'No,' said Terry. 'They do. They would be able to tell you.'

'And how long have you been working on Lucky?'

'Approximately three months.'

'Have you actually conducted any buys from Lucky? Any buys of drugs?'

'Yeah, yeah,' said Terry confidently. 'They've got records of those at the drug squad.'

'So what you're saying is you've been working as a paid police informer?' clarified Gregor.

'Yes,' said Terry.

'Working on Lucky?'

'Yes.'

'At the direction of members from the drug squad?'

'Yes.'

'Okay. Can you tell me who your handler is?'

'David Miechel.'

'Right. And how do you spell his name? Do you know?'

'I wouldn't have a clue,' said Terry.

'And how long have you been dealing with Dave – David Miechel?'

'Two years since I've worked for the drug squad.'

'And are you a registered informer for any other person or any other member of the police force apart from David Miechel?'

'And Paul Dale,' said Terry. 'He's the sergeant there.'

'Is it correct to say that Paul Dale and David Miechel are —'

'Partners,' finished Terry helpfully.

'And all work together?' asked Gregor.

'Yes, yes, yes,' said Terry.

'And have you actually received reports or payments of money?

'Yes.'

'From these police members?'

'Well, not actually them. But from the bosses up above.'

Terry Hodson told Gregor and Daly about the $10 000 payment a couple of months earlier in recognition for some major jobs he had helped with. He said that he had also been an informer for the Tactical Response Group. 'I've passed on a lot of information over the last two years.'

After Terry Hodson established his informer cred, the interview moved to the events of the previous evening. Terry said that Lucky had picked him up from his home in Kew and dropped him near the school around the corner from the Dublin Street house. When Gregor asked what sort of car Lucky drove, Terry Hodson said it was like a tradesman's van.

Terry pointed to the small plastic bag that was among his possessions that the detectives had laid out on the interview room desk. 'He went and got me that sample of coke there.'

'So can you tell me what actually occurred?' asked Gregor.

'Lucky's dropped me off at the school —'

'And what was the purpose of being dropped off there?'

'Apparently he's got a dealer around the area, who had got some coke. He went and got the sample, came back with it. I tested it.'

'How did you test it?'

'Snorted it,' said Terry. '... Asked him to go back and get me an ounce ... an ounce of cocaine ... so I could see it wasn't just powder. It had to be the proper thing. And he said, "Not a problem." It took him approximately – well, I don't know – fifteen to twenty minutes to get the sample ...'

'And where were you when you met this person?'

'I was in the school playground ... where I was arrested.'

'Where was Lucky when you were in the playground?'

Terry said that Lucky had left him in the playground while he went to get the sample.

'In his van?' asked Acting Superintendent Daly.

'In his van,' agreed Terry. 'Then he came back in the van. I tested it and then he left again, in the van, to go and get the ounce so that I could have a look at it which is the normal thing to do. And the next thing I know, I'm arrested.'

When Gregor asked Terry what he was going to do with the ounce, somewhat piously Terry replied that he would test it and then report back to his officers so that they could tell him the next step to take.

Gregor asked if Dale and Miechel knew about the buy and Terry said that he hadn't mentioned it because he didn't know that it was going to happen before Lucky called for him at 6.30 p.m. He assured the officers that he was covered because he had a special form to make drug purchases.

Gregor asked Terry when he had last spoken to anyone at the drug squad.

'I think it was Thursday,' said Terry. Miechel had rung him on the department-bought mobile. 'I spoke to Dave and we arranged to meet at the Boathouse. We have different locations where we meet, and I met with him and Paul.'

'And what was the meeting about?'

'About Lucky and the ecstasy tablets that he's – he's in with a crew that they're dealing in import tablets and I've been ... getting samples and letting 'em know what's what – because apparently they're working on a job ... they never tell me exactly. And I'm just told to go. "Can you buy this? Can you buy that?" And find out about this, that, and the other.'

Murray Gregor began to close in on Terry. 'So when was the last time you saw Dave Miechel?'

'Thursday.'

'Are you sure about that?'

'Yes.'

Gregor asked Terry who else at the drug squad he dealt with. Terry named a number of other police officers. Then Gregor switched back to the previous evening, once again establishing Terry's story about Lucky picking him up in the van and driving him to East Oakleigh. He got Hodson to go over his story and gave him a map of the area so that he could show where Lucky had dropped him and where he had waited.

Terry traced the route that he said Lucky had taken, coming off the Princes Highway. Terry said that he had been waiting near some sheds at the school when an officer with a dog had come his way. 'He said, "Don't move! Get on the ground!" So I did what I was told.'

'And what happened after he did that?' asked Gregor.

'He says ... "Why did you go into the house?" And I said, "What house? I don't know." And he put the handcuffs on me. Took me out the front here.' Terry pointed to the map. 'And then this other officer came in the divvy van and searched me and found the sample in my top pocket. He says, "What's this?" I said, "Cocaine." He says, "You're under arrest".'

Gregor again went over the route that Lucky had taken to drive into the area, and for the third time made Terry repeat his Lucky-dropped-me-off-at-the-school story.

'Now I notice that you weren't carrying a wallet ...' said Gregor.

'I never do,' said Terry.

'Or any money,' said Gregor, letting it sink in that a story of a drug buy from a guy who had no cash might not be kosher.

'No.'

'Any particular reason?'

'Inside my wallet is Paul and Dave's phone numbers. I just never like to carry anything with me ...'

'Do you know Paul or Dave's phone number off the top of your head?'

'No, I wouldn't. It's programmed into the phone – the work phone.'

After going back and forth over details of Terry Hodson's story, Gregor then asked him if at any time during the evening he was running or attempting to evade capture.

'No.'

'Or walking fast?'

'No.'

'Did you move from the location you were arrested at?'

Terry said that aside from relieving himself around the back of the shed, he hadn't moved more than ten metres in any direction while he waited at the school.

Gregor asked again if Terry had been in Dublin Street and Acting Superintendent Daly pointed to it on the map.

'No ... I told you where I was. I was down near the school.'

Gregor then listed a number of names of people associated with Operation Galop who were connected to the Dublin Street house. Terry denied knowing any of them.

Gregor cut to the chase. 'I put it to you that you attended at [house number] Dublin Street, Oakleigh in company with Senior Constable David Miechel and, at that – at those premises, you forced the front door in. What have you got to say about that?'

If Terry Hodson thought the two ESD cops were buying his story, he must have been surprised at this. He stammered his reply. 'Sorry? I'm – I'm not being facetious but I – I – I don't know anything. I haven't seen David Miechel.'

'I put it to you, you were, in fact, in company with David Miechel.'

'Well I'm ...'

'Last night.'

'I'm afraid I disagree with you, okay.'

Gregor persisted. 'As I said, I put it to you that you attended at [house number] Dublin Street, Oakleigh in company with Senior Constable David Miechel, last night, where the front door was kicked in. What have you got to say about that?'

'No.'

'I further put it to you that yourself, or Senior Constable Miechel, broke the porch light at [house number] Dublin Street, Oakleigh, prior to forcing the front door. What have you got to say about that?'

'No,' Terry said.

'Did you at any time last night, force entry to any of these premises?'

'No, I did not.'

Gregor repeated Terry's assertion that he was dropped off at the school by Lucky. 'I put it to you that you, in fact, got to that location by driving your BMW motor vehicle ... What have you got to say about that?'

'No comment,' Terry said, switching into crim mode.

'I put it to you that the black BMW is in fact parked currently in Oakleigh Street, Oakleigh, opposite the school where you were arrested last night. What have you got to say about that?'

'No comment.'

'And in fact, I put it to you that the keys contained in this property receipt which you earlier identified as keys belonging to you, in fact, open that vehicle which is located in Oakleigh Street. What have you got to —'

'No comment.'

Gregor showed him the wallet containing credit cards in the name of Terence Hodson.

'Yeah, that's mine,' muttered Terry.

Inside the wallet was a piece of paper with the name Dave and a mobile phone number. Terry said that the phone number belonged to Dave Miechel.

'I put it to you ... do you agree that I located this wallet and items in your motor vehicle which is located in Oakleigh Street, Oakleigh?'

'No comment.'

'When I checked the boot of the motor vehicle, there was a ... wooden partition which was partly dislodged. I removed the wooden partition and I located a pair of brown leather-type gloves and a black beanie which has got what appears to be eyes cut out of it. What can you tell me about these items?'

'No comment.'

Gregor listed all the other items that he had found in Terry's boot, behind the wooden partition: the cardboard registration plate, the army-type web belt, and the holder and pistol.

Terry 'no commented' his way through the list. He also answered no comment through all the questions about the pistol having its serial number filed off.

It was around 6 a.m. when Murray Gregor told Terry Hodson that Dave Miechel had been arrested at the scene of the robbery. Terry continued to play dumb.

'Does it surprise you?' asked Gregor.

'Yeah,' Terry said.

'Why would Senior Constable Miechel be in the same area as you last night?'

'I wouldn't have a clue.'

Gregor asked Terry if he had anything to add. Terry said he didn't. Gregor told him he'd be charged with a number of offences including burglary, possession of a drug of dependence, possession of an unlicensed pistol, and possessing articles of disguise.

An hour after the interview Acting Superintendent Daly drove Terry back to his BMW – probably the highest-ranking chauffeur Terry had ever had. After dropping Terry at his car, free to go home, Daly joined Murray Gregor in a sweep of the surrounding streets, looking for Dave Miechel's motorbike. They found it one street away from the Dublin Street drug house. An examination of the gear sack revealed, among other things, Dave's wallet with all of his identification cards in it. The bike was lifted onto a tow truck and taken to the Oakleigh police station.

•

While Terry Hodson was being interviewed, Operation Galop went into full swing. There would be no rest for anyone at the

MDID that night. I stayed at the office making sure the warrants were ready to go, and coordinating with the bosses on duty and my crew as to how we were going to manage what had happened at the Dublin Street house. It was around 3.30 a.m. by the time I left the office with two other detectives. We went to the Moorabbin police station and a couple of us ran a briefing about how we were going to execute the multiple warrants we had.

When we finally left to get the operation under way, I headed to the principal address of Azzam Ahmed in Besant Street, Moorabbin. I arrested his father and took a set of keys we found at his house around to the Dublin Street house. We wanted to find as much evidence as we could to link Azzam Ahmed to the drug house. I stood at the front door, checking all of the keys to see if one fit, but none did.

By 9.30 a.m., I was back at the offices of the MDID, processing the arrests of our targets.

•

Despite the flurry of police activity, following the arrest of Miechel and Hodson it seemed that whatever had been taken from the Dublin Street house had vanished. Terry didn't have anything on him aside from the small amount of cocaine the arresting officers had found. Dave went to hospital in just the clothes he was caught in.

The mystery was solved when I got a phone call around 11 a.m. on the Sunday morning. The guy whose house we changed the tapes in had found two bags full of drugs in his backyard that morning. He had my number because I was the one who had originally asked him if we could use his house.

'Hey Paul, I've found some bags in my backyard. Looks like they've been thrown over the back fence. What should I do?'

I was snowed under at work dealing with the arrests. 'Look, mate, there are cops at Dublin Street at the moment searching the house. Can you go round there and ask for Murray Gregor or Dick Daly? Don't touch the bags. They'll deal with them.'

With so many cops around, two suspects in custody, and a whole bunch of drugs missing, it's a wonder that no one thought to look over the fence in the first place. And because no one thought to look over the fence, nearly 30 000 ecstasy tablets lay out all night in someone's backyard.

An hour and a half later, the drugs had been seized and logged as exhibits.

Police also retrieved the surveillance tape from the man's house. The tape showed two grainy figures breaking the front verandah light. Due to the quality of the tape, the identity of the figures couldn't be determined.

The morning after the Dublin Street break-in Superintendent Anthony Biggin was contacted by Acting Superintendent Dick Daly from Ethical Standards – the same Dick Daly who had conducted the interview with Terry Hodson at the Oakleigh police station the night before. Daly asked Biggin to clear out Dave Miechel's desk.

It is worth noting the exact wording of Superintendent Biggin's statement because it will become important later on: 'At 12.20 p.m. with the assistance of Detective Sergeant Martin Duggan I then removed all items from the desk and placed them in a cardboard box. I also seized a two-drawer filing cabinet on issue to Miechel. I then secured these in my office, and retained the key in my possession.'

The following day Biggin also seized another filing cabinet that was on issue to Dave Miechel. 'I removed the four-drawer filing cabinet on issue to Detective Senior Constable Miechel. I removed this cabinet from the general floor area and secured it in my office which I locked and retained the key.'

Around midday on the Monday, Dick Daly arrived at the MDID office and Biggin gave him Terry Hodson's informer management files. Later, they would accuse me of stealing Terry Hodson's informer management file. Yet, in his statement, Biggin says he handed it over to ESD. There were only ever two copies of the informer management files for Terry. One was the blue folder and one was kept by Jim O'Brien – it was this one that we added the information reports into in the weeks after the break-in.

•

A week after the robbery we were all called into the Ethical Standards Department to give statements. We had been working around the clock trying to clear up the mess and salvage as much as possible in regard to the investigation. We had retrieved the pill presses and the 30 000 ecstasy tablets, and we had arrested and locked up all the main players. Even so, one of our own had gone down and that left a pall over the office. Despite limping to the end of the race, Operation Galop was still the biggest ecstasy drug bust in the history of the Victoria Police.

In among the frantic week, ESD were badgering us for information, which added to the pressure. Dave's empty desk was a constant reminder of the shock that one of our own had done something so unfathomable. Everyone in our squad was spoken to by command and told to give honest statements to ESD. That attitude made us bristle. Here we were, giving our all to clear up the mess, and we were being thrown into the same boat.

Nonetheless, we agreed to go on the following Friday to give statements. Widely known as 'The Filth', ESD was thought of as the cops out to get other cops. We were driven there and then separated and taken into different rooms. Despite being there to help, we all felt like we were suspects.

Afterwards, we all met at the pub. Sam Jennings was the last one to arrive, and when she finally got to the pub she told us that an officer had walked into the interview room and told the detectives to leave. When it was just her and him, he told her what to say in her statement. He had picked the wrong person to target as 'the weakest link'. In her pub re-enactment, she told us how she'd held up her hands and told him that she didn't know anything about what he was telling her to say – about the Hodsons and their daughter Mandy – then told him that she wasn't comfortable being alone in the room with him, and requested permission to ring her boss.

Sam was incensed. We were all ropable and congratulated her for standing her ground with The Filth. Good on her.

After that, I needed time away from it all. We had been working long and hard and I'd had little time off. Inasmuch as I couldn't understand what Dave had done, it was a bit of a straw-breaking-the-camel's-back thing with ESD starting to do damage control by pointing the finger at our squad, and trying to make members of my crew say things that weren't true. You don't hang your colleagues out to dry.

I had a baby at home and it was a time to withdraw and spend time with the people who really mattered – my wife and son. There is a perspective about life when you have your baby son sitting on your lap, that the world will right itself, and that the tilting out of alignment will tilt right back.

CHAPTER 10

Dangling carrots and clichés

Acting as Terry Hodson's lawyer, Nicola Gobbo rang Andrew Hodson a week after the Dublin Street break-in with a request. Would he ask his father to contact Detective Inspector Peter De Santo?

Andrew Hodson later wrote in a police statement: 'I then spoke to my father and advised him to contact Peter De Santo. I assumed at the time that Peter was still working at ESD. I had no problem with giving my father this advice because I had dealt with Peter De Santo in the past and I felt comfortable with him.'

So, according to Andrew Hodson, Nicola Gobbo was setting Terry up with Ethical Standards a week after the robbery. To dob me in. Of course, she never mentioned anything to me about this when, a few weeks later, she offered to be my lawyer too.

I had no idea Terry was using Nicola. While I knew she had done bail hearings for a couple of the Dublin Street cohort, I had no idea that she was acting for them. She certainly never said anything about Terry to me. If I'd have known that, I would not have sought advice from her.

•

Terry Hodson didn't know he was being taped – in fact, the two cops interviewing him told him he wasn't. On 3 October 2003, Detective Inspector Peter De Santo and Detective Senior Sergeant Murray Gregor sat down with Terry and his son, Andrew, for a chat.

'Will I be getting locked up tonight?' Terry said, opening with his greatest fear.

De Santo hedged. 'Don't know. You're asking me the hard questions at the moment.'

'It's only ...' Terry hesitated.

'Oh, look,' said De Santo, 'I don't think we'll venture into that at this stage as far as turning around and saying what we're going to do and what we're not going to do with it.' He clearly wanted Terry to sweat it out.

Carrots must be dangled slowly and hypnotically.

A cop's favourite interview is one where the guy sitting opposite you is up shit creek without a paddle – in other words, where the cops hold all the cards. Such an interview is a bit like advertising: first describe a problem, then offer the perfect solution. It's a time for clichés and euphemisms. De Santo and Gregor went to the metaphor library and borrowed up big:

You can go for gold.
I'm not firing blanks.
Give it to you straight up.
Got a front ticket.
Come on board.
Along for the ride.
A front seat ticket.

'We're from a task force who are doing all the drug squad problems,' De Santo explained. He listed his street cred by naming four police officers he'd recently charged with corruption, then indicated his offsider. 'Murray's from what they call the corruption area of ESD and they're handling Saturday night.'

'Right,' said Terry, who had met Gregor the night he was arrested.

Terry agreed to talk, and immediately made himself comfortable by chatting about cops he knew in the drug squad.

De Santo handed Terry his card. 'I know ... you've been under a fair bit of pressure this last week.'

'Yeah.'

'The offer still stands; if you want to ring me in particular about anything ...'

Terry took the business card.

Murray Gregor took over the interview. After some preliminaries, he told Terry that the Ethical Standards Department would be happy if he could assist them.

'Certainly not!' Terry said.

Gregor laid his cards on the table. He told Terry that if he didn't cooperate, he was up against the very best investigative techniques the Victoria Police had to offer.

Terry told him that his first concerns were for his family.

Gregor reminded him he had another concern as well. 'Obviously the charges ... trafficking a drug of dependence commercial quantity, okay.'

'I didn't ...' began Terry.

'Okay, I'm just telling you, all right.'

'All right, yeah.'

'I don't need you to comment in relation to whether you know anything about that ... because I'm not interviewing you.'

'No.'

'I'm just *telling* you.' Gregor didn't elaborate on what the difference was, then moved in to complete the coup de grace. 'All right, so I'm just putting you in the picture so you know exactly what the situation is and what your position might be, all right. I'm not firing blanks at you ... You're looking at being charged with trafficking commercial quantity ... ecstasy.'

'Yep,' said Terry.

'Okay, um, as you know the potential sentence if you're convicted on something like that is —'

'I can tell you what it is now,' De Santo jumped in.

But Terry knew the drill. 'About twenty-five years,' he said, glumly.

Gregor reminded Terry that there were also the other charges to consider. 'Aggravated burglary ... The possession of pistol, all that sort of, all that palaver. But obviously the top end, the

DANGLING CARROTS AND CLICHÉS

main thing we're looking at, okay, is the trafficking commercial quantity ... and possession, all right.'

'Yeah,' said Terry.

'You know exactly what's happened on the night and I can understand you're in a position where you're ... concerned in relation to which way you might want to move ...' Gregor let it hang for a moment. 'Look, I can tell you now, the bottom line is if you don't come on board, I'm not going to lose any sleep over it.' It was his job, he explained, to investigate corruption within the police force, and since Hodson wasn't in the police force, it was Dave Miechel who was the focus.

'You're along for the ride, okay,' said Gregor, 'and you've got a front ticket.'

'Yep,' said Terry.

'Front seat ticket,' said Gregor.

'Yep.'

'Obviously your barrister has spoken to you and ... explained the options to you, what's available to you if you get on early,' said Gregor.

'Mmm.'

'If you get on board early with us, you know, that will obviously be taken into account down the road. I'm not offering indemnity.'

'No,' said Terry.

'Or anything like that. I can't because you're a front runner ... And you're up to your neck in it.'

'Yep,' agreed Terry.

'But obviously your assistance ... would be acknowledged down the road. It might not be by us, but also ultimately by the court, all right.'

'Yep.'

'But you can take your chances and you can go for gold,' Gregor said, further displaying his fondness for popular phrases, 'but I can tell ya, I wouldn't like to be in your situation.'

Terry knew the score. 'Well, I'm damned if I do and damned if I don't.'

'Yeah,' agreed De Santo.

'But Terry, can I ask you this?'

'Yes.'

'And neither of us are wearing any tapes, all right.'

'Yep.'

'I'll tell you that now. I haven't got a tape on or anything like that,' De Santo said. Which, of course, didn't mean the conversation wasn't being recorded.

'Neither have I,' said Gregor.

'This is conversations between us and it's in this room. You've been got at since Saturday?'

'No, not yet,' replied Terry.

De Santo spoke. 'Right. You had a threat held out at you prior to the Saturday in the event that something went haywire that you're a fuckin' dead man walking.'

'Yep.'

'Because of the business you were doing and who you were doing the business with,' said De Santo, '... we've got to consider you for protection ... I mean, look, the bottom line is you go down for this.'

De Santo told Terry that he would probably get eight years just for carrying the pistol. 'You're not the first person to have sat in that chair in this situation, right. There's been other people that have ... sat there and there's others we've looked after. And there's other people that we have looked after their welfare of their family and everybody else ... You know the circles you move in; you're playing with all the A-grade players.'

'Yeah,' said Terry.

'Are you scared of the A-grade players or the A-grade cop players you're playing with?'

'The cops,' replied Terry.

'Well at least we've confined it to that.'

'Yeah.'

With a lot of coaxing from De Santo and Gregor working tag team in the interview, Terry suggested that someone else was responsible for planning the Saturday night burglary. The two detectives tried every trick in the book to get Terry to name the other person. He hedged, then De Santo dug the boot in. Figuratively.

'Terry, how old are you?'

'Ah, fifty-six.'

'Your health's not the best.'

'No.'

'All right,' said De Santo, letting the meaning sink in.

It did.

'I know it could be a death sentence,' said Terry finally.

'Is that the way you want to live out the rest of your life?' asked De Santo.

'I've got two daughters and a son,' said Terry.

'But that's where we've come in with an alternative for you.' De Santo helpfully suggested that Hodson 'forget about the brotherhood bullshit' and leant in closer to tell Hodson that anything that he said was not admissible and it was just between those in the room.

De Santo asked Terry what his cut from the robbery was supposed to be.

'A third,' Terry told him.

'A third. So it was a three-way split?' clarified De Santo.

'Yep,' said Hodson.

Instead of asking the obvious – how could someone who wasn't there command a third of the proceeds from two who have taken all the risk? – De Santo began a rant against the MDID.

'... You've got this mindset that you're playing with the drug squad, that the drug squad are all fuckin' heavies ... here's a heavy and that they've threatened you and in what regard they've probably threatened you, I don't know. Whether they've put pistols to your head or whatever, I don't know, to say if you double fuckin' cross you, you're dead ... I think these two are acting independently of everybody else. I mean what he's been up to prior to all this, well you could just about write a book on and you'd know that. Him, he hasn't been so, he's only come on the scene down there what, in the last twelve months, this one, hasn't he? He hasn't been there too long, but he hadn't mucked around obviously to get in the swing of things I think.'

'This was the first ... I know you might find it hard to believe,' said Terry.

'First one with David?'

'I swear to God.'

This part of the conversation made it clear that Terry had dropped my name prior to the interview – I was the one who'd only been there in the last twelve months. The fact that he was reticent to say my name again might suggest that he knew he was being taped and he didn't trust the detectives.

Reading the transcript of the interview, I can picture Terry sitting with De Santo and Gregor, who had no idea what he was like. If the police weren't interested in one thing, Terry would immediately up the ante. That was how he operated. De Santo and Gregor didn't understand that Terry was a professional manipulator. His mind would have been ticking over, doing exactly what he did with us all the time. I reckon he would have been thinking: *What can I give them that they don't already have? They've already got Dave, so what buttons can I push?*

Terry knew how to capture police interest. He knew that cops wanted the big bust and because De Santo had started the interview by naming all the cops he'd put in jail, Terry would have known straightaway that De Santo wanted the heads of cops on a plate. He knew police talk and he knew exactly what was being offered to him.

That was when he started mentioning the 'three-striper' – or, in police parlance, a sergeant. Terry went fishing. He threw out the mention of the 'three-striper' and got what I imagine he wanted – an immediate salivation from De Santo and Gregor. And, like a dog with a bone, they bit and – to mix a metaphor – swallowed it hook, line and sinker. Terry raised the stakes. They already had a senior constable – a two-striper – in the bag in Dave Miechel, so Terry did what he always did: went one up, and offered them a three-striper – me.

'And how was it introduced to you? Was it introduced to you ... through Dave, or was it introduced from the three stripe?' asked Gregor.

'Both.'

'Done at a meeting?'

'Yep.'

'One of the meetings. How long ago?'

'About a month ago.'

Then the two detectives asked Terry a crucial question but didn't let him answer – although waiting for an answer could have exposed his story as a scam. One of the reasons that we hadn't been able to install listening devices in the Dublin Street house was because the drug-house babysitter, Tayluh Jones, rarely – if ever – left the premises. She was there to mind hundreds of thousands of dollars' worth of drugs and couldn't leave them unattended, and that meant we were never able to gain access to the house. So when the two detectives asked Terry if he had planned the robbery in advance, no one thought to discuss how anyone planning to rob the Dublin Street house would have to know in advance when Tayluh the babysitter would not be there.

'How did it come that you had to act on Saturday? Was that planned how long beforehand? Was it?' asked Gregor.

'It wasn't,' said Terry.

'Was it spur of the moment like as in we got to go today or —' Gregor began.

'Did they give you the nod it's on for today?' finished De Santo.

'Mmm,' replied Terry.

'Tell me, Terry,' broke in De Santo, 'you haven't been cunning ... and recorded any of the conversations you had with them, have ya?'

'Well, I never had any cause to,' said Terry.

Andrew Hodson – who had been silent this whole time – must have laughed because De Santo told him that even though he found the notion amusing, he had to ask. And with that, they lost track of that particular line of questioning regarding how a robbery could have been planned for the house that was almost never vacant.

When Terry explained how he bought and sold drugs under licence for the MDID, De Santo suggested that money was skimmed off the top of the deals. Again, De Santo seemed to put words into Terry's mouth – except Terry didn't bite. 'Yeah, I mean if you had two thousand pills to move or if you're doing an evidentiary buy for a thousand pills.'

'No, no, no,' Terry objected.

'No?'

'No, no. I was allowed to buy them. And given authorisation to sell them.'

Undaunted, De Santo pressed on. 'Okay, but when you say there's a divvy up, there's obviously extra money that's been made where you've – it's just been split, has it?'

'Yeah, well I was allowed to put money on the top, so I bought them for $20 and sold them for $22 to —'

'The drug squad,' finished De Santo.

'Well, not to the drug squad.'

'Oh, to whoever.'

Here, Terry was clearly alluding to the permission that he was given to move the large quantities of drugs that he had purchased with his own money. De Santo's line of questioning from the transcripts made it sound like he was suggesting that Terry was sharing the profits with Dave Miechel and me.

Then De Santo started talking about a deal, and made his bias perfectly clear: he'd protect anyone who could give him a copper's head on a platter. Terry Hodson, who had spent all of his adult life wheeling and dealing, gave him mine.

'But … we've got to assess if we can put an offer on the table to you for protection, right … What would you have that would stand up and show that you're telling the truth – and I'm not saying that you're not – show that you're telling the truth here about the discussion for Saturday night?' De Santo said.

'Oh, I haven't got anybody,' said Terry.

'No?' asked De Santo.

'No, no.'

'You got any meetings with him or the other bloke that were unscheduled?'

'No, no.'

'On Saturday when the call came for you to do it, who did the call come from? Which one? The little one? Did he say that the big one knew about it or ... did he say the big one knew about it?'

'Mmm.' Again, Terry failed to commit to a response and De Santo didn't press him.

De Santo went on to suggest that the mystery three-striper had his own problems, big time.

Terry tried to be helpful. 'I think it's only going to be a matter of time before he gets in touch.'

'And reinforce what he's already stated?'

'I'd say so.'

At this stage of the interview De Santo turned to Andrew Hodson, who had been pretty silent throughout, except when the police left the room and he thought he could speak freely.

'What do you reckon of all this?'

'Well, you know my love for your kind,' Andrew replied.

'Sorry?'

'You know my love for your kind.'

'Yeah, well that's how we first met, wasn't it?'

'That's right,' said Andrew. 'But fuck 'em.'

'Oh, that's what I'm saying,' said De Santo.

'Fuck 'em,' repeated Andrew.

'That's what our job is,' said De Santo. 'You blokes live on your side of the fence, right. We live on our side of the fence. What we hate more is blokes wanting to live on our side of the fence —'

'Playing on our side,' finished Andrew Hodson.

'Masquerading on our side of the fence, but they're actually your side of the fence,' De Santo said, then paused and added, 'With all due respect. I'm not trying to be rude.'

'No,' said Andrew.

'Our job here is to lock them up and put them away and put them away for a long time. And that's why there's no doubt about it. We do deals with people left in the predicament that you're in at the moment.'

Gregor asked about the planning leading up to the burglary.

'What was the cover story?' he asked.

'Just about Lucky,' said Terry, referring to Lucky Pantelopoulos.

After more back-and-forth chat, De Santo finally got Terry to admit that Saturday night had been a last-minute thing and that Dave Miechel had called him. Terry denied doing any kind of reconnaissance beforehand. He said that they had met at the nearby school.

'Was anyone carrying a scanner?' asked Gregor.

'No,' said Terry.

De Santo then told Terry he wanted to go and talk to his commander to see what else the police could 'put on the table' before they left.

Terry asked what exactly he was going to be charged with. No doubt he wanted to know what he had to bargain out of.

Possession of a commercial quantity of drugs, trafficking a commercial quantity of drugs, steal and possessing an unlicensed firearm.

There was a general agreement that Terry Hodson was facing ten years in prison, if not life.

'Look at it this way,' said Gregor, 'you're looking at a substantial time.'

'Hamburger with the lot,' agreed Terry.

De Santo left the room to confer and Terry and his son talked. They didn't appear too worried, and discussed legal terms and maximum sentences like seasoned professionals.

When De Santo returned, he and Terry discussed protection for him and his family, then Terry asked what would happen if he came on board.

'Well ... I would say at this stage we'd still go the same way. Sooner or later, you're probably going to have to cop something for it, but before I say that, I may mean you're going to have to say yep, I was involved in it, I did this, I did that. So we can walk up to the Director and say this is where you're at. The way it will probably be done is probably maybe under inducement.'

'It'll be done in an induced statement,' said Gregor, 'in that we put on the tapes, and inducement is given to you and that anything you say or do cannot be used against you.'

'Cannot be used against you,' parroted De Santo.

'Mmm,' said Terry.

'Basically, that covers you, all right. We do 'em all the time,' said Gregor.

'Quite regularly,' agreed De Santo.

'All right?' said Gregor. 'So you can tell us you bloody murdered the bloody pope and we can't do anything, use it against you, all right.'

CHAPTER 11

Putting together the brief

Back at the Major Drug Investigation Division offices, we were oblivious to the behind-closed-doors meetings conducted by the Ethical Standards Department.

On Thursday, 2 October 2003, five days after the Dublin Street burglary, my colleague Detective Senior Constable Samantha Jennings gave a statement to ESD. She gave her background at the MDID, and described how she had been leading Operation Galop and how she had been allocated to bring the operation over to my crew about two months earlier. She gave a brief background of the investigation, then brought her narrative around to changing the tapes at the surveillance house. She wrote in her statement that on the Friday night she was heading to an appointment in Geelong and had the Saturday off; she hadn't had a day off for two weeks. She and Dave Miechel were the last at the office and before she left he offered to change the tapes the following day so that she didn't have to drive back from Geelong to do it. She told Dave about the spare set of keys that were kept in my desk drawer and watched as he fetched them.

Sam talked about the night of the robbery. She had received a phone call from a member of our crew asking her if it was some kind of joke that the Dublin Street house had been compromised. She recalled ringing me and said that I clarified that something had happened and that Dave was in the hospital, bitten by a dog. She said she assumed he had been bitten by one of the dogs guarding the drug house.

Sam said that she had been told the previous day of the possibility that there was a relationship between Dave Miechel and Terry Hodson's daughter, Mandy. Sam said that while she knew Dave had a girlfriend, she had never met her. 'I would describe him as a real loner,' she wrote in her statement. 'He is a very hard person to talk to. He is just very quiet. I have never socialised with Miech or met his friends.'

Sam added something of note in her statement. Later, drug dealer Azzam Ahmed would claim that he had hundreds of thousands of dollars in his house on the night of the burglary. No money was ever located, and the suggestion, often repeated in the media as fact, was that somehow I ended up with it. It would be this nonexistent money that was later rumoured to be the source of me offering huge amounts for hit men.

From Sam's own statement: 'We always expected that there would be drugs in the house, but weren't sure how much money, if any, would be in the house. It wasn't till the Saturday night when I reviewed the telephone intercepts that I ascertained that there would be a large quantity of money taken to Sydney in exchange for drugs. I don't know whether this call was made on the Friday night or the Saturday night. I don't know if any of my fellow crew members had listened to this call prior to me listening to it. So as far as what money or drugs would have been located at Dublin Street on the Saturday night, I would have had no idea and to my knowledge, neither would any of my crew members. We would certainly have expected something to be there, but as far as amounts, there was no way of telling.'

Sam finished her statement like this: 'I would like to add that Operation Galop was an extremely complex and time-consuming investigation and although I was not daunted by the task of being given the job, I was nevertheless requiring a lot of guidance. I found Sergeant Dale to be extremely helpful, patient and thorough during the handling of this investigation. Sergeant Dale showed a lot of confidence in my abilities by letting me make decisions and assisted me with those decisions. At no time do I feel that any decisions made by Sergeant Dale were negligible or compromised the investigation. I feel confident in his abilities and leadership.'

Sam signed her statement at 2.26 p.m. at the Corruption Investigation Division at the Victoria Police Centre in Flinders Street.

Just over two hours later, at 4.44 p.m., Sam Jennings signed an amended version of her statement with the same senior constable who took her first statement. This one, however, was made at Ceja – an anti-corruption task force. Sam began this new statement by acknowledging that she had made a statement earlier in the day and now, only hours later, she wished to add more information. She didn't state whether this was by her own choice, or if someone had requested her to do so.

As a detective, I always tried to get all of the information in the first statement because the more statements and the more additions a witness made they tended to discredit their ability to recall the facts.

Sam Jennings would eventually make five statements over six years.

Sam opened with a description of a reconnaissance mission that our crew had done on the Dublin Street house a month earlier. She described how she had accompanied Dave and me and two other crew members into the backyard of a house, and looked over the back fence into the Dublin Street house.

'Here was easy access to the address from this property. D/S/C Miechel jumped the back fence whilst I remained in the property behind. I kept watch whilst he listened at the back window of the address. He came back a short time later and said he could hear a sound similar to a hand operated pill press in the back room. He was never out of my sight during this. We both attended back to Sergeant Dale.'

Sam Jennings described a couple of nights' surveillance on the Dublin Street house. She described jumping the fence on a second occasion with other crew members and hearing the distinctive clunk of the pill press every few seconds.

Sam said that the curtains were closed at the house and it was hard to get the lie of the land. She asked the tech support at work if she could get copies of the house plan so that she could see the layout. She described showing the plans to Dave Miechel. She added that Dave had the numbers and passwords so that he could monitor the phone intercepts. While generally the location of drugs at the Dublin Street house was not mentioned, on a couple of occasions phone intercepts had been picked up that there were drugs hidden in the freezer, food cupboards, and the range hood.

'Any person monitoring these calls would have knowledge of these locations where the drugs were supposedly kept,' finished Sam.

If you had to guess, reading both the statements, the extra information would have been as a result of the line of questioning being pursued at the time. Sam didn't give a statement then, two hours later, slap herself on the forehead, head back to a different task force and say, 'Oh, I forgot a couple of things.'

Sam would give a third brief statement when she handed over the grainy surveillance tapes from the surveillance house, and then it would be four years down the track before she formally spoke to investigators again. Again, I assume, not as a response to a forehead-slapping moment but, rather, in response to a specific line of questioning as police tested the extent to which their theories – or assumptions – might stand up. I was a cop too. I knew how it worked.

But more about that later.

•

In the two months after the burglary, we spent our time compiling the brief of evidence for all of the Operation Galop players. We all worked closely together.

In light of Terry Hodson's arrest, there was a mad scramble to look back on the paperwork to see that it was in order. All of a sudden, there were bosses scurrying around making sure they dotted their i's and covered their butts. If Terry was in fact buying drugs from Lucky Pantelopoulos, was there a corresponding section 51 form authorising him to do so? Of course, the nature of Terry and his rampant drug buying to keep us active on cases meant that we didn't have all the corresponding paperwork up to date. In fact, I couldn't think of any division – unless it was a pure paperwork division in fiction land – that would have had all its paperwork up to date.

There were a lot of section 51 forms which allowed indemnity for a one-off drug buy. They had to be initiated by a senior sergeant or above, and technically there needed to be one for each and every time Terry had purchased drugs for us. Information reports were completed and filed in Terry's informer management file – which was no doubt looking a lot thicker than the one ESD had received the day after the break-in.

Our bosses had always known what we were doing and when we were meeting Terry. My crew always told the bosses when Terry alerted us to his drug buys. He did have some indemnities to allow him to buy some drugs. I was confident my crew had followed the correct protocols.

I too spent time transcribing my day-to-day scribbled notes from an exercise book into my official diary, in order to get them up to date. We all did this once a week and had to show it to our bosses in order to claim overtime and meal allowances. The official diaries were A4 sized and too bulky to carry – not to mention the fact that they were emblazoned with the official police insignia, which wasn't good when we were in plain clothes trying to blend into the community.

•

One problem that surfaced soon after the break-in was that detectives from the Ethical Standards Department began getting up in court, challenging our evidence. And not only that, they were even asking for closed hearings that excluded MDID detectives from our own cases – hearings like that of

Tayluh Jones, the drug-house babysitter, and Azzam Ahmed's girlfriend. In hindsight, if Nicola Gobbo was the lawyer for all of them, no wonder they didn't want me in the room. And you also have to wonder if Terry would have used her as a lawyer if he had known she was acting for all the Dublin Street crew and had told them about him.

There was clearly more going on than simply Dave and Terry being arrested. Behind-closed-door deals were being done without our crew's knowledge and, unbelievably, some of these people who were up to their eyeballs in traffickable quantities of drugs – which carried a life sentence in prison – were offered indemnities.

We felt that ESD were sabotaging all our hard work. I even complained to Superintendent Biggin that I was attending court only to be removed by Acting Superintendent Daly and Murray Gregor.

There was a feeling of unease around Daly and Gregor when they spoke to me. Of course, because we saw ESD as the enemy, it was always a little strained anyway – but this was something more.

Giving indemnity to the young drug-house babysitter Tayluh Jones, an ice addict, was an interesting decision. I wonder if they ever stopped to ask her *why* she arranged to go out on the Saturday night of the robbery when the house was full of hundreds of thousands of dollars in drugs and it was her job *not* to leave. All of our reports and surveillance stated that the reason we couldn't install listening devices was because she rarely left the house. And then, suddenly, a friend who she won't name – despite the promise of indemnity – called her and said, 'Hey, come out for a drink,' and, without hesitating, she went.

Tayluh Jones would later know *two weeks* before the Hodsons were murdered that they were going to die. But she wouldn't share this with the police.

Not until long after they were dead.

•

When Tayluh Jones sat down for her formal interview on 15 October 2003 – nearly three weeks after the robbery – it was clear that deals had been struck. The third paragraph of her statement included the following: 'I also make it on the understanding that this statement will not be used as evidence in relation to the criminal (drug) charges pending against me or any other person as the result of an investigation conducted by members of the Major Drug Investigation Division known as Operation Galop.'

When asked to describe her movements on the night of the break-in, she said that she got called by a friend to come and visit either in Prahran or South Yarra; she couldn't remember which and didn't want to name the friend. She said she left the house at 6.30 p.m. and returned by 8.30. It's not in her statement, but a quick look at the street directory shows the distance between East Oakleigh and South Yarra as around 20 kilometres – at least half an hour one way by car, or an hour to get there and back.

And she was only gone for two hours.

Leaving a house that she never left.

To visit a friend for just an hour.

Leaving a house full of drugs.

What did Tayluh Jones know?

Why did she leave?

Alas, someone given indemnity in exchange for a statement was not, in this case, pushed for details.

Tayluh spent the bulk of her statement listing in great detail all of the drugs that had been in the house. And while, later, allegations would be repeated in the media that hundreds of thousands of dollars supposedly went missing during the break-in, she said something very important at the end of the statement: 'The Drug Squad located the only cash in the house when they did their search. There was no other money in the house on this day.'

In the meantime, Terry Hodson was talking to ESD at a covert location. On 7 October he sat down with Detective Senior Sergeant Murray Gregor and Detective Inspector Peter De Santo. It was 4.15 p.m.

Without stating the exact nature of whatever inducement they had given Terry, Murray Gregor referred to it nonetheless.

'Terry, as previously explained to you, the inducement I gave you is still in place.'

'Yes,' Terry replied.

De Santo handed Terry a red pen and the two cops encouraged him to mark on a map his movements on the night of the Dublin Street break-in.

Gone were the cagey responses from the previous interviews; Terry was fired up and prepped. For several minutes, the trio discussed some people Terry said he had seen walking nearby as he and Dave Miechel left the drug house.

'You couldn't help but miss us, walking that way,' said Terry. They were only about four metres away when they all passed each other.

'Did he have a balaclava or was it a beanie?' asked Gregor.

'He wore – you know, the police one? The black one you're supplied with,' said Terry.

De Santo spluttered a bit when he heard that.

Terry said that he and Dave had gone up to the school yard, around the corner from the Dublin Street house.

'That was where you were arrested, was it?' prompted Gregor.

'Yes, yeah. The exact spot.'

'Yeah?'

'Then we see the police van —'

'You're both at that location?'

'Yes.'

'And could you see it from there?' asked Gregor.

'Yeah, coz of his light. He had his spotlight on.'

'... [A]nd what did Dave say?'

'He said, "No, don't panic. Don't panic." He says, "It's not unusual for a divvy van to put his spotlight on." He says, "Get rid of the balaclava and the gloves."'

'I just threw the gloves and the bally into the back of the car,' said Terry.

'So you've left from where you're standing?' asked De Santo.

'Yeah.'

'Is it correct to say the police car's driven past with the spotlight on?'

'Yep. That's come down here,' said Terry, pointing to the map.

'You've then left David. You've left Miechel and gone to your car ... or you were at your car?'

'No. I went to the car. He —'

'Went to the car when he's told you to do this?'

'Yep. He stood by the sheds.'

Terry described returning to his car and throwing his gloves and balaclava in the hidden back compartment in his boot. 'And threw it, pulled it down and threw it in there but I didn't shut it up properly because you could see activity up on Dublin Street, with the police cars.'

Terry was a little vague about what happened next, and neither cop asked him why – if Terry was at his car and he knew the Dublin Street house was swarming with cops – he didn't simply drive off rather than walk back to the sheds, where he was nabbed a short time later. Or why Dave – who was up the road at the school, free and clear of the robbery scene – would go back to the house that had police cars with flashing lights out the front of it, only to be caught nearby.

Inspector De Santo: 'So he walked in the direction of the school and ...?'

'Yeah.'

'The steps?' said De Santo cryptically.

'Yes.' Terry seemed either to know what he was talking about, or agreed with him anyway.

'You were – had your briefing on?'

'Yes,' said Terry, 'that's it.'

'For want of better words.'

'Yes.'

'... [L]ast saw of him?'

'Yes, that's the last I saw of him.'

Terry then described how he waited a good ten minutes at the school until a cop came and arrested him. '... [T]he next thing is, the police dog's charging at me and an officer telling me to get on the ground.'

Again, De Santo didn't press Terry as to why, if he and Dave had escaped capture at the drug house, they had both hung around to be captured shortly afterwards.

When pressed about the small amount of cocaine found on him that night, Terry admitted snorting some to help him relax before he met Dave.

Gregor filled in the next bit about Terry being taken to the Oakleigh police station. He asked Terry about the story he'd told that night when Gregor and Daly had first interviewed him.

'Yeah, that was barefaced lies,' admitted Terry.

'How'd you come up with that story?' asked Gregor.

'Well, I'd been arrested with the coke and I knew I'd been working on Lucky for three months and not realising that Dave had been pinched, I thought: *Well, here's a good reason why I should be here.*'

'Something which might stand up to scrutiny or an argument later on?'

'Yeah.'

Terry said that he had seen an ambulance arrive and one of the arresting officers had told him that Dave had been bitten.

'I thought: *I'm in big shit … that's the truth.*'

Terry told them that he had asked the sergeant at Glen Waverley to get in touch with me. 'I told him that I was a registered informer and I couldn't discuss anything, but if you could get the sergeant.'

'And you were released, have you had any contact with Dave Miechel or Paul Dale, directly or indirectly?' asked Gregor.

'I haven't had any contact with Dave Miechel, but I got a call on Saturday night at 5 p.m. and I believe it was from Paul.'

'And what was said?' asked Gregor.

'They asked to speak – my wife answered the phone. They asked to speak to me. They had an urgent message.'

'To speak to who?' interrupted De Santo. 'Terry or Terry Hodson or —'

'Terry,' said Terry.

'So the person indicated it was an urgent message?' repeated Gregor.

'Yes. Yes. The guy said I – I never – I didn't recognise the voice, let's put it that way. And the message was – we're – we're all family, and we look after each other and there's no reason to go on board with anyone.'

'Did you respond?' asked De Santo.

'Yeah. I says, "Everything's fine."'

'Any response from that?'

'No,' said Terry.

'What? They just hung up?'

'Yep.'

Terry said that his wife, Christine, had thought she heard STD pips when she answered the phone.

Gregor brought the questioning around to the reason Terry had come forward. 'Just to clarify things, Terry, you agree that ... a message was communicated to you via a third person? As a result of that, you attended at the ESD offices last Friday on the third of October where we had ... a conversation about ESD's interest in pursuing David Miechel and any other police member that was involved in this.'

'Yes.'

'As a result of that, we agreed on, I'll say a "game plan" in the event that anybody asks us what was the purpose of your attendance at ESD and what the outcome of that meeting was?'

'Yes.'

'And the agreement by all parties, being the three of us here, was that we would say that you politely told us that you didn't want to assist us and you were prepared to take your chances.'

Murray Gregor went over what they had discussed at the previous meeting. Terry had apparently told them that he had met with Dave and they had discussed the drugs that were being kept at the Dublin Street house.

'He said that they were bringing in 20 000 Es down from Sydney.'

'You were aware that these dealers in this target address were large-scale dealers?' said De Santo.

'Right,' agreed Terry. 'It wasn't a bloody two-bit operation!'

'And the investigation that the Major Drug Investigation unit had under way, had a lot of police resources into it and it was one of their major investigations.'

'Well, Dave did tell me that – no, sorry – Paul told me that Jim O'Brien – it was his biggest job. He – and when it was gonna get done, he'd be pissed right off.'

'That Jim O'Brien would be pissed right off when it had been – the place – the job had been – I won't say sold out but the ... target house had been burgled?' asked Gregor.

'Yes. Yes.'

'Do you know what the operation ... was called?'

'No, I don't.'

'All right.'

'I really don't.'

'All right.'

'They didn't tell me. They only told me what they wanted me to know.'

'All right. Just recapping. There was an agreement between the three of you that the proceeds were gonna be split —'

'Three ways,' finished Terry.

'And that they expected at least a couple of hundred thousand in there?'

'Yes.'

Murray Gregor took the interview back to specifics of the robbery. He and De Santo tried to pin Terry down on the size and weight of the bag used in the break-in. Terry admitted carrying one of the bags, but he said that once inside the drug house he didn't see Dave.

'I only saw him when we went in the door and when we come out.'

Minutes later, Murray Gregor decided to stop the interview. 'We had grand plans to be doing a statement straight after this, but I don't think ... any of us are in the position ... to do that because we've been going for a fair while and we're all probably pretty mentally—'

'Drained?' finished Terry.

'Drained,' agreed Gregor. 'So what I intend to do at this stage is, from my notes, I will draft a statement up coz I've taken fairly – quite extensive notes just in relation to what we discussed and obviously I'm gonna have to then sit down with you and go through it again to make sure we've got everything right as per the script, as you've told it.'

'Yep.'

Inspector De Santo concluded the interview.

CHAPTER 12

The first arrest

Detective Senior Sergeant Murray Gregor from Ethical Standards was the one who knocked on my door at 5.45 a.m. on Friday, 5 December. He was accompanied by a bunch of other detectives. I'd been on leave for a week or two and I was due to return to work that day. My wife answered the door and led the horde of police officers into the kitchen.

As Murray Gregor handed me the search warrant and read me my rights, alongside the shock I registered the thought that reading someone their rights as soon as you walk through the door – before you even said why you were there – was unusual. It meant that they were going by the book.

While Gregor stayed with me, the other detectives began searching my house. They went into my closet and took my police uniforms – taking back police property was a pretty good indicator that their minds were made up before they even entered the door. It didn't matter what I said in my defence.

Gregor told me that I was under arrest for conspiracy to commit burglary and theft, and conspiracy to traffic a commercial quantity of a drug of dependence.

All on the word of Terry Hodson – a guy who'd sell his own grandmother.

Not only was being arrested in my own kitchen on an uncorroborated statement from a criminal beyond belief, it was really bad investigative work. Even from a legal point of view, you can't convict a co-accused just on the word of someone else charged with the same crime.

But that's all they had.

I was taken into the ESD offices at the Melbourne World Trade Centre and at 7.30 a.m. sat opposite Murray Gregor and another detective in an interview room. Gregor fired questions at me about how I'd conspired with Dave Miechel and Terry Hodson to rob the Dublin Street house. I denied all allegations.

While they questioned me, I was asking a set of my own questions in return.

Them: *We put it to you, Mr Dale that you …*

Me: *Who said that? Where did this come from?*

'Someone's obviously told you this crap,' I said. 'Now, if … Hodson's told you this stuff, the only thing I can think of for him to say something like this would be to try and benefit any sort of problems he may have. I don't know whether he's got any problems, but … why would they tell you this? Why would they try and say I had any involvement in this whatsoever …?'

I could tell that they were uncomfortable. They also looked embarrassed because when I asked for the source of their information we all knew that there was only one source. And it wasn't a reliable one.

Terry.

Around 8.15 a.m., Gregor announced that he was going to suspend the interview.

Just after 11 a.m. I was taken to the Melbourne Custody Centre until my appearance with Terry Hodson and Dave Miechel before a magistrate in the Melbourne Magistrates' Court. While I never saw Terry, I was put in a cell with Dave.

My first words were shouted: 'I know why you're here, but what the fuck am I doing here?'

'Dunno,' he said with a shrug.

He wouldn't look me in the eye. Which wasn't unusual. But …

He let me rant until my fury was spent.

Two cops together in a cell. Both of us were aware that every breath we took, every word we spoke would be fully monitored, so after my initial rant we settled into a silence, broken only by small talk.

My anger at Dave delayed my reaction to being put in a prison cell. Had Dave not been there for me to yell at, I would have looked around the bare concrete walls and at the bare concrete seat, and looked over at the stainless steel sink and dunny, and panicked.

After I calmed down, my delayed response kicked in. I began to tremble.

A cop in a cell.

A very dangerous place.

In the blink of an eye, my world had turned upside down. I was supposed to lock up crooks. *Not be locked up.*

And despite a long history of locking up crooks, my work stopped when their cell door shut. I had no idea about the other side of the cell door.

And now I was finding out.

•

As soon as I was arrested, my first thought was that I needed Nicola Gobbo – I wanted the best. When I first met Nicola Gobbo, she was one of the highest-profile barristers around. Her list of clients read like a who's who of the Melbourne drug trade. When people found themselves on the wrong side of large-scale drug charges, Nicola Gobbo was their lawyer of choice. She handled most of the big drug cases, and I had been charged with conspiracy to traffic large quantities of drugs – one of the most serious drug charges on the books, carrying a maximum sentence of life in prison.

I rang her from the ESD offices.

I had no idea at the time that she was acting for Andrew Hodson and had taken on Terry and had liaised with Peter De Santo for Terry to come in. She would have known full well that to liaise with Ethical Standards could only mean that Terry was cutting a deal. To then agree to meet with me as my lawyer and pretend she was there for my best interests was crazy. I also had no idea that she was acting for Azzam Ahmed and brokering deals for Tayluh Jones the drug-house babysitter, helping Ethical Standards close a net around me.

As well as Nicola Gobbo, I had access to Tony Hargreaves, who had the contract with the Police Association; he had been the preferred police lawyer for twenty years. So as much as I needed Nicola Gobbo, I also needed the Police Association to fund my legal case, and Tony Hargreaves had a terrific reputation. I had to try to get bail and get myself out of this situation.

Nicola and Tony met with me at the Custody Centre. Their legal advice was to not make a premature bail application. They said that if bail was refused it could take months to get another hearing, which meant months in jail. They said we should wait and see what the police case against me was, then counter it.

Here was I incarcerated, and at that moment the two people I trusted most in the world with my freedom were Nicola and Tony. As difficult as it was, I took their advice and was remanded into custody into the Port Phillip Prison.

The first visitor I had was Nicola Gobbo, who came as my lawyer. I couldn't have any other visitors until my visitor list was approved. For the uninitiated, a visitor list has to be compiled and okayed, then the prison does a background check on each person on the list, then contacts the police and also the people on the list to get their okay as well. The whole process takes time, but a lawyer doesn't have to go through the process and can visit any time.

Nicola was a sight for sore eyes in those early days. She told me that she wanted to represent me and that she understood that the Police Association was funding Tony Hargreaves's work, but that she would do it pro bono. We both knew that my case was going to be high profile and I think Nicola wanted to be a part of that. She offered to act as my barrister, working with solicitor Tony Hargreaves. While it was generous, this offer caused me some dilemma because I knew that Nicola wasn't exactly on the Victoria Police Christmas-card list on account of her getting bail for all the drug bigwigs. I didn't know if the Police Association would allow me to use both Tony and Nicola.

As we talked in the prison visitors' room, Nicola made notes about my bail application to take back to Tony Hargreaves. Nicola took all of my legal notes that I'd made in solitary confinement to take to Tony Hargreaves. But she didn't take them to Tony: she took them straight to her police handlers. I never followed up with Tony because I never thought I had to. I only found this out later at the Royal Commission in 2019.

•

Ten days in a cell felt like a lifetime. I spent the stretch in the Port Phillip Charlotte Unit – which is the Port Phillip equivalent of Barwon Prison's notorious Acacia Unit.

Ten days.

Twenty-three hours a day. Sitting in a cell with the only light of day coming through a tiny reinforced window that faced a brick wall. I was a physical person. I went to the gym most days. To lock someone in a shoebox where you could barely move. You couldn't speak to anyone. You couldn't go anywhere. Your food was passed through a slot in the door. Your anxiety levels went through the roof. No family. No human contact.

No nothing.

Except walls.

And a boiling kettle.

A couple of years earlier, I had investigated a murder in this very unit. A guard had left a door open and an inmate had been bashed to death. I knew this kind of thing happened. Hence the constant boiling water. If that door opened I would not hesitate to throw boiling water at the person who walked through.

Constant fight-or-flight mode and the attendant adrenaline rush gave you the jitters. Always on guard. Watching the door. You couldn't eat. You couldn't sleep. You were hyper-vigilant all the time. I lost ten kilos in ten days.

Other inmates howled like wolves for my blood.

Dale? Dale?

You're a fuckin' dog!

We're gonna kill you.
Dale? Dale?
I never answered.

•

Ten days later I was granted bail, and Tony Hargreaves presented me with a $10 000 bill for his services, which I paid with money I borrowed from Mum and Dad. I would be reimbursed if the Police Association took on my case.

This is why I decided not to solely use Nicola Gobbo as my lawyer. The Police Association didn't just take on any member's case: there was a whole set of criteria that needed to be filled before you made an application. You had to appear before a panel of Police Association executives. You had to sign a waiver and promise to be candid in your responses. The panel examined the case against you, questioned you, and then made a decision if the case against you had merit. In other words: if they thought you were guilty, they wouldn't fund your case.

I followed this process and the Police Association agreed to fund my case. Their decision to fund my case was a huge lift to me – it meant that a jury of my police peers had read the brief and come to the same conclusion: that the case against me was not watertight.

So I made the decision to go with the Police Association and use Tony Hargreaves and whatever barrister he chose, and not to formally use Nicola in court. I explained to Tony that I would continue to seek her legal advice and he was fine with that. Nicola was happy with that arrangement too.

Thus began my formal representation with Tony, and my informal but equally as valued representation with Nicola Gobbo. The biggest difference between the two was that Tony was always official and businesslike. My relationship with Nicola was very different: she would catch up for a chat and was always available for advice. That was the way she operated.

Navigating the minefield of legalese was made easier by having Nicola as an interpreter. She was happy to sit at a café over coffee and give me examples of other cases that might have a bearing on mine. I found her counsel incredibly valuable. She would also prove valuable as a sounding board after all the hearings I would eventually attend. Another thing she did was discuss the legal ramifications of what was being said about me in the press.

Right from the start, the media picked up on the corrupt cop story and never let it go. What I found unbelievable was that the media could create an impression of guilt so easily.

Disgraced ex-detective
Allegedly corrupt policeman
Detective X
Former detective Paul Dale, accused of ...

I quickly found out that you didn't have to have been declared guilty by the courts for the media to make you guilty in the minds of the public.

Nicola feared that her office was bugged, so she never met any of her clients there. Because we always met at restaurants and coffee shops, the police would later put a spin on our relationship, saying that it wasn't a legal one because of the places we met, but she met all of her clients in those sorts of places. We never caught up just purely for social reasons; there was always a legal reason for our meetings, although over time we became friends and parts of our conversations would be social.

Later, I would be charged with talking to her about the Australian Crime Commission hearings, on the grounds that she wasn't my lawyer. But I was certainly under the impression that she was acting as my lawyer and I had been seeking her legal advice, albeit on a pro bono basis, from the first day I was arrested.

CHAPTER 13

The 'spark' between Mandy and Dave

On Christmas Day 2002 – ten months before the Oakleigh robbery would change everything – Dave Miechel and another cop went to the Park Hyatt hotel in Melbourne to pass on their season's greetings to the Hodson family, who were all staying there, celebrating the festive season by ordering a room-service Christmas lunch.

Mandy Hodson would later identify this as the first time she noticed 'a spark' between her and Dave. In hindsight, this visit was unwise, but we had never been able to treat Terry Hodson as the typical informer. The fact that Dave went to see the Hodsons for Christmas was simply a way of appreciating the relationship and the information Terry had given us.

In her statement, Mandy said that she went shopping and bought Dave some expensive gifts. If Dave was given a gift from the Hodsons for Christmas, the correct protocol would have been to refuse to accept it – but Terry was a hard guy to refuse.

The fact that Dave was in the presence of Mandy also wasn't a good thing. Dave had arrested her a year earlier and he was, therefore, the police informant against her in the charges that hadn't come to court yet. (The police informant was the officer who would give evidence in court on a charge.)

Mandy later described the 'spark' that grew from that meeting; I'm not in a position to comment on this because I wasn't there. Dave certainly never mentioned Mandy to me, ever. I had never met Mandy, and she was of no interest to me. I had never met anyone else in the Hodson family except for Terry's wife, Christine.

I had never heard Dave mention any friends and had no idea who he socialised with. He never mentioned a girlfriend apart from on that Grand Final day when he turned up at my house, but I didn't see her and didn't know her name. His social life wasn't something I needed to or wanted to know about.

What I do know is that after Terry was caught robbing the Oakleigh house, the Hodsons had weeks to put together a story that would give Terry an easier ride through the serious charges he was facing.

When Mandy was first questioned by police the day after she discovered her parents' bodies, she told them that she had never met me, and that she had seen Dave Miechel at her parents' house on one occasion when he was playing cards with her mum and dad.

Of course, she was either lying about Dave then or later. As with many statements attached to this case, it's hard to tell.

A couple of months after the robbery, Mandy had replaced Dave in her affections with a new beau called Mickey. When he later gave a statement to police, this is what he had to say: 'She told me that she signed a statement about having slept with a policeman by the name of Dave ... the only rumour that I had heard was that the policeman who had arrested her, she had slept with. It didn't make sense to me ... Mandy told me that she had made the statement to help her dad.'

So who knows?

•

When Acting Superintendent Dick Daly spoke to Terry Hodson on New Year's Day 2004, three months after the break-in, Terry told him that both Mandy and Andrew wanted to 'provide information' to the police, just like their dad. By that stage, they'd all had three months to come up with a story.

On Monday, 5 January 2004, Terry Hodson spoke to Daly about a security concern. He said that a guy named Frank had come to his house a few days earlier, looking for him. Mandy had covered for her dad and told Frank that her father was locked up, and therefore not at home.

When talking to the superintendent Terry was a little cagey about Frank's real identity, but admitted that Frank came from Brunswick and had connections with the Mokbel family. This had to be a real threat to Terry, because while it would take police much longer to establish the connection to Mokbel as the distributor of the drug house Terry had robbed, Terry himself would have known that he had crossed Big Tony big time.

Detective Murray Gregor did a bit of digging and found out who Frank was. And what his connections were.

Frank wasn't the only man who came looking for Terry in early January 2004. Hodson also told Daly that Jayson Rodda had been in the street outside his Harp Road house and spoken to Mandy as she left. Apparently, he had given Terry 'advice about his security'. Jayson Rodda and Terry had a long history – most of it revolving around Terry informing on Jayson over and over, and Jayson falling for it over and over. And not only that, Jayson Rodda – like a lot of other crooks – had made allegations against MDID detectives arising from an operation for which Terry Hodson had been the informer.

As well as muddying the waters after an arrest, pointing the finger at a cop also delayed any court cases arising from the arrest, and the crook was virtually guaranteed bail rather than waiting a couple of years in jail while the allegations against so-called 'crooked cops' were investigated. By 2003, this had almost become a spectator sport.

According to Acting Superintendent Daly's statement, Gregor took Mandy Hodson to the CID office for an interview on 7 January 2004 – right after Terry Hodson had told the police of two men who had both been headed off by Mandy in front of the Harp Road house. Yet her statement, dated 22 January, did not mention this.

CHAPTER 14

2004

On 22 January 2004, Mandy Hodson gave a statement to Murray Gregor at the Balwyn police station. In it, she described her relationship with Dave Miechel which, she said, had grown to be far more than arresting officer/drug trafficker.

Mandy explained that in August 2001 she and her brother, Andrew, had been arrested for trafficking ecstasy. She said that she had never met Senior Detective David Miechel prior to the arrest. She also said that despite the charges being around two-and-a-half years old, they were still outstanding – meaning that the case had never made it to court.

In her new statement she covered the Park Hyatt room-service Christmas of 2002 and how she had bought Dave gifts from her parents. Mandy said that she could tell by Dave's behaviour that he was interested in her, and she saw him again a week later when he came to a New Year's Eve celebration at her house in North Balwyn. Her parents were there and Dave came around for a few drinks. Things didn't go well, Mandy explained to the police interviewing her. 'I got drunk and for some reason I told Dave to piss off and he left.'

But the good thing about telling someone to piss off is that it gives you something to talk about next time you see them. Accordingly, she said, when she saw Dave again, this time at her parents' house, watching TV with them, she was able to apologise for her behaviour.

A couple of weeks after that Dave arrived at Mandy's place, having packed a picnic lunch. She said he wanted to take her for a picnic on the back of his motorbike. Not liking bikes, she refused, but offered to cook him dinner that night instead.

She described her feelings for the police officer: 'At first, I wasn't really interested in Dave, but I found him to be a really nice person so I got more interested in him as time went on. It was obvious that Dave was very interested in me. Dave was a person with few words. I did nearly all the talking. He was very secretive regarding his personal life. Dave talked about doing up his Valiant Chargers and Mini Minors he had back home in Cobram. Dave also told me he had a trail bike. I asked Dave if he had a girlfriend. Dave said he had one about two years ago.'

It was during this statement that Mandy first introduced the nickname 'Killer' when referring to me. I have never been known by anyone as Killer, nor have I ever met Mandy, but she didn't let this get in the way of her carefully established story that matched the one her father was already telling ESD.

'Dave used to train at the gym with Paul Dale who Dave referred to with the nickname "Killer". Dave told me he was having a competition with Killer in who could reach 100 kilograms in body weight. Dave told me that Paul was on steroids. I never met Killer, but Dave showed me a photograph in which Dave pointed out Killer with other detectives.'

Mandy had said that she had never been to Dave's house and didn't even know where he lived. So I guess we would need to assume that Dave carried around photos of the cops he worked with to show his girlfriends ...

Using the name Killer also made me sound ruthless, and Mandy used the name throughout the rest of her statement. 'Dad told me that he had been caught doing a burglary with Dave. It was either on this day or a few days later that Dad told me Killer was also involved. I was really angry. I went home and cried for four hours solid and I threw some of the things Dave had given me over the back fence.

'I also found out that Dave, Killer and my dad were arrested and charged on the same day. Some days later, I found out that Dad was helping out the police investigating the burglary that he did with Dave and Killer. After talking to Dad, I decided to cooperate as the police thought I was somehow involved in the burglary, which I am not.'

Hmm. Is it just me, or is this another Hodson dealing her way out of charges?

To add further weight to Dave's complicity – just in case ESD believed his story about being caught doing legitimate surveillance of the Dublin Street house – Mandy told Murray Gregor that Dave had come into the shop where she worked in Burke Road, Camberwell, in late November.

'That was the first time I had seen or heard from him since his arrest. I was very surprised by Dave's visit. I told Dave to sit down and wait for me to finish ... I was pretty angry with Dave. I said, "I should bash you – what you have put me through – you're a fuckin' idiot – why did you do it?" Dave just shrugged his shoulders and goes, "Phrww." And I said, "No, not phrww." I said, "If I'd known you were going to do this, I would've belted you and my dad. How fucking stupid can you be?"... Dave said, "Oh, this is going to sound a bit stupid, but I probably did it more for you than your dad." I said, "What'd you do it for me for? Have I ever asked anything from you other than your love and affection?" Dave replied, "Nah." I then said, "Then why did you do it?" I then got upset and cried and Dave cried as well.

'Dave then handed me a card with Al Pacino on the front from the movie *Scarface*. On the back of the card, it says something like, "I've never fucked a man over who didn't deserve it and I got my name and my balls". Dave then said, "Now this card has a double meaning." He goes, "Just give it to your dad – your dad will know." I kept the card, which Dave handed to me in a brown paper bag. This surprised me because I had given this card to my dad a few years previously.

'I could see the scar on Dave's face where he was hit at the time of his arrest. I said to Dave, "You know you're fucked – you're probably looking at ten years – like is it really worth it?" Dave shook his head and said, "I've gotta do what I've gotta do." I said, "Do you know anything of a bag containing money going missing?" I had heard this in the news reports. Dave replied, "Nah, they got everything." I said, "Well, apparently, according to the paper, they didn't find this bag with the money in it." Dave replied, "Well, I haven't got it." ... I told Dave I still loved him and that I might see him again one day. I then gave him a kiss on the cheek and he left ... I later dropped into Mum and Dad's and I told them that Dave had dropped in to see me ... I gave Dad the *Scarface* card and the message regarding the card having a double meaning.'

So, all up, Mandy's statement implied that Dave sat with her, cried with her, listened as she told him she loved him, and then gave her a card which threatened her father.

Sound realistic? You be the judge.

•

Acting Superintendent Dick Daly again acted as chauffeur when Terry Hodson had to attend the committal hearing on the Oakleigh burglary charges. On Wednesday, 17 March 2004, the superintendent, along with Senior Sergeant Murray Gregor, collected Terry from his house and took him off to court, via a café near the Victoria Market. Over coffee, the three men talked about expediting the completion of the court proceedings of the charges that Terry was facing. Terry was keen for this to happen.

Two days earlier, Gregor had received a phone call from Terry. Someone had smashed a bottle against Terry's front door. Terry also thought someone had moved the sensor on his side fence. The surveillance tapes didn't show anything.

At the Wednesday hearing, the next court date was set for 19 May.

But it would never happen.

Terry Hodson would be dead by then.

Murray Gregor would later write in his statement that Hodson was to appear at his own case in the Supreme Court for a plea of guilty in August 2004. 'Terry Hodson had verbally agreed to give evidence against Dale and Miechel. Hodson had been advised via OPP to his solicitor that his assistance in the matter would be communicated to the court at his plea, which would obviously substantially reduce any sentence he would receive.'

I wonder just how much his sentence would have been 'substantially' reduced in exchange for a statement against me.

•

On Tuesday, 20 April, Acting Superintendent Daly visited Terry Hodson at the Harp Road house to discuss security issues surrounding his 19 May court case. Terry told him that he had received two phone calls to his secure mobile phone – an occurrence which was unusual. Daly made a note of the numbers. Hodson also told the police officer that he had received a visit from an acquaintance named Brett who had come to the Harp Road house and had stayed quite some time. In the end Terry asked him to leave, using the excuse that his wife needed to vacuum the house.

If Daly was worried at the line of crooks beating a path to Terry's door, he didn't detail it in his statements.

And it wasn't just the lightweight disgruntled crooks from the seedy drug world who were closing in on Terry: there were some real heavyweights in the running as well. It is worth having a look at just who came into Terry Hodson's orbit. Because Terry was playing the dangerous game of providing police with information about his rivals, his enemies, as you'd imagine, were dangerous. In the shifting sands of loyalties it can sometimes be hard to see all of the connections, but with the people who Terry had crossed it was pretty clear.

Journalist Adam Shand had been recorded talking to Carl Williams on a phone tap. Carl was miffed because he'd found out that Lewis Moran had put a hit out on him and somehow Terry Hodson was involved in it. But it wasn't just the hit Carl was miffed about.

It was the price.

According to Shand, Carl was angry at the paltry figure Lewis Moran was prepared to pay for his death. Someone of the stature Carl imagined he had would be worth hundreds of thousands of dollars. The bargain-basement hit price of $50 000 was insulting. That's only 400 bucks per kilo, complained Carl. He felt he should be worth at least double that.

While Carl didn't sound too worried when he was talking to Adam Shand on the phone tap, that didn't mean that he would take the Moran/Hodson threat lying down. Carl wasn't like that. If he felt threatened by anyone, that person didn't tend to live very long.

And if he didn't feel like raising a sweat to exact his own revenge, he was in almost daily contact with a notorious hit man, Rod Collins, who Carl had known since he went to school with Rod's daughter, Leonie. The two had remained friends and caught up all the time.

And, of course, the web widened.

In 2004 Rod Collins's girlfriend was a woman called Joan McGuire – mother of Danielle McGuire, who was the girlfriend of Tony Mokbel.

So if Big Tony was upset about Terry Hodson robbing the drug house and – if the rumours were true – doing him out of a lot of money, he only needed to have a chat to his father-in-law for advice.

Then the web tangled even more.

Nicola Gobbo admitted a Hodson/Mokbel connection. In a police statement, she wrote: 'I first met Terry Hodson when I appeared for his son Andrew Hodson at his bail application over drug charges in early 2002. Andrew had been referred to me via Tony Mokbel. Terry attended the County Court for Andrew's bail application which is where I first met him.'

But it wasn't just major players in the Victorian gangland who might have wanted Terry dead. He had given the MDID information about a major drug cartel in South Australia with connections to South America and the Colombian drug cartels. The South Australian detectives utilised Terry's information and made some big arrests in one of the largest cocaine seizures in Australian history.

Mokbel.

Carl.

Collins.

Colombians.

The list was endless.

Because the police had listening devices and phone taps in place on all of Carl Williams's phones, Acting Superintendent Dick Daly heard about the conversations between Adam Shand and Carl Williams and drug trafficker David McCulloch on Tuesday, 11 May. The men were overheard discussing the leaked document in which Terry Hodson was named. Lewis Moran had been gunned down six weeks earlier, on 31 March. It would be reported that Tony Mokbel paid $150 000 for the hit and Carl Williams would later be convicted of commissioning the murder.

While in the press every leaked document was hinted at as coming from me and the elusive, supposedly missing blue folder, this particular document that the cops thought they could tie back to me ended up being from a legitimate source 'provided to persons outside of Victoria Police legitimately for an unrelated legal matter' – according to the statement of the guy running the case, Detective Cameron Davey. Which was my point right from the beginning: Terry's informer number was on all of the defence briefs and people had been putting two and two together for ages.

But now every document that surfaced about Terry and his informing – documents supplied legitimately, if unwisely, by the Victoria Police – was blamed on me.

Just saying.

While Dick Daly acknowledged in his statement that Carl Williams was talking about Terry Hodson, he didn't say whether or not he was worried. Worried that Carl Williams was discussing Terry.

Carl Williams, whose enemies were dropping like flies.

CHAPTER 15

Following Carl

By early May 2004 there was often surveillance on Carl Williams. Covert crews followed him about his business, watching from their cars while he met colleagues at the local Red Rooster or any of his other favourite haunts.

On Wednesday, 5 May, a team of four covert cops observed Carl Williams and his dad, George, park a silver Mercedes in Lonsdale Street in the city then walk over to a café to meet Nicola Gobbo, who was waiting out the front. The three met for about forty minutes, then Nicola left and walked in the direction of the County Court, while Carl and his dad stayed at the café for another twenty minutes.

Then they began a series of stops – one at a pub and one at an address in Prahran, and then one in Brunswick. Finally, George dropped Carl at a pub at 5.15 p.m., and the surveillance cops sat outside until their shift ended at 9 p.m.

A day in the life of Carl Williams: meet with the lawyer, make a few quick stops about the place, end up at the pub.

After leaving him to his own devices on the Thursday, by Friday, 7 May, the surveillance teams were at it again, dogging Carl's every move.

At 11.13 a.m. Carl Williams, dressed in blue jeans and a light-blue jumper, carrying a jacket, was observed leaving his mother's house in Primrose Street, which was also under constant camera surveillance. Carl drove off in a gold Nissan Maxima.

While he was driving to meet hit man and friend Rod Collins, Carl Williams's phone records showed that he spoke to journalist Adam Shand en route. *What was Carl telling the journo on the way to meet the man who would later be accused of murdering the Hodsons*, I hear you ask. Funnily enough, he was talking about Terry. At 11.15 a.m. Carl chatted to Shand about the document he'd seen recently in which Terry Hodson was implicated in the contract on Carl's life.

Twelve minutes later, Carl pulled into the Red Rooster at Maribyrnong and got out of his car. Two minutes after that he met with Rod Collins. The two were videoed as they spoke in the car park. Collins was wearing a black jacket and dark-blue trackie daks. Five minutes later the two men moved over to Williams's car and climbed inside. They were joined by what surveillance cops described as an 'unknown female', who was undoubtedly Rod's partner, Joan McGuire, who – phone taps showed – had a doctor's appointment and Rod went with her. The doctor's surgery was opposite the Red Rooster. Williams drove off with Collins and the woman, and was seen dropping them both off in West Footscray six minutes later.

All up, Williams and Collins had been together for fourteen minutes.

A couple of hours later Carl was spotted again. He was at Windows Restaurant on the corner of Lonsdale and Exhibition streets in the city with his wife, Roberta, Roberta's sister, Michelle, and another associate. Twenty minutes after the surveillance had resumed, the foursome was joined by Rod Collins wearing a blue beanie. He had a conversation with Carl and then the two men moved through the restaurant, out of sight of the watching police. Twenty-three minutes later Williams and Collins returned to the group.

At 2.51 p.m. Roberta Williams left the café to chat with a man out the front.

Then gangland figure Lewis Caine arrived and followed Roberta into the restaurant, joining the group at the table.

Rod Collins hung around the group along with Caine, Roberta, Michelle, and Carl, before leaving the restaurant at 4.02 p.m. Two minutes later Antonios 'Tony' Mokbel was reported getting into a black Mercedes sedan in Lonsdale Street. He was carrying a beige shoulder bag, and wore a beige baseball cap and a red windcheater. He was later identified by the surveillance cops as the man seen talking to Roberta earlier.

After Mokbel and his man-bag had disappeared off into the afternoon, Rod Collins came back into the restaurant at 4.08 p.m. He had missed his son-in-law, Mokbel, by a couple of minutes.

Throughout the afternoon there would be small breakaway groups that would leave the table for a couple of minutes at a time. The surveillance crews didn't say what they were doing. At 4.25 p.m. the surveillance stopped watching the rogues' gallery, packed up and went home.

The meal would prove to be a last supper for Lewis Caine.

A day later, he would be murdered.

He met with a crook called Evangelos 'Ange' Goussis and a mate of his to discuss the planned assassination of underworld lawyer Mario Condello at the behest of Carl Williams. But things became confused and Lewis Caine ended up dead.

Killed by a shot to the face.

What was going on between Carl Williams, Lewis Caine, Rod Collins and Tony Mokbel is anybody's guess. But if anybody was to guess, it was common knowledge that when a group like that met there was a murder shortly after. The Purana task force – established to bring down this particular group of criminals – knew this all too well.

The hit man Rod Collins was there; so was Carl Williams, who later admitted organising the hit on the Hodsons. Then who should make an appearance but Tony Mokbel. Let's examine those connections.

By bungling the Oakleigh robbery, Terry Hodson had enabled the seizure of hundreds of thousands of dollars' worth of pills – pills that were to be sold by Tony Mokbel. Thus, Mokbel potentially lost millions of dollars in drug sales. Of course, the MDID would have seized the drugs anyway, but that was hardly a consolation to Mokbel. Tayluh Jones the drug-house babysitter would later admit that Azzam Ahmed had exaggerated the amount of drugs in the house to Mokbel and alleged that $700 000 had also been stolen. The drug-house crook had clearly jumped at the opportunity to explain away probably a million dollars in cash and drugs. So Mokbel would have been a million times more angry.

Carl Williams had admitted to journalist Adam Shand that he had recently seen documents suggesting that Terry Hodson had been in on a plan with Lewis Moran to kill him. According to Shand, Carl was more incensed at the paltry price put on his head than anything else. But incensed nonetheless.

So here at the one table was Carl Williams, who held a grudge against Terry Hodson because of the alleged contract with Lewis Moran. (Not that Carl had to worry about Lewis Moran anymore – he had arranged his murder on 31 March. Which was exactly how Carl dealt with his enemies.)

Tony Mokbel had lost hundreds of thousands of dollars when Terry exposed the Dublin Street drug house.

Rod Collins was a hit man and Tony Mokbel's father-in-law, not to mention a longtime friend of Carl's.

Without any help from me, any or all of these men easily had motive to kill Terry. And they had lunch together ten days before Terry was murdered.

Innocently eating together?

Or plotting yet another murder?

Another significant thing is the date that this meeting took place. A month earlier, Lewis Moran had paid for his hatred of Carl with his life: he had been gunned down at the Brunswick Club. Later, it was suggested that Tony Mokbel had offered $150 000 (by surprising coincidence, the exact amount that I was accused of offering for the Hodsons) so that Carl Williams could organise the hit. Williams was later convicted of this. Mokbel was acquitted.

But still ...

A week after the Williams/Mokbel/Collins meeting, the Hodsons were gunned down.

And, again, the focus stayed on me.

And only me.

CHAPTER 16

Saturday, 15 May

Andrew Hodson said that he visited his parents on Saturday, 15 May. He said that he and his twelve-year-old son got to their place at 12.30 p.m. They stayed about half an hour, and he told police that he 'went somewhere for a couple of hours then returned'. After he arrived back later in the afternoon, he said that he stayed until about 6.30 p.m. 'Everything was fine. Mum and Dad were happy although Dad was complaining of a sore back. They made no mention to me about any concerns. They had no plans to go anywhere over the weekend. They never mentioned anyone coming over to visit.'

A number of neighbours who lived near the Hodsons heard loud, sharp 'cracks' or bangs around 6 p.m. on the Saturday evening. If Andrew's statement was correct, he would still have been at the house at the time.

Neighbour 1: 'At some time between 5 p.m. and 6 p.m. that afternoon whilst I was in my backyard, I heard a loud, sharp sound. It was an unusual sound. I would describe it as like a crack. Not long after the first crack, maybe a second or a couple of seconds later, there was a second crack sound. I heard either two or three crack sounds in total. The sound got my attention because it was so unusual. I didn't know what the noise was. It was not a car backfiring.'

Neighbour 2: 'I heard what sounded like a shot about 6.15 p.m. which was early evening but didn't pay any attention. You hear bangs and cars all the time on our busy street.'

When Nicola Gobbo was later questioned about Andrew Hodson, she was asked if she went out to dinner with him on the fifteenth. She admitted that she had. She'd written about the dinner in her diary. They'd dined in Chinatown. So Andrew must've gone from his parents' house out to dinner with his lawyer. Interestingly, later at the Royal Commission, during Senior Sergeant Jim O'Brien's testimony, *Age* journalist Tammy Mills reported this: '[Azzam] Ahmed knew about the murders before they occurred, the commission was told. He warned [Tayluh] to be seen out on the night of the murders, while Ahmed's alibi was Ms Gobbo.'

At 9.36 p.m. on the Saturday night Carl Williams rang Darren Lunny from Channel 9 to talk about the Hodson/Moran threat to his life – since Lewis Moran had already been gunned down, only the Hodson part of the threat was still valid.

Except that by then the Hodsons were probably dead as well.

Unlike on TV cop shows, the exact time of death can never be estimated to the minute, or even the hour. If the bangs and cracks heard earlier by neighbours were indeed the sounds of the shots that killed the Hodsons, Carl might have been simply ringing Lunny on a Saturday night to chew the fat. If the Hodsons were killed a little later in the evening, the phone call might have been an alibi.

At first, Carl grizzled about the police not taking his death threats seriously.

'And then with the threat to kill, like you know with the other one, the one they threatened to kill me, or well, [an informer] went to see Terry Hodson and offered fifty thousand to Lewis Moran. So obviously they [the police] were aware of that ... of what was going on ...'

He also told Lunny that he had been threatened by a cop the last time he had been arrested. 'And then ... when they did arrest me, the copper said to me, "Ya gonna be killed. We're gonna kill ya, maybe not today, but ya gonna be killed. We're gonna get ya. Mark my words. You dog. We're gonna kill ya."'

Carl Williams obviously took offence to the alleged police death threat and lodged a complaint to the Chief Commissioner.

He lodged four complaints – all of which, according to him, were ignored.

With the clock ticking towards 10 p.m. on a Saturday night, Carl then whinged about how Chief Commissioner Christine Nixon had had him banned from Crown Casino. A suspicious person might think Carl was trying to keep Darren Lunny on the phone.

CHAPTER 17

The Harp Road crime scene

A neighbour's statement: 'The following day, Sunday 16 May 2004, I spent all day outside in the garden. At some time after dark, I was still in the front garden working. I had the outside light on. It was after 6 p.m., but I'm not certain of the exact time. While in my front garden, I heard a man yelling and swearing, saying the f-word a lot. The yelling was coming from the direction of the west. I initially thought that there must have been a domestic, but there was only one voice; a man's voice. There was about three bursts of this yelling and I thought it sounded like a man was outside because it was so loud. The yelling lasted for a couple of minutes.'

Andrew Hodson had just discovered his parents' bodies.

After Sergeant Paul Ritchie arrived at the Harp Road house at 6.30 p.m. he described the Hodson siblings as such: 'Andrew Hodson appeared to be in a highly agitated state. He stated: "My parents have been fucking killed! Call ESD. This is an ESD matter." Hodson also smelt strongly of intoxicating liquor. He also stated the premises had security video cameras operating ... I then had a short conversation with Mandy who was a lot calmer than her brother.'

One can only imagine the screaming and yelling outside around 6 p.m., then the methodical ransacking, gun-searching, drinking and cocaine-snorting inside the house, which preceded the 'agitation' seen by the police arriving half an hour later.

Following closely on the heels of the local constabulary were officers of all ranks. When Inspector Peter De Santo arrived,

Andrew Hodson was quick to point the finger: 'Fucking Dale's done it!' he declared. 'They've been executed, both shot in the back of their heads face down in the back room. He's left his fucking calling card: a spent shell was on the back of Dad's head. It's been placed there.'

Acting Superintendent Dick Daly and Senior Sergeant Murray Gregor arrived just before 8 p.m. According to Daly's statement, Andrew had apparently calmed down.

'I don't blame you blokes for what has happened,' said Andrew, 'but you have to make sure that you get that bloke.'

Just after 8 p.m. Daly spoke to Mandy Hodson. 'After expressing my sympathy to her, she explained what had happened: "I spoke to them on Friday. Dad invited us around for a casserole. I tried to ring them today. There was no answer. I came around. Andrew was here putting the rubbish out. I had the remote. We opened the garage door and the dogs were in the garage. We went around to the courtyard. The door and gate were unbolted. I heard the TV. I looked in and saw them lying on the floor."' After giving her comprehensive overview, Daly said, 'Mandy Hodson then became very emotionally upset.'

•

When crime scene examiner Senior Constable Peter Cox got to the Harp Road house at 8.25 p.m. on Sunday, 16 May 2004, he walked up the driveway, passing Christine Hodson's red Holden station wagon and Mandy Hodson's BMW parked behind it. As he walked past the cars his movement activated a sensor light above the garage door and a floodlight lit up the driveway.

Being one of a long line of cops to arrive at the murder scene, Cox entered through the open garage door. It was a large double garage with workbenches, tools, wood, and other household items. Cox saw the time-lapse video recorder on the top of a shelf in the garage. He found no tape in it, but he took swabs of the stop and eject buttons.

After an examination of the garage, Cox entered the house to begin the collection of forensic evidence inside. The house was well kept and tidy, and there were no outward signs of what had occurred in the TV room out the back. There were no signs of forced entry.

Did that mean that Terry or Christine had let their killer into the house?

Cox found all the windows locked; there were security grills on the windows at the front and side of the house. The gate to the side yard was padlocked.

Since the Hodsons had video surveillance of their house courtesy of the police-installed system, Cox located the videos which could be vital evidence, even though the one from the machine – the most recent – was missing. In a linen cupboard in the hallway were six videotapes labelled *Monday*, *Tuesday*, *Wednesday*, *Thursday*, *Friday* and *Sunday*. There was also an empty video case. The fact that *Saturday* was missing suggested that the killer had known the intricacies of the surveillance and had known where to find the recorder in the garage. Cox collected the remaining videotapes as evidence.

In the lounge room four drawers had been pulled out of a dresser and stacked neatly. Had the killer searched the house?

In the kitchen Cox noted an alert system that lit up when the sensors were activated in both the lounge room and the driveway. The unit had been muted. On the kitchen table was an empty bottle of Cascade beer. Cox swabbed it for fingerprints. With little more to see in the main section of the house, he made his way through a small extension area that was used as a bar room. Through the bar room was the entry to the TV room where Terry and Christine lay, dead.

There was no sign of forced entry in the TV room and Cox set about his examination. First, he did fibre trace lifts from the backs of the two bodies.

Interestingly, Cox also found two more sets of videotapes, each labelled with the days of the week. The first set had Monday through to Saturday, and the second set, found next to another time-lapse recorder, had Sunday through to Friday. Like the set from the linen closet, this set was missing Saturday.

Cox worked around the bodies of Terry and Christine Hodson, collecting their cigarette butts and swabbing their wine glasses. Then he moved outside to the garden. There was a fence separating the yard from a fernery and garden bed area which Cox entered through an open gate. There, he found some scuff marks in the soil and mulch near the back boundary fence, which he thought could have been made by the heel of a shoe. Not only was there a scuff mark in the mulch, but a pot plant near the marks had been partially knocked over. Could someone have escaped over the back fence?

If so, the police could have questioned Mandy Hodson. She used to live over the back fence. Indeed, Terry had even built a gate in the back fence to allow her easy access. She would have been more than familiar with the layout and access.

Cox took soil samples to match against the shoes of possible suspects. He also took a trace evidence lift from the top of the fence. Not only were there scuff marks in the soil, Cox found scuff marks on the horizontal uprights of the wooden paling fence, and a vine growing along the fence which looked like it had been pulled out of the way. A later examination showed corresponding scuff marks on the other side of the fence, which was the home of an elderly woman.

Cox finished his examination of the crime scene, not realising that he would be back two days later to examine all of the hidden cavities that Mandy Hodson would admit were in the house. But not before she had removed most of their contents.

•

An hour and a half after Cox arrived at the Harp Road crime scene, so did the deputy director of the Victorian Institute of Forensic Medicine, Dr David Ranson. With a career spanning three decades, Dr Ranson was an eminent expert in the field of forensic pathology. He had been contacted by Charlie Bezzina of the Homicide Squad. Accompanied by Bezzina and the State Coroner, Graeme Johnstone, Ranson was shown into the Harp Road house. Like everyone else that night, he entered through the garage door and made his way through the lounge room into the TV room out the back.

The bodies of Terry and Christine Hodson lay face down with their feet towards the two-seater sofa and their heads facing the television. Christine lay closer to the door.

Dr Ranson noted that Christine was 'dressed in pink and white slippers, white trousers with star logos on the back pockets, and a pink top. Extensive blood staining could be seen at the sides of the pink top and the sides of the arms. The arms were flexed at the elbows with the hands lying underneath the chest between the front of the chest and the floor. The hair was blonde in colour and two areas of apparent skin defect could be seen over the back of the head which was uppermost. There appeared to be some blackening around these defects. Blood was also present in this area. Extensive blood was present over the floor around the face ...'

Dr Ranson examined Terry Hodson's body. He too noted the spent cartridge that Andrew Hodson had thought was a calling card: not on the back of the head, but over the back of the right shoulder of the dark blue shirt. Another spent cartridge lay on the floor to the right side of the head. A further spent cartridge could be seen on the floor towards the right side of the body, adjacent to the skirting board beneath a small table on the far side of the room. Ranson noted two cigarette butts on the floor – one near Terry's hand and one near Christine's right shoulder.

It looked like they had both been smoking when they had been shot.

Ranson reported well-developed rigor mortis in both bodies. Lividity was also well formed and he concluded that it was consistent with them dying where they now lay. Their body temperatures were the same as the ambient temperature: they had been dead for a while. Unlike TV forensic pathologists, real-life experts are loath to narrow down the time of death because there are so many variables, and any anomaly could lead detectives in the wrong direction.

•

At 9.42 p.m. Senior Constable Alan Pringle arrived at the Harp Road crime scene. Pringle was a firearm and tool-mark examiner attached to the Victoria Police forensic laboratory at Macleod. While Pringle gathered up evidence with regard to the shooting deaths, he was to miss an obvious piece of evidence that Mandy Hodson would find a couple of days later in bizarre circumstances.

Like Ranson, Alan Pringle saw the cigarette butts on the floor – one near each of the bodies. Pringle collected the cigarette butts, which were later found to have DNA consistent with having been smoked by the pair.

Pringle saw the three cartridges that were noted earlier by Dr Ranson. He collected the cartridge case from Terry Hodson's right shoulder, another from the floor near Terry, and another from under the side table. That was three fired cartridge cases for the four head shots.

One was missing.

•

During the evening, forensic officer Peter Ross arrived at the crime scene. While he swabbed Andrew Hodson's hands for gunshot residue, Andrew explained that he had touched his mother and father on the back of the head and kissed them both on the head. If Ross found that strange – considering the Hodsons' head injuries and the extensive bleeding around the heads – he didn't add it to his notes. He found no traces of gunshot residue. But if the Hodsons had been murdered the night before, that meant that whoever killed Terry and Christine had had the chance to go home and wash or shower, which would remove all traces of gunshot residue.

•

Around 2 a.m., Andrew Hodson took one of his parents' German shepherd dogs, Rosie, to a vet in Bundoora. Police had called first and asked the vet to collect a blood sample from the dog. The vet concluded that Rosie appeared fit and healthy, and displayed no signs of being concussed or poisoned. The vet took a blood sample, which was collected the following Monday.

Another vet, earlier in the evening, had examined Molly. Unlike Rosie, Molly was listed as 'tremoring, panting and appeared very agitated'. The vet found dilated, minimally responsive pupils, and bruising consistent with blunt trauma to the head. The vet concluded that Molly 'may have been suffering the expected response after a major stress event or physical trauma. Intoxication was considered as the main differential.' The vet collected a blood sample.

The examination of the guard dogs was important because much would later be made of who the dogs would and wouldn't react to. Even senior police officers in their statements said that if they were going to visit Terry they made sure he had the dogs tied up or put out the back before they ventured up the driveway. One neighbour interviewed in the days following the murders said that the Hodsons' dogs barked a lot and nearly drove her insane. However, on the Saturday night she didn't hear them bark at all.

The Hodson children all agreed that Molly was the aggressive one, while Rosie was younger and more friendly. It made sense that if an intruder did need to subdue the dogs, Molly would pose the greater threat.

No mention was made of Christine Hodson's nine-year-old poodle called Ty.

As a point of interest – and I'm no expert – if Molly the dog was 'intoxicated' when examined in the small hours of Monday morning, and the Hodsons were killed possibly as early as 6.00 p.m. on Saturday evening when the neighbours reported hearing shots fired, how long would alcohol stay in her system?

CHAPTER 18

The investigation

Andrew Hodson leapt forward at the crime scene and declared, 'Fucking Dale's done it!' He steadfastly refused to admit to investigators that his father had any other enemies but me and Dave Miechel. But while detectives looked in my direction, they also looked very closely at the Hodson offspring.

Because of the rumours that Terry Hodson had informed on all of his own children, the police rightly had to investigate whether any of them held a grudge. They also looked into Andrew Hodson's association with Tony Mokbel. The police, however, found no basis for charging any of his offspring in relation to the murders.

When Mandy Hodson told the Homicide detectives that her brother had removed the gun from the crime scene, the detectives retrieved it and charged Andrew for possession.

In early June, Ethical Standards Department detective Peter De Santo had a conversation with Andrew. Two days later, warrants were granted to tap a number of Andrew's phones. A warrant was also obtained for a surveillance device to be placed onto Andrew's car.

Detectives also visited Carl Williams – who was, by then, in prison – to talk to him about the telephone intercepts that had him talking about Terry Hodson to a journalist not long before Terry was murdered.

Homicide detectives Charlie Bezzina and Cameron Davey interviewed Tony Mokbel, who was a picture of helpfulness. No, he didn't know Terry Hodson. Yes, he knew Andrew Hodson –

they'd been in jail together. Yes, he had met up with Andrew a few times since they were released. No, he had no hard feelings against Terry. No, he was not aware of any ill feeling between Mandy Hodson and his girlfriend, Danielle McGuire, over drug territory. No, he had no ill feeling towards Mandy. No, he didn't fund Andrew Hodson's bail application. Yes, he was a guarantor for Andrew's bail application. No, Andrew Hodson did not work for the Mokbel family. Yes, he knew Azzam Ahmed and the Ahmed family very well. No, he had no involvement in the drug press operation at the Dublin Street house. No, he didn't know who killed the Hodsons – and if he did, he wouldn't tell the police anyway.

•

The big questions in the investigation remained: Who would Terry and Christine Hodson have let into the house? Who would they have watched TV with, relaxing with alcohol and cocaine? Who would they have been totally not threatened by so that Terry didn't feel the need to have his handgun by his side, like he usually did when he watched TV in the back room?

Indeed, who might he have put the gun *away* for?

Who would have known about both sets of video surveillance tapes in order to remove them from the scene?

And what happened to Christine Hodson's poodle? It's not mentioned at the murder scene. Did someone kill the couple and then take the poodle? And if they did, why? And the other two guard dogs – one showing signs of intoxication – were they tested over a period of hours? How long would a dog show signs of intoxication for? A blood sample was taken at 2 a.m. on the Monday morning at a veterinary clinic. Was one taken at 3 a.m. to show how the level of alcohol was reducing in order to calculate when it was given in the first place? How likely was it to still show early Monday morning if, indeed, the killings occurred on the Saturday night? And if the alcohol was administered much later on, why? Who would go to the effort of getting a dog drunk?

CHAPTER 19

Who knew?

In statements given to detectives after the Hodsons were murdered, a number of people admitted knowing that something was going to happen to Terry.

What is most interesting is *when* they knew.

For the official police story to work, it has to work in both directions. They would later claim that a week before the murders, I asked Carl Williams to organise a hit man.

But ...

Tayluh the drug-house babysitter had made a statement saying that she knew that Terry Hodson was marked for death *two weeks* beforehand, and that the source of the information was Azzam 'Adam' Ahmed. Read what she has to say for yourself:

> About two weeks or so before the murder of the Hodsons, I was over at Adam's house one night. On that night, we were talking and the subject of the burglary came up and we were talking about Hodson and Dale and Miechel, as we did. Adam then told me that something was going to happen to Terence Hodson. Adam never mentioned Christine's name at all. I can't recall the exact words he used but I was left in no doubt that there was an intention to kill Terence Hodson. Adam never mentioned any names to me about who was involved in the plan. I formed the opinion that Adam had been told of specific information about a plan to kill Terence Hodson. I do not believe that Adam just made an off-the-cuff comment that Hodson might be killed. I didn't question

Adam any further about what he knew. I didn't really want
to know ...

A day or two before the murders, I was talking on the
phone to Adam ... on that occasion, he told me to be out
on the Saturday night. He told me to make sure that I was
seen by people. I didn't ask Adam why he told me to be out.
I suspected that he was telling me to be out and be seen
because there was an intention to kill Terence Hodson on
that night.

That Saturday night, she did as Ahmed told her and went
clubbing in Albert Park. In the small hours of Sunday morning –
around fifteen hours before the bodies were discovered – she got
a call from Ahmed. In her statement, she says that Adam told
her that the thing they had spoken about was done.

She took it to mean that Terry Hodson was dead.

And these were the people the police were doing deals with.
People who knew.

Acting Superintendent Dick Daly also suggested he knew
something was in the wind on Tuesday, 11 May – the Tuesday
before the murders. In his statement, he said that he went to
the Investigation Support Division of ESD, 'where I listened to
telephone calls involving persons named Carl Williams, Adam
Shand and David McCulloch with reference to a document in
which Terry Hodson was named ...'

While he admits discussing this turn of events with the head
of the Purana task force, he doesn't mention any particular
concerns. Journalist Adam Shand talked regularly with Carl
Williams and would eventually write a book about Williams
and the gangland wars, called *Big Shots*. David McCulloch
was a drug boss who had, in 2002, delayed his trial for several
years by making corruption allegations against Victoria Police
officers.

Interestingly, in the world where I was accused of tipping
off everyone about everything, Adam Shand admits to being
tipped off that the police were listening to his conversations

with Williams. 'The cops had warned my editor that I was being picked up in telephone intercepts talking to Carl and that I should be careful,' he wrote in his book.

•

As well as Tayluh Jones and Azzam Ahmed discussing the murders two weeks before they happened, and some police members thinking something was in the wind, Terry Hodson himself had predicted his own end.

His youngest daughter, Nikki, told police that her mum and dad had been talking for a while about how they would probably be killed. In her police statement, she wrote the following:

> Dad has always said that he was a dead man walking because of the statements he'd made. Dad sat us all down at Christmas time and said that he had done things during his life that he wasn't proud of. He said, 'I've made my bed and now I've got to lie in it.' Dad was certain he was going to be killed; it was just a matter of where and when. Both Mum and Dad accepted that they couldn't change what was probably to come. Dad had said if it wasn't the crims, it would be the police that would get him and Mum. I only assume that Dad believed police might kill him because he'd made statements against Miechel. I've got no idea why Mum had accepted that she was going to be killed. We as a family were never ones to be morbid. We knew that he was probably going to get knocked. He was offered witness protection but he would not take it which is something I couldn't understand. He chose to stay at home with Mum.

It is interesting that Terry Hodson said if it wasn't the crooks it would be the police, meaning that even he felt that he had more chance of being offed by the crooks who, by then, everyone knew he had double-crossed.

CHAPTER 20

My second arrest

A bunch of police colleagues and I did a trip once a year to get away from it all, get on the grog and catch up with each other's news. This trip to Bendigo was organised months earlier by one of my mates.

My wife had a good friend who lived in Bendigo and she decided to come up with me and stay with her friend while we had our boys' weekend. She drove me up and dropped me at a local footy game, said hi to my mates, then left with our son to stay with her friend.

I was really looking forward to letting loose because times had been really tough: I had gone from being a detective sergeant to being suspended without pay. I was on bail for major drug trafficking charges, I had spent ten days in solitary confinement at Port Phillip Prison, and I was seeing a psychologist on a regular basis to deal with the anxiety and depression that came with being treated the way I had been treated. To add to this, I was working six days a week digging ditches to support my family, earning about twelve bucks an hour.

A weekend away with the couple of copper mates who still spoke to me was just what the doctor ordered.

•

When Charlie Bezzina knocked on my door at 5.45 a.m. on Monday, 17 May, I knew it couldn't be good news, since no good news arrives at that time of the morning. Charlie was a respected Homicide detective and he and I had worked together in the Homicide Squad. I had always liked him.

'The Hodsons have been killed,' he told me. 'I've been instructed to come here and arrest you.' He was respectful – and, I think, a little awkward, as if it wasn't his decision.

'When did it happen?' I asked numbly.

'Probably Saturday night,' said Bezzina.

'But I was in Bendigo all weekend,' I protested. 'There's no way I can be involved.'

'We still have to go back to the office to sort this out,' he said.

'But there's nothing to sort out!' I was angry. 'I was in Bendigo all weekend with other police officers!'

'And I was with him!' my wife cried. 'Paul and I were in Bendigo all weekend!'

Bezzina sighed. He was an experienced investigator. This wasn't how things were done. If I really was a suspect, an investigator of the calibre of Bezzina would have built up a systematic case from a distance before he came anywhere near me.

'It will be a media circus!' I said, knowing full well that if I appeared at the St Kilda Road police headquarters the media would splash my picture all over the papers. Again.

'Let's talk about it in the office,' he said.

I chose that moment to absolutely dig my heels in. 'I'm happy to sit down right here,' I said, pointing at my kitchen table, 'and I'll write a minute-by-minute description of my entire weekend. You've got no right to take me anywhere.'

I rang my solicitor, Tony Hargreaves, and explained what was going on. 'I don't believe they have the power of arrest,' I told him.

He asked to speak to Charlie.

'It's the way it's gotta be,' Charlie told him.

While every part of me screamed against going with the detectives, I knew deep down that Charlie was just doing his job. And, bottom line, I respected Charlie fully.

I also understood that he was simply following orders from cops much higher up the chain than him. He would later say in his memoirs that it was his decision and he wanted to come to me first so that he could honestly say that he had left no stone unturned.

•

The strain of the last six months had taken its toll. If you heard that people you liked had been shot in cold blood, under normal circumstances you could take in the horror, lament their passing, grieve for them, laugh about funny things they said or did, then come to the understanding that they were gone. But I had been targeted every which way but loose. I had been thrown in a cell, leaving my wife and small son behind. They had tried to pin a major drug charge on me, and the fact that Charlie Bezzina was standing at my door the morning after the Hodsons' bodies had been discovered did not bode well for my liberty.

The presence of Bezzina and other detectives from the Homicide Squad at my door spoke volumes about where the investigation was going to focus. Just like my first arrest, they had a search warrant and left my wife in tears, holding the baby, as I was arrested and taken in for questioning. As with the first search, they found nothing at my house to suggest that I had anything to do with anything.

Mine wasn't the only house that was searched. Dave Miechel, suspended from duty following his arrest the previous September for the Oakleigh robbery, also received an early-morning visit. While I got Charlie Bezzina, he got Sol Solomon.

Dave too was taken into the Homicide Squad for an interview. His interview started at 7.50 a.m. and ended ten minutes later. He answered 'no comment' to every question.

I didn't blame him.

•

The same day I was arrested and taken from my home, a much stronger suspect was allowed to carry on his business.

On Monday, 17 May, Carl Williams had a telephone conversation with drug boss David McCulloch. McCulloch was another crook to benefit from the 2002 situation at the drug squad. He was given bail and his case was delayed for years because he made corruption allegations against several police officers. When he was finally sentenced the judge admonished him for making false accusations leading to a futile two-year investigation into legitimate police investigations. McCulloch had taken things further than just making allegations to try to delay his court appearance: after he was granted bail he used the media to pressure the government into calling for a royal commission. He went to great lengths, including hiring private detectives to try to muddy the waters around the charges against him. Ultimately his tactics didn't work, but a lot of police hours were wasted following up the allegations.

At 10.09 a.m. Carl Williams rang David McCulloch.

'You read the newspapers?' asked McCulloch.

'Yeah, Hobson,' said Carl, mispronouncing Terry's last name like he usually did. He used variations like Hodgeson and Hobson and Hodgkins.

'Yeah, unbelievable, isn't it?' said McCulloch.

'Yeah,' agreed Carl.

'So he's a bloody wild old city.'

'They didn't have 'im under very good police protection,' said Carl.

'... Funny you sayin' that,' said McCulloch. 'I was thinkin', who knows with the level of corruption, who knows what sort of situation's transpired there.'

'Yeah.'

McCulloch mentioned that a journalist had already been in touch with him and told him she would ring Carl.

'I'll tell her ... I think it's great!' said Carl. 'More people who give evidence against should be killed.'

'Well, y' you know, yer, you're just ... saying that in jest,' sputtered McCulloch. 'But what you're saying is there's a lot of evil people out there ...'

'That's right,' agreed Carl.

'And —'

'It's come back … to bite 'em on the arse.'

'It's karma.'

'Yeah … was the wife giving evidence too?' asked Carl.

'I don't know. I'm not sure.'

'Must have been someone he knew, though, to let a – to be let in the house, eh?' said Carl.

'A couple of radio comments on it and they're saying that there was no sign of forced entry.'

'Yeah.'

'… It's certainly a bloody very interesting development, particularly in view of the fact that there's been corrupt police that he was alleged to be workin' with,' said McCulloch.

'That's right,' said Carl.

'On bail recently.'

The two chatted about radio commentary on the murder.

'Could be ESD or anything. Who would know?' said Carl.

'Could well – it's a very, very interesting situation all round, isn't it?'

'Isn't it, yeah,' agreed Carl.

McCulloch explained the rumours he had heard about the 'massive protection' on Terry Hodson and that maybe the police were cost-cutting and that had led to the murders.

'I don't know,' said Carl.

'And so, weekend. You have a quiet one?'

'I went out all weekend,' Carl told him. 'I went out Saturday, Saturday night, Sunday. Sunday morning.'

The two men then made plans to catch up for a coffee.

On Tuesday, 18 May 2004 – two days after Terry and Christine had been found dead – David McCulloch and Carl Williams spoke again. While the two discussed who had been barred from Crown Casino and who hadn't – clearly a favourite topic with Carl – they soon moved around to talking about something that they couldn't or shouldn't have known.

'Why did the ESD tapes go missin' from the Hodsons' house the day of the murder?' asked Carl.

'It's amazin', isn't it? Is that what's comin' out now?' said McCulloch.

'But they were set up across the road from the house to face the front door. But they're gone missin' is the rumours,' said Carl, citing some pretty specific rumours.

'It's amazin', isn't it?' McCulloch repeated.

'They malfunction on the day of the murder,' said Carl.

'Malfunction. Isn't it amazing?'

'Yeah,' agreed Carl.

'It's amazing how these malfunctions happen within the police force, isn't it?'

'Yeah,' said Carl.

'It might well be that there's one or two at Ceja that are just NQR – not quite right,' McCulloch said, back on his police corruption theme.

On 18 May, Carl was banned from licensed venues in the eight eastern suburbs within the Stonnington City Council. The reason? Because he was of 'notoriously bad character'. So instead of looking at Carl Williams as a possible suspect in the Hodson murders, the police were busy with the important task of banning him from clubs and bars around Melbourne.

CHAPTER 21

Stooks and the forgotten bullet

Even though on Tuesday, 18 May, journalist John Silvester had written a widely published article in *The Age* that said, 'Police said Hodson was a carpenter and had built secret cupboards and storage areas for some of Melbourne's biggest drug dealers', the police processing the crime scene and searching the house didn't think to check for such hidden storage areas, known in the trade as 'stooks'.

After the police had processed the scene and cleared it, they gave Mandy Hodson the set of keys to the Harp Road house. She took her new boyfriend, Mickey, with her when she returned to the house where her parents had lost their lives.

I will let 36-year-old Mandy tell you in her own words how she came to find the missing fourth shell casing.

Mandy: 'Later, when the police returned the keys for the house to me, Mickey and I went through the house. We went into the back room where Mum and Dad were found. When we were in there, I was laying on the floor trying to show Mickey how Mum and Dad were found. As I was down on the floor, I saw a shell, under a side-table against the wall with a small seat pushed under it.'

Given that she knew its possible value as evidence in the murder of her parents, you might think she would ring the police. But she didn't.

'I don't know why I didn't call the police straightaway,' she later wrote in her statement. She had spoken to Homicide detective Charlie Bezzina earlier that day and dobbed her brother in for taking the gun from the crime scene. She decided to go and visit her brother to tell him that she had told the police about the gun and that he would have to hand it over to them. While she was at his house, she gave him the shell casing and told him to hand it over when he handed over the gun. Killing two birds, so to speak.

After her session on the floor mimicking the position of the bodies of her slain parents, Mandy searched the house. Her father had built a number of stooks into the house. While not a word you would find in a dictionary, in the Hodson house stooks were hidden cavities where things could be stashed. Even though the police had processed the crime scene, these stooks were built to fool the coppers, and fool them they had.

Having the house to herself, Mandy raided the stooks. First there was the one in the ceiling of the TV room that held the sawn-off shotgun, then there was the one at the end of the passageway near the TV room that was more like a hidden room; that was where Terry stored the drugs and the guns that he sold on to others. There was another stook in one of the bedrooms, behind a bookshelf. There was one in the kitchen in the fridge cavity where Terry kept drugs and money, and there was one in the garage where Terry kept tins of money. There was a stook in the toilet and one in a pelmet over a wall mirror where Terry kept drugs. The house was a veritable treasure-trove.

Mandy knew that neither Andrew nor Nikki knew about the stook in the garage where the tins of cash were kept. She raided these and found between $50 000 and $60 000 in cash. She took it and used some of it to pay for the funerals and spent the rest. She also removed the drugs from the toilet stook.

After the stooks were discovered, crime scene examiner Senior Constable Peter Cox returned to examine the hidden cavities. He photographed the cavity above the step in the TV room and the concealed space next to the study. He also photographed items from these.

Well, the items that Mandy hadn't taken.

CHAPTER 22

The investigation

At the Homicide Squad, Detective Charlie Bezzina was in charge of the Hodson murder investigation. Such was the wide-ranging effect of Terry's informing and life as a drug dealer, Homicide detectives would eventually interview 150 potential suspects.

Despite these overwhelming numbers, there were forces within the Ethical Standards Department that seemed determined to focus on me.

Helping Bezzina was another Homicide Squad member, Detective Senior Constable Cameron Davey. Davey joined Bezzina at the Harp Road crime scene and was present when Andrew Hodson's hands were swabbed for gunshot residue. Thanks to Cameron Davey's statement, I learnt just how quickly the detectives looked in my direction. He said that it was around 3 a.m. on the morning after the bodies of Terry and Christine were discovered – which gave them just enough time to obtain a search warrant and be on my doorstep a couple of hours later.

Detective Cameron Davey's subpoenaed notes:

01.53 – Exit Scene

01.55 – escort undertakers with the deceased to the State Coroner's Office

2.10 – State Coroner's office. Deceased logged. 83s completed.

02.35 – C1 [Code 1 meaning that he was on the road]

02.40 – Suspects: Dave Miechel, Paul Dale.

Aside from arresting me, members of the Homicide Squad did begin a proper investigation. They spoke to the local resident who said that she'd heard what she described as two or three large sharp cracking sounds a couple of seconds apart on Saturday, 15 May between 5 and 6 p.m. She thought that maybe someone was setting off firecrackers. She thought it was a different noise from a car backfiring, but noted the noise because it was unusual.

One lead that hit the press two weeks after the murders was that one of the documents being passed around that contained Terry Hodson's informer number – 4/390 – was in the hands of the ABC. It was reported to say: '4/390 (Hodson) met on Tuesday in garage with [name deleted] who wanted 4/390 to knock Carl Williams for Lewis Moran for $50 000.' Detectives couldn't ask Lewis Moran about this because he had been gunned down on 31 March.

Since Carl Williams had indeed found out that Lewis Moran had asked Terry Hodson to kill him, it would seem to the average joe that he might just have had his own motive in respect to Terry. It was later reported that Tony Mokbel had ordered the hit on Lewis Moran, carried out by Ange Goussis, who was paid $150 000 for shooting Lewis Moran at the Brunswick Club.

While the police had Carl Williams under surveillance for some of the days in the lead-up to the murder, documents that I subpoenaed describe two surveillance teams following him on 5 May and 7 May, but then nothing. This would later become significant as the police tried to build their case against me.

•

Journalists found themselves on the other side of the fence, giving statements to the police. Veteran *Herald Sun* crime reporter Geoff Wilkinson told detectives that on 1 June he had been approached by another journalist, Jeremy Kelly, who showed him a document written by Dave Miechel, dated 3 June 2002, marked Highly Protected. Kelly asked Wilkinson's opinion as to whether the document was genuine. Having contacts high up in the police force, Wilkinson rang Assistant Police Commissioner Simon Overland directly and reported the presence of the document. He handed a copy on to police. And then helped Kelly with his story.

Interestingly, the document was later traced back to a 'legitimate source', meaning that the highly sensitive information had most probably been attached to a brief – just like such documents were in the bad old days before I pointed out the danger in doing this. Apparently Jeremy Kelly had requested a copy of the information report from Carl Williams, who obligingly got his dad, George, to fax it to him.

The police traced the document from Williams back to his associate, David McCulloch. Subpoenaed police documents read: '[A]n investigation has been conducted into how McCulloch came to be in possession of a copy of IR 44 from the Hodson Informer Management File and it has been established that this particular Information Report was provided to persons outside the Victoria Police legitimately, for an unrelated legal matter.'

Hmm.

Still, despite the circulation of Terry Hodson's informer documents that were provided 'legitimately', they were nonetheless dangerous to Terry. And despite the 'legitimate' circulation of them, the Office of Police Integrity engaged former Federal Court judge Tony Fitzgerald, who named me as 'the most obvious suspect' in the theft of the blue folder – one they said had disappeared from our office.

I was always suspicious of this story. Our office was literally crammed with blue folders. If they couldn't find Terry's, maybe it was under a pile. Or maybe it never went missing at all. Jim O'Brien had one in his office and we all added paperwork to it in the week after the Oakleigh break-in. Superintendent Biggin wrote in his statement that he handed over the other informer information file to Dick Daly on the Monday after the break-in. There were only ever two files and they are both accounted for in the statements of senior police officers in the aftermath of the drug house break-in.

•

Detectives Cameron Davey and Charlie Bezzina met with Mandy Hodson and her boyfriend, Mickey, who told them about the gun Andrew Hodson had removed from the crime scene on the night of the discovery of the bodies. The two detectives paid Andrew a visit and took the gun and the magazine. He also handed over the shell casing that Mandy had found when she was lying on the floor showing Mickey how her dead parents had been found.

On 11 June the police went back to Mandy Hodson for another statement. Earlier, the gun and the bullet casing had been handed into forensics for testing. In her written statement, she described how she and Andrew came to find the gun.

Her statement differed from Andrew's in that he said she disappeared and went to find the gun. Here's her version: 'On Sunday 16th May 2004, Andrew and I arrived at my mum and dad's place and found them in the back room. I knew that my dad always had a gun with him, but at first I didn't even think to look for it. Andrew asked me where it was and I said that if it wasn't in the room with him, then the only other place he would keep it was in the bedside table. So Andrew and I both went into the main bedroom and I opened the top drawer and pulled out a gun. It was a black handgun and I think it is an automatic. I gave it to Andrew and he took it and put it down his pants. I said to him, "shouldn't you hand it over?" and he said, "no, I'll take it because dad wanted me to have this." He put it down the front of his pants. Then we went back to the kitchen area and waited for the police.'

Considering that it only took the police six minutes from notification of the murders at 6.24 p.m. to arrive at the Harp Road house at 6.30 p.m., I wonder if this search for the gun took place *before* they called the police or after. Her sister, Nikki, said in her statement that Mandy rang her between 6.25 and 6.30 p.m., so there's also a phone call to fit into that six minutes.

Mandy then detailed how immediately after finding her dead parents she snorted cocaine, and then took her father's specially made 22-carat gold-plated straw. She also pocketed the Tupperware container of cocaine that sat on the small table at her mother's end of the couch.

After describing the cocaine snorting at the death scene of her parents, Mandy wrote about how she had come to find the missing bullet casing.

The detectives asked Mandy's boyfriend, Mickey, for his version of events. According to Mickey, he and Mandy hooked up in March. He'd heard around the nightclubs that she was a 'dog' or a police informer, but he didn't think so. He'd met her years earlier, when he was doing the nightclub scene to 'chase sheilas', but things had hotted up when she saw him in a photo from a friend's New Year's Eve celebrations. She told the friend to tell Mickey to give her a call.

Before he met Terry and Christine, Mickey heard Mandy had to go to court. 'Mandy told me that it was to do with her old man and something that he did involving a house in Oakleigh. I asked her about the rumours of being a dog. She told me that she signed a statement about having slept with a policeman by the name of Dave. Mandy didn't expand on this and you have got to understand that I didn't want to know about any of her past lovers and stuff like that. I think Mandy assumed that I had read all the papers and was aware through rumours and gossip. The only rumour that I had heard was that the policeman who had arrested her, she had slept with. It didn't make sense to me.

'Mandy also said that she had a few blues with her dad about making the statement because it went against everything that he had taught her and brought her up to believe. Mandy told me that she had made the statement to help her dad.'

Mickey knew about Andrew taking the gun from the crime scene. 'Mandy has told me that Andrew grabbed the gun from the dresser drawer in the bedroom and stuffed it down his pants. He has later told me that he was walking funny at the scene because the gun was down his pants. He didn't say why he took it. I told Mandy that there were only two things that came from guns: trouble and dead people.'

Even though he had only been going out with Mandy for two months, Mickey had picked up on the family's dislike of sister Nicola's husband, Peter Reed. 'I have never met Nicola's husband before or seen him. I know his name is Pete and he got pinched with Craig Minogue and the Russell Street bombing crew. Terry and Chrissy didn't like Pete. Mandy has told me that Pete didn't like them and they didn't like Pete. You suspect it may have had something to do with Pete not agreeing with Terry breaking the code and turning police informer. It was never spelled out like that, but I just assumed.'

Mickey talked about the time frame on the night Mandy and her brother discovered their murdered parents. He took a page in his statement to write about how he needed to be on time for dinner at 6 p.m. at Terry and Christine's. He said that he watched the clock all day, and at six on the dot he got a call from Mandy telling him that her parents were dead.

'I asked if she was joking. Mandy kept on crying and I realised it must be true. I just hung up the phone and drove straight there. I arrived at Harp Road at 6.30 p.m. on the dot.' He didn't elaborate on why he watched the clock all day, only to be *not* at the Hodson house at the allotted dinner time.

Mickey's story differed from Mandy's as to how they found the missed shell casing. While Mandy said she was lying on the floor showing Mickey the position her dead parents had been found in, Mickey said that they found the casing while Mandy was cleaning the floor – which at least sounded less odd.

'She was down on her hands and knees scrubbing the tiles,' he said. 'I was looking at Mandy and then I noticed a shell lying on the floor underneath a small Chesterfield chair that was right in front of the TV. I told Mandy ... not to touch it. I handed Mandy a screw ... to pick up the empty shell and we put it straight into a clip lock bag and rang Charlie Bezzina from the Homicide Squad.'

In Detective Cameron Davey's statement, there was no mention that Mandy had contacted Homicide after finding the bullet.

Mickey said that he knew Mandy had a shooter's licence because he had seen it, but he didn't know if she owned a gun.

When the police pointed out that the call records showed the call from Mandy came at 6.20 p.m., not 6 p.m., the young man said that he must have made a mistake.

Andrew Hodson was subsequently charged and convicted for removing the gun from the crime scene.

•

One suspect the Homicide Squad put a lot of effort into chasing was a guy by the name of Mark Smith. In September, Detective Cameron Davey and another detective from the Homicide Squad flew to Queensland and executed a search warrant on Smith's house. Smith was already in custody in Melbourne, but in his house in Queensland they found thirty-one pages of MDID information reports, from Terry Hodson's informer management file. The reports were from 2002 and contained the old informer number – 4/390 – that I had changed when I got to the MDID.

Some of the faxed copies that were found at Smith's house had 'duplicate' written on them, which indicated they were from our working copies, while others had 'original' on them, indicating that they were from the officer in charge of the folders – in other words, from the files we gave to the bosses. One of the information reports had not come from either the working copy of Hodson's file or the boss's copy.

A trace on the fax number the documents came from led straight to Tony Mokbel.

A notorious killer later shot Smith with a gun that Carl Williams gave him.

•

In the aftermath of the Hodson murders, the rest of Melbourne's underworld didn't stay idle. If Carl Williams was upset at the paltry $50 000 that Lewis Moran had allegedly offered for his offing, he'd have to be chuffed with the rumoured $300 000 that Mario Condello was later accused of offering.

It was the beginning of a hit man's tit for tat.

On Wednesday, 9 June 2004, two would-be hit men were arrested at Brighton Cemetery, a couple of minutes' walk from Mario Condello's house. Carl Williams was also arrested and charged with conspiracy to murder Condello.

Condello pledged forgiveness to the media and told one journalist that for the first time he had 'heard the birds singing in the trees'. But while he might have heard chirping, he was also plotting his own revenge. A couple of weeks later, on Thursday, 17 June, Condello and his lawyer George Defteros were arrested for conspiracy to incitement to murder Carl Williams and his father, George.

A couple of months later, Carl Williams was sentenced to a minimum of five years in prison for trafficking a commercial quantity of drugs.

The DPP would later drop the case against George Defteros.

Mario Condello wouldn't make it to trial. He was gunned down in his driveway right before it began.

CHAPTER 23

Dale v Chief Commissioner of Police

On 30 September 2004, the Chief Commissioner of the Victoria Police, Christine Nixon, sacked me. The notice of dismissal expressed concern over my association with Tommy Ivanovic and my association with Terence Hodson. It read in part:

I, Christine Nixon, Chief Commissioner of Police, having regard to:
• your integrity;
• the potential loss of community confidence in the force if you were to continue as a member of the force;
• having supplied you with a written notice pursuant to s.68(2) of the *Police Regulation Act* 1958; and
• having taken into account all submissions made by you;
am reasonably satisfied that certain aspects of your relationship with known criminals [Tommy Ivanovic] and Terry Hodson, make you unsuitable to continue as a member of the force. I believe that the findings I have made significantly undermine your integrity. I also believe that there is potential for loss of public confidence in the force were you to continue as a member.
I reach this conclusion having regard to your relationship with both [Tommy Ivanovic] and Hodson. However, I am also reasonably satisfied that you are unsuitable to continue as a member of the force when considering your relationship with

Hodson viewed alone. Accordingly, I dismiss you pursuant to the powers vested in me by s.68(1) of the *Police Regulation Act* 1958.

Your dismissal is effective from this 30th day of September 2004.

To be dismissed like this after my long career in the police force was such a slap in the face. The Police Association stepped up straightaway. I presented my case to them and they offered to help me fight the dismissal all the way to the Supreme Court.

•

On Friday, 25 February 2005, *Herald Sun* reporter Peter Mickelburough wrote an article entitled: 'Ex-detective only suspect'. Attached to the article was a quarter-page-sized photo of a smiling Terry and Christine Hodson.

But rather than meaning I was the only suspect in the Hodson murders, as the headline suggested, the article was about how Tony Fitzgerald had conducted an inquiry and found that I was the most likely suspect in the so-called theft of the blue folder.

Mickelburough reported that the state opposition was calling for a royal commission into police corruption, organised crime and the underworld killings. At this stage, none of us knew that when a royal commission came, it would be much more explosive than this.

On 1 June 2005, I fought back by challenging my dismissal. And not only did I challenge the Chief's dismissal of me, I also said that her public statements against me suggested a 'reasonable apprehension of bias'.

I was horrified to have been charged with the Dublin Street robbery, even though the cop part of me understood they had to go through the due process.

Back then, I trusted the due process.

In the beginning, I fully expected that the Oakleigh robbery would play out through the court, and the truth would come out and I would be back doing my job as a detective.

Silly me.

But once the Hodsons were murdered, there was no due process. Terry's statement underpinned the police case. While his death prompted them to drop the Oakleigh charges against me, it also left the case hanging forever in midair. While some would suggest that I wanted Terry dead, the opposite was true. I looked forward to my day in court, which would expose his story for what it was: an uncorroborated yarn to save his own skin. And this was, in fact, proven as soon as the charges were dropped.

If they had anything else – anything at all – do you think they would have dropped the charges?

•

So, in the end, I won the dismissal battle but lost the war. The more I thought about it, the more I realised that I couldn't be a member of the Victoria Police anymore. I'd seen coppers who had been charged with things before, and those who won returned to work under a cloud. No matter what happened, I realised that things could never be the same again. Not only that, I was also bitter about the way Victoria Police treated their own. I had spent ten days in prison and there was no reason for that.

So I realised that once I was vindicated, I couldn't stay.

Straight after I won the case, I handed in my resignation.

CHAPTER 24

Tayluh's next statement

Ten months after the Dublin Street drug house burglary in July 2005, the drug-house babysitter, Tayluh Jones, was brought in to give another statement – this time to Detective Murray Gregor.

Gregor played her three listening-device recordings and she identified them as conversations that she'd had with Azzam Ahmed. The first phone call was taped when Tayluh returned to the house on the night of the break-in. At that stage she hadn't been inside to see what was missing. The second phone call was to report to Ahmed that most of the drugs had been stolen. In that call, Tayluh told him she thought a guy called Peter must have been responsible. She told Gregor she had first suspected the man named Peter because he was an ex-con who came round all the time to buy drugs. Just before the break-in, Peter had been asking lots of questions when he visited the house. He had also rung Tayluh on the night of the break-in – while she was out of the house.

The third phone call had occurred in the time between Tayluh arriving home and the police leaving the premises and returning later with a warrant. Ahmed had told her to pack up the drugs that were left and he would arrange a taxi to come round and collect it all. She did that, but the police arrived before the taxi.

The second-last paragraph of Tayluh's statement was the most important, considering what would be alleged later on. Any Google search of the Oakleigh break-in will show most news articles reported that $700000 in cash went missing on the night of the robbery. Despite the fact that Terry and Dave were caught at the scene and everything they took had been recovered from the bags thrown over the back fence.

Tayluh said in her statement: 'Over the time we had the house in Dublin Street, there would on occasions be large amounts of cash in the house. About two weeks prior to the burglary, there was $1 000 000 cash inside the house which was there for a short period before it was sent to Sydney in exchange for drugs. I helped Adam count this cash and package it. After this money went to Sydney, there were no further large amounts of money to my knowledge inside the house.'

Considering how thorough Tayluh was in her inventory of the drugs kept in the house, you'd think she would have noticed $700 000 lying around.

Azzam Ahmed would later claim the police had ripped him off by taking the money, but it was only his word that the money was there. Tayluh disagreed. Of course, if Ahmed was right about the money being there before the robbery and it wasn't there after the robbery, but all of the stolen goods were recovered at the scene, then the only person who left the house *before* the robbery was Tayluh on her mystery trip to Prahran, or maybe South Yarra, to meet the friend whose name she didn't want to say.

It is also worth considering something else at this point. Later, it would be revealed that Tony Mokbel and Azzam Ahmed had a big falling out. Ahmed had told Mokbel that a much larger quantity of drugs – and $700 000 – had been taken by police.

Sorry, Big Tony, but while I'd love to give you your drugs and cash back, the bloody coppers took it all. Every single cent. Every single gram. Best just write off the loss.

Well, you would say that, wouldn't you? You'd shout it from the rooftops.

CHAPTER 25

The Queen v Dave Miechel

In May 2006 Dave Miechel finally had his day in court. He had never wavered from the story he told me from the back of the ambulance. During the court hearing, Dave's account was summarised. He claimed to have 'been to a "friendly's" house to change tapes. He was working on a job in Dublin Street ... He saw a suspicious male near the target. He approached the male and asked for details on what he was doing. The male then ran off and the applicant chased him through the school grounds. The next thing he knew was that a Dog Squad member was behind him and a dog was biting him. He told the Dog Squad member five times that he was in the job. The Dog Squad member stood about ten feet away and did not call off the dog. He was not going to lie there and get bitten. He got up and started to run away. The Dog Squad member hit him with his torch and he was handcuffed.'

The defence team called in Dave's dad and his uncle who was a minister. They also called in a cop who had known Dave since the academy. All agreed that until he was found at the scene of the Dublin Street break-in, Dave was a hardworking, dedicated cop who had led a blameless and law-abiding existence.

The jury clearly didn't believe Dave's account and they found him guilty of burglary, theft, trafficking in large commercial quantities of MDMA, methylamphetamine, amphetamine, dimethylamphetamine, and ketamine.

Maybe it was because of the DNA found in a beanie discarded near where Dave was felled by the police dog and handler. Maybe it was that both he and Terry were caught at the scene. Maybe it was Mandy's statement that Dave came into a café where she worked and allegedly told her he did it for her and her dad.

On 18 August, Justice Betty King sentenced Dave to fifteen years in prison, saying that he had to serve a minimum of twelve years before being eligible for parole. While I get that cops are held to a higher standard, Dave's sentence was higher than most received by the cream of the drug-dealing world – higher than Carl Williams's latest sentence, higher than Mokbel's. And remember that he was a first offender and never had a second to profit or benefit from the crime.

It is also worth wondering what Terry Hodson's sentence would have been had he lived and gone to trial. Just what would the drug dealer with a long police record have got compared to his co-accused? I'd bet London to a brick that Terry's punishment – or lack thereof – would have proven exactly what his finger-pointing was worth. In 2019, Terry's lawyer Rob Stary would tell the ABC's *Four Corners* program what went on behind the scenes. 'We brokered a deal where he would plead guilty to burglary and theft committed in the company of two other police officers, and then he would give evidence against those police officers including Paul Dale, and we'd come to an agreement with the prosecution that he would not serve a term of imprisonment.' Not a bad deal, considering the police had already proven that I was not in their company that night.

After he brokered the deal, Stary was replaced by Nicola Gobbo.

So, just to clarify: rather than a long sentence, there would have been no jail for Terry. He and Dave were both caught at the scene and he should have served at least the fifteen years Dave got – if not more, since he had a long criminal history. He gave them my name and was able to wriggle out of the entire mess. What's in a name? Freedom.

Speaking of sentences: other detectives convicted in the first shakedown at the drug squad had made a lot of money and lived the high life, and didn't get as much of a sentence as Dave Miechel. It is worth pausing to make some comparisons.

Just a couple of months before Dave's trial, an ex-drug squad cop called Ian Ferguson was convicted of trafficking a commercial quantity of heroin, and of money laundering. He was said to have lived the life of Riley, profiting to the tune of $630 000. The DPP suggested that the fruits of his labour included two properties, five luxury vehicles, a tractor and a boat. He was ordered to pay the Victorian government nearly a million dollars.

He was sentenced to twelve years' imprisonment with a non-parole period of eight years.

Colleagues of Ian Ferguson in the old drug squad, detectives Stephen Cox and Glenn Sadler, were tried on similar charges of trafficking a commercial quantity of heroin. Cox got seven years with a four-year minimum, and Sadler got ten on top with six on the bottom. All three ex-detectives were ordered to repay large amounts of money as their profits from crime.

And Dave got fifteen years with a twelve minimum.

Fifteen years.

And if you think that's odd, let's compare Dave's sentence to those given to crooks. In September 2004 Carl Williams was found guilty of trafficking in a commercial quantity of drugs including MDMA, ecstasy and cocaine. He got seven years with a five-year minimum.

And Dave got fifteen years.

Now to Antonios Mokbel – Big Tony. In 2006 he was charged with 'being knowingly concerned in the importation' of a traffickable quantity of cocaine into the country. He got twelve with a nine.

And Dave got fifteen years.

Dave, who got caught at the Dublin Street house, bitten by the police dog, bashed by its handler, and never profited for one minute from his crimes, got fifteen years.

What I wonder about most is that if the Victoria Police offered huge inducements to everyone to get me, *what did they offer Dave*? Whatever it was, he clearly refused to say that I had anything to do with the Dublin Street robbery, and he paid with a higher sentence than other cops who had made hundreds of thousands of dollars and lived the high life. And was given a higher sentence than career criminals like Williams and Mokbel.

Fair?

You be the judge.

CHAPTER 26

The Australian Crime Commission

The Australian Crime Commission (ACC) is a federal government body that – according to their website – 'was established under the *Australian Crime Commission Act 2002* as a statutory authority to combat serious and organised crime. We report directly to the Minister for Home Affairs and are part of the Attorney-General's portfolio.'

Remember that for later. *Federal body, serious and organised crime.*

While most people – including me, once upon a time – have never really had anything to do with the ACC, or even know what they do, it's worth mentioning some worrying things about them. For starters, they operate under a weird code of secrecy. If you get a summons to appear before them, you can only share that information with your lawyer. So, say you get summoned and your wife asks you why you are travelling to Melbourne for a couple of days, it is actually *illegal* for you to tell her that you are appearing before the Australian Crime Commission.

Yes, folks. Illegal.

Even newspapers are really limited in what they can print about this secret commission. The one thing that I did know about the ACC was that they were a powerful investigative body. I had heard a bit about them from police members who had gone across to work with the ACC on secondment. The ACC was initially successful in breaking the code of silence in outlaw motorcycle gangs by giving people the right to speak freely while offering indemnity from prosecution.

I knew they had a lot of power to conduct coercive hearings.

In their own words, 'the ACC can draw on coercive powers which enable it to obtain information that cannot be accessed through traditional policing methods' which allows their examiners to 'summons any witness to appear ... require that witness to give evidence of their knowledge of matters concerning the criminal activities involving themselves and others upon whom an investigation or intelligence operation is focused ...' They point out that their coercive powers are 'protected under the secrecy provisions of the *Australian Crime Commission Act*'.

Yes, that's a lot of words used to say you *don't* have the right to remain silent; witnesses are protected; everything is hush-hush. Unless, of course, your name is Paul Dale and they decide otherwise.

In hindsight, I don't know why the ACC even held the hearing, since it was outside of its charter of investigating serious and organised crime. It is also outside its charter of investigating state crime with federal implications. For the ACC – called in by the Victoria Police – to use their coercive powers in a murder investigation is, in my opinion, a very dodgy use of those powers. In my three years in the Homicide Squad we never called in the ACC to question our witnesses and compel them to testify without legal representation. A good reason why we never would have called in the ACC for assistance in a murder investigation is that murder is actually outside their charter. The crime of murder is not a law governed by the state – it comes under common law with origins in seventeenth century England.

When I was in Homicide we did our investigations the old-fashioned way: gathered evidence, presented our case and got a conviction fair and square.

On 23 February 2007, I was served with a summons to appear before the ACC. An ex-colleague of mine, Wayne Cheeseman, served the summons. When I saw him come into my work, I thought: *Hey, there's Cheesy!* I went out and greeted him like old friends do.

'Cheesy, what are you up to?' I asked, patting him on the back.

Cheesy looked towards the floor. 'Actually, I'm with the Australian Crime Commission now,' he said, reluctantly, 'and I'm here to serve a summons on you.'

He must have seen my face fall.

'I offered to do it because I knew you,' he explained in a quiet voice.

I accepted his small act of kindness. Still stung, though.

On Wednesday, 7 March 2007, the Australian Crime Commission held a hearing to examine the circumstances surrounding the deaths of Terry and Christine Hodson.

For me, the most dangerous thing about the ACC was that they did a really good job of convincing you that nothing you said in the hearing would ever be used against you, and it would be kept secret.

You had to answer every question, but while your fundamental right to silence was taken away, they told you that you were protected. If you did say something that was self-incriminating, they offered a blanket indemnity.

The examiner – Judge Hannaford, who was a federal court judge – made this very clear right from the start. He pointed to various police members in the room and told me that they couldn't take away any information and use it in any way.

So I stood before Judge Hannaford at the beginning of my ACC questioning, having been through several Office of Police Integrity hearings, interviewed by ESD, arrested on several occasions, and every time I thought there might be an end to this I would receive yet another summons to appear before a private hearing or an open hearing. By the time the ACC summons arrived, I hoped this might mark the end of this constant pursuit of me.

After the first ten minutes at the ACC hearing I was almost put at ease. The judge's very clear explanation takes around ten pages in the transcripts. He described to me all the ways that the commission could be trusted and said that I could talk openly and honestly.

Here's a sample. Judge Hannaford: 'I will again advise you as to what happens with the evidence that's received ... the *Australian Crime Commission Act* provides that you must answer all the questions that I require you to answer ... there is no entitlement that's available to you which would allow you to avoid those particular obligations ... those particular obligations apply notwithstanding the fact that an answer ... might tend to incriminate you or might tend to render you liable to the imposition of some penalty. However, the *Australian Crime Commission Act* does extend to you a legal protection from self-incrimination in respect to any documents or things that I might direct you to produce to me.'

He then explained that I could have protection from answers for some questions, or could have general protection. 'I will then further reassure you that what that then means is that absolutely nothing that you say to me during the course of this hearing will be able to be taken from this room and produced in a court as some evidence in any criminal prosecution proceedings against you, nor will it ever be taken from this room and produced as some evidence in any other proceedings for the imposition of some penalty against you. Mr Dale, do you understand the concept of self-incrimination?'

'Yes,' I replied.

'Would you like therefore to have the benefit of the general protection from self-incrimination that's available to you?'

'Yes, I would,' I said. I opted for the blanket indemnity because by now I didn't trust anyone, least of all the police.

'Mr Dale, you having sought the general protection from self-incrimination, can I now advise you that you do have the benefit of a general protection from self-incrimination in respect to all of the evidence that you're required to give me during the course of this Examination. Now just to reassure you as to what that now means. It now means that absolutely nothing that you say to me during the course of this hearing can now ever be taken from this room and produced in a court as some evidence against you in any criminal prosecution proceedings against you, nor will it ever be able to be taken from this room and produced as some evidence in any other proceedings for the imposition of some penalty against you and that protection will also extend to every document or thing that I might require you to produce during the course of this hearing. Do you understand? Do you have any questions of me about that?'

'No,' I said. But if I knew then what I know now, I would have asked lots of questions. First, I would have asked him if he was aware that all his promises could be overturned with the stroke of a pen at the whim of anyone who wanted them to be. And then I would have asked if it would surprise him that when I was eventually arrested in 2009, 'secure' ACC documents would be included in affidavits by the Victoria Police to oppose my bail application. There are allowances in ACC documents to be used against you if your answers are incorrect, but it wasn't used against me for what I said at the hearing – it was used against me when I was charged with murder. And, finally, I would have asked him if my 'secure' testimony could be included in the documents supplied to hit man Rod Collins, charged with the same crime as me, so that they could be circulated through the prison system to people who would threaten to kill me and cut the throat of my wife.

Yes, these are all the questions that I would have asked him if I'd had any awareness that all his promises that I would be protected by the ACC meant absolutely nothing.

But the wisdom of hindsight makes me digress.

After being promised and assured of indemnity and security, I felt confident to speak freely to the ACC hearings.

When I was later presented with twenty-three charges stemming from what I said at the hearing, I found out the hard way that the esteemed commission's promise of indemnity and secrecy was a big fat lie.

While I tried to cooperate as best I could, a number of questions about what I was doing on specific dates and times four years earlier were impossible to answer. I asked to refer to my police diaries, which had been confiscated on the day of my arrest in December 2003. The assistant to the commissioner said that she wanted to get my fresh view of things and refused me access to my police diaries. I challenge anyone to answer specific questions about events four years earlier in such circumstances.

CHAPTER 27

Courting Carl

Carl Williams said it best when he was being pushed by the Office of Police Integrity to implicate me. 'They keep passing messages on through the Prosecution though. Dale, Dale, they keep pushing the issue of Dale, so I don't know why they're pushing it or I don't know what's happening. Have you blokes been pushing or ... do you have any idea why they're pushing it?'

Well you may ask, Carl.

•

On 24 April 2007, Detective Senior Constable Cameron Davey took a statement from Carl Williams at Barwon Prison. The timing of this statement was interesting. It was just a couple of days before Carl Williams stood before Justice Betty King to plead guilty to three counts of murder and a conspiracy to commit murder charge. He must have been feeling expansive ... or maybe he was hedging his bets, feathering his nest, having a bet both ways. And since the very first line of his statement says, 'I make this statement in the belief that no part of it can be used as evidence against me,' he made it clear that deals had been done before Cameron Davey ever arrived at the prison.

Here's how I think it worked. Someone who was not Cameron Davey did a bit of horsetrading with Carl before Davey came onto the scene. Then Cameron Davey arrived at Barwon and took Carl's statement.

Why, you might ask.

Here's my theory. It involves an investigative strategy called Chinese walls. Setting up so-called Chinese walls is a way to separate some cops from decisions and strategies. For example, if the powers-that-be made Senior Constable Cameron Davey the informant (the guy in charge of the investigation) but did deals he didn't know about, that put a Chinese wall between him and the deal. He could later stand in court, hand on heart, and swear that he had no knowledge of any inducements offered to witnesses. And he would be telling the God's honest truth.

But it didn't mean inducements weren't made.

They were just made at a distance.

Behind Chinese walls.

Later, when I subpoenaed documentation from the Victoria Police, I found the transcript of an interview between John Nolan and Paul Atkins from the Office of Police Integrity talking to Carl Williams at Barwon Prison on Wednesday, 24 January 2007 – three months *before* Davey took his statement.

Carl didn't waste any time. 'The prosecution want to do some deal with me ... I don't know if you're aware of it.'

'Yep,' said Nolan.

'They want to give me ... a plea and they're talking about they're wanting me to give assistance on anything they said, but they keep pushing the issue of Paul Dale.'

'Yep.'

'Yeah, I ... told them that if they want me to give assistance against Paul Dale, probably the police are interested in assistance against Paul Dale ... and probably ... you blokes are interested in giving assistance against Paul Dale.'

Carl explained that he had spoken to his lawyer and she had suggested to call them in for a chat. But the gangland killer wasn't silly. His first question: 'What's in it for me?'

Nolan and Atkins let him talk. He lamented the fact that 'they' had been stuffing around with a possible sentence if he pleaded guilty.

Carl admitted to high-level meetings between his lawyer and the cops. 'Peter had a big meeting with ... Paul Cochrane, with

Peter Faris. Paul Coghlan, Jim O'Brien, all of them. They had a big meeting and they come and said 35 from the day I come in. And Peter come up here and he said to me by the time he left the office and got somewhere, they'd told him that it was 35 plus what I'd done, so I'm up to 37. Then he went, "Oh, don't worry," and he talked to Horgan and said, "That's just too high," ya know. That's with no assistance obviously.'

'Yep,' said Nolan.

'And I said, "Tell him ... 30 minus what I've done and I'll be able to start talking about anything, ya know ... and he came back to me, and they said 33 minus what I've done. I said, "Well, now we're starting to get somewhere."'

'Yeah.'

But Carl was clearly peeved. 'Now they've come back up to 35 plus what I've done, so they're just talking in riddles with us.'

Nolan asked who was involved in the deal and Carl said that his lawyer was in talks with Jim O'Brien, who was then with the Purana task force, and the prosecution.

Carl then listed all of the charges – murders and drugs – that he'd been convicted of and the sentences that he had received. It took quite a while. He finished by listing all of the murder charges that were coming up.

The next several pages in the transcript contained a cat-and-mouse game of I-might-know-something versus unless-you-are-prepared-to-tell-us-we-can't-discuss-a-deal.

Carl finished with a hint that he might have knowledge of drugs and murder, but declared, 'If I was going down that track, I wouldn't be doing it for nuthin, ya know.'

Nolan hedged.

Carl pushed. 'Well, the prosecution ... they're coming to me asking about Dale. They're not coming to me asking about any other copper.'

More back and forth before Carl finally started talking about the Hodson murders. 'I wouldn't have a clue who carried it out. I only know who ordered it ... well, I was told ...'.

'Paul Dale?' asked Nolan.

'Yeah.'

When Nolan tried to press Carl for details, the killer was blunt. 'You gotta tell me what's in it for me before I'm gunna give you anything that I know.'

Nolan tried to explain his difficulty. He couldn't offer Carl a deal if Carl didn't tell him what he had. Carl's situation was the reverse: if he told the cops what he had, it would cease to be currency.

The crook's catch-22.

Carl then showed a bit more of his hand. 'Twenty-three for the murders, if you're gunna talk about a sentence, if you're gunna talk about Dale ... my solicitor says that's more valuable than anyone, ya know. And any other statement is pretty valuable information about Dale, ya know.'

Nolan finally conceded. 'I suppose the ace card the police would want is a name for the Hodson murders. I'd expect that would be a high bid.'

At the end of the meeting, Carl was adamant. 'You know these trials or whatever, but I'm not gunna do something fuckin' ridiculous, 35 years, ya know. It's gotta be something reasonable. Ya know, 23 years or something like that, ya know. That give me some sort of light at the ...'

Exit Nolan, stage right.

Deals struck.

Enter Cameron Davey.

In the interview room at Barwon Prison, Carl sat opposite Davey and gave his implausible account. The first time I met Carl Williams was under the strict instructions of my superiors and it included a full briefing and debriefing. Not so, according to Carl in his statement. He said that we met alone at the Brunswick Club in a most unlikely story that was obviously swallowed hook, line and sinker by the cops who wanted it to be true.

While I know Carl's story was crap, it should have sounded unlikely to the average punter too. Here's what he said. Judge for yourself.

Carl: 'I am not sure of the time of day that the first meeting happened but I went there alone. I only talked to Dale alone. This first meeting was not long after I was released. We just sort of touched base. He was telling me that he could keep an eye out for me. In return, Dale expected to be paid for any information that he gave to me. I took this to mean that he would keep an eye out for what was going on with the police with investigations and things like that. Dale didn't give me any information during that first meeting and I gave him no money. I think we were both suspicious of each other at that time and remained so.'

Seriously?

As if a cop would approach Carl Williams as a stranger and put his hand out for cash.

Another unlikely anecdote that Carl told Davey was that I met with him again and showed him evidence that someone was trying to set him up. Carl sanctimoniously finished that story with: 'As a result of reading that report, I dropped off Jimmy and did no more business with him. Dale didn't give me the report, he just showed it to me.'

Again, as if! We all knew what Williams did if he got a whiff that anyone was double-crossing him – he killed them.

Next Williams described paying me for the statement that I had made for Tommy Ivanovic. He said that if he paid me that I would be more likely to give evidence for Tommy in court. Only problem with that little peccadillo was that I never gave evidence for Tommy in court.

Was never asked to.

Was never likely to.

I never even offered to give a statement for Tommy Ivanovic – I was asked to by the Homicide Squad.

But then again, Carl never let the truth get in the way of a statement that gave him indemnity for a double murder ... not to mention nearly two million dollars in cash and prizes. But more about that later.

Carl wove the first meeting Dave Miechel and I had with him into his fantasy narrative, but added a detail that should have screamed make-believe. He agreed that we had spoken about his problems with Jason Moran – he had indeed told us that Jason was the one who shot him – but he added a detail that was extraordinary.

'Dale said they could kill Jason for $400 000. It was to be $200 000 for each of them. I told them they were dreaming. Miechel was part of this conversation.'

Okay.

So Dave and I were supposed to have suggested to Australia's most notorious criminal that we could not only do a hit for him but charge him close to half a million dollars to do it.

Come on.

You have to wonder whether Cameron Davey, sitting across from a guy charged with cold-bloodedly killing át least four of his enemies, saw any irony in the killer's comments. Carl Williams had proven that he was more than capable of arranging murders.

While he was at it, Carl threw numbers around like tennis balls. He said that he had paid me $30 000 to $40 000 over the years to provide him with information, and that I had offered to pay him $150 000 to kill the Hodsons. And he could happily confess to his part in the conspiracy to commit a double murder because he had negotiated an indemnity – which meant he could say whatever he wanted and the only repercussion was the amount of cash the Victoria Police would throw in his direction.

In other words, if his story was true – which I knew it wasn't – they would let him off conspiracy to murder Terry and Christine.

Maybe the police thought he'd cop a long sentence for the four murders he admitted to and they were happy to give him a couple for free.

Who knows.

At the end of his statement, Carl Williams said that while he told me that he was happy to help out if I needed him to, he actually had no idea who was responsible for the murder of the Hodsons.

Carl's final word on the subject: 'I have never met any of the Hodsons. I know that there was a son who spent some time in jail, but I never met him. I have never had any dealings with any of the Hodsons. I do not know who is responsible for the murder of the Hodsons. All I am able to say regarding their murders is what I have provided in this statement.'

Then he signed that his statement was true and correct.

Of course, he signed all of his statements that way, regardless of whether the next statement contradicted the last and proved it not to be true and correct at all. Carl played fast and loose with the truth, but it never seemed to bother the police who would wheel and deal, wine and dine him for his latest 'true and correct' version.

•

On 27 April 2007, Carl Williams pleaded guilty to the murder of Jason Moran on 21 June 2003, the murder of Mark Mallia on 18 August 2003, and the murder of Lewis Moran on 31 March 2004; and, finally, conspiracy to murder Mario Condello between 29 May and 9 June 2004.

On 7 May 2007, Justice Betty King sentenced Carl Williams to a minimum of thirty-five years in prison. In her final summing-up, she told the court that the unnamed driver in the Lewis Moran murder had made a statement that implicated both Carl and Tony Mokbel as being joint procurers of Lewis Moran's murder.

According to the driver, in the weeks leading up to Lewis Moran being gunned down at the Brunswick Club, he had met with one of the hit men, Evangelos Goussis, and both Mokbel and Williams at a club owned by Mokbel in Brunswick. While the driver said he didn't accept the contract straightaway, he was told to call Mokbel or Williams if he changed his mind. He said that when he agreed to do it, Williams offered to pay half the money and Mokbel the other half after the job was done. A week after the murder, the driver said that he and Goussis met Mokbel in a hotel car park, where Mokbel handed over an envelope with $140 000 – ten grand short of the agreed amount.

Justice Betty King said that the driver's evidence was untested before her, so she wasn't in a position to judge it, but she was damning of Carl Williams's account: 'I find that the evidence that you gave, in the main was unbelievable, even incredible at times. It was, in my view, designed to ensure that it would provide no evidence against any person other than those who are already dead, convicted or have pleaded guilty to various offences. You denied any involvement or knowledge of involvement of Mokbel in the murder of Lewis Moran ... You, accordingly, dispute the contents of different statements made by ... the driver in Lewis Moran's murder, as well as the secretly recorded conversations of the shooter in the conspiracy.

'In relation to your evidence in respect of this matter, and the other matters to which I have referred ... not only do I consider you a most unsatisfactory witness, virtually incapable of telling the truth, except for some minor and largely irrelevant portions of your evidence, I find that the manner in which you gave evidence was arrogant, almost supercilious and you left me with a strong impression that your view of all of these murders was that they were all really justifiable and you were the real victim, having been "forced" to admit at least some of your involvement, by the statements of other members of your group who had cooperated with police.

'Accordingly, I do not accept that the arrangement for the murder of Lewis Moran occurred in the manner that you have described. However, equally I am unable to be satisfied to the required standard that the circumstances under which the driver, Noel Faure and Ange Goussis were employed to murder Lewis Moran were as described by the driver. The driver has not been tested is any way before me, and it is difficult to place great reliance upon the untested word of an accomplice, at least for the purposes of sentencing.'

I think that was Judge Betty's way of calling Carl a big fat liar, only she used longer words and lots more of them.

So, even the judge mentioned Mokbel and Williams organising a hit six weeks before the Hodson murders. Working together.

And despite the strong suggestion that Carl Williams and Tony Mokbel teamed up to organise the murder of Lewis Moran six weeks before the murder of Terry Hodson, the cops of the Petra task force – established to investigate the murder of the Hodsons – pursued me with vigour.

Not only that, they courted Carl to do it.

Sometimes the logic of this case twists and turns like a mad snake, then twists all the way around and bites itself on the bum.

CHAPTER 28

The Petra task force

While Charlie Bezzina, Sol Solomon and Cameron Davey had investigated the Hodson murders from the start, there was internal friction within the police hierarchy that would ultimately claim the scalps of some high-ranking officers.

Right from the beginning, this case echoed down the corridors of power of the Victorian state government, because the minute Terry Hodson was caught with Dave Miechel at the drug house break-in there was a tangible link between cops and crooks. And once Terry had pointed the finger at me, it wasn't just about one cop who got too close to an informer and made a bad decision. Two cops made it look more organised and widespread. Made it look like police corruption. And police corruption was very high on the agenda of the state government and the upper echelons of the Victoria Police.

In his memoir, Charlie Bezzina said that Assistant Commissioner (Crime) Simon Overland regarded the Hodson investigation as important. 'It was basically his baby because he was hell-bent on crushing the slightest suggestion of corruption, let alone allegations of any police involvement in a double murder,' wrote Bezzina.

Bezzina described his weekly meetings with Overland, and another assistant commissioner, an ESD investigator and a member of the Office of Police Integrity. These weekly meetings would later be the subject of an embarrassing moment in court for one of the participants, although we'll get to that.

A week before the Carl Williams prison interview by Cameron Davey, Charlie Bezzina was informed that Overland had created the Petra task force – a secret group to take over the Hodson investigation. Instead of asking Bezzina to head it up, the seasoned Homicide detective was overlooked in favour of his two team members, Sol Solomon and Cameron Davey. According to his memoir, Bezzina took this decision as a huge vote of no confidence in his abilities and it proved to be the beginning of the end of his career.

Needless to say, it came as no surprise when the Petra task force seemed to focus on me as the main suspect and ignore others staring them in the face. Sometimes literally across an interview table.

Deals and indemnities that had been done in the aftermath of the Oakleigh break-in must have impeded them, but by then it was too late.

While they went over old ground, they also got old witnesses to say new things. Improbable things, but new.

•

On 28 June 2007, drug-house babysitter Tayluh Jones gave yet another statement to police. She had given her initial statements on the understanding that they could only be used to pursue those responsible for the break-in. Now she gave permission for the statements to be used by police investigating the murders of Terence and Christine Hodson.

Tayluh gave more of her background in this statement. She talked about being a drug user and getting addicted to ice courtesy of Azzam Ahmed, who supplied her, mostly for free. She admitted to having a casual sexual relationship with Ahmed, who she called Adam.

Keen to help in the production of pills, Tayluh did whatever Ahmed asked her to do. She had rented a couple of places before the Oakleigh house. Ahmed made his money by buying high-grade ecstasy tablets from an Israeli connection in Sydney, then bringing the pills to Melbourne, where he and Tayluh would use a coffee grinder to reduce the pills to a fine powder. Tayluh would buy glucose tablets to grind into powder. Once the glucose was mixed with the ecstasy, the pills would be re-pressed. That way, the original pills could be doubled in number.

In this new statement, Tayluh again said that there was very little cash kept in the Oakleigh house. 'On the day of the burglary, the only money that I was aware of at the house was a few thousand dollars. That money belonged to Adam. I think it was between $5000 and $10000. I knew that the money was in the house prior to the burglary. That money was kept in my bedroom from memory, and the money was not stolen during the burglary, but it was located by the police during the search of the house the next day.'

Tayluh said that during her phone conversations with Ahmed after the break-in, but before the police had returned with their warrants, at no time did he ask her to check to see if a large amount of cash was missing.

While Ahmed would later claim that the mysterious $700000 was kept in a cavity space above the stove, Tayluh had a very different story.

'After the burglary, after the uniform police had left, but before I was arrested, I checked that hiding space above the kitchen cupboards and the drugs from that spot had not been stolen. There was no money in that space then. I had checked that space a few days before the burglary and there was no money in that space either. There was no cash located in that space during the search by the police. I can't recall Adam ever hiding money there that I'm aware of.'

Tayluh was happy to talk about the connection between Azzam Ahmed and Tony Mokbel. She knew they were connected and she had met Mokbel while she was involved in making pills with Ahmed in 2003. While Tayluh said Mokbel had never come to the house in Dublin Street, she did remember that after the burglary, 'there was bad blood between Adam and Tony. They both accused each other of owing the other money. I didn't know if this was related to Operation Galop or something unrelated.'

She remembered it wasn't until four months after the break-in that Ahmed first raised the idea that there was money in the house. In February 2004, after they had both received bail, she met him at a pub.

'During that meeting, Adam told me that there was $700 000 at the house at the time of the burglary. Adam told me that the money was stolen during the burglary. I had no knowledge of that amount of money being at the house at the time of the burglary. Apart from Adam telling me that the money was at the house and stolen during the burglary, I have no reason to believe the money was there ... Adam talked about the money from the house at Dublin Street regularly. Adam thought that Paul Dale and David Miechel had the money ...'

Well, he would, wouldn't he?

Just say that Azzam Ahmed had $700 000 and one of his drug houses was ripped off – by the police, no less. He could squeal loud and often about those copper bastards who took the cash, and tell anyone – say, the person whose cash it might have been – that it was all the police's fault. Perfect laundering.

It's not like Tony Mokbel – or whoever's money it was – could come after the Victoria Police for restitution.

Tayluh then made an odd addition to her statement. Remember, this statement was made *four years* after the robbery. A reasonable person might find the next bit strange.

Judge for yourself.

'After my arrest during the police search of Dublin Street, I saw Paul Dale come to the house for a short time. He was doing something with a set of keys at the front door. This stands out in my memory because I remember that Dale looked quite nervous and I couldn't understand why. Later, after I had been taken to the police station to be interviewed, prior to Detective Sam Jennings interviewing me, Dale spoke to me for a short while in the interview room. He just asked me if I was OK. This was the first time he had introduced himself, and the first time

I knew him to be a policeman. When I saw him at Dublin Street with the keys, I thought he might have been a locksmith. I have never spoken to Dale since that time.'

Huh? She met me twice briefly on a night four years earlier when her house had been burgled, then raided by dozens of cops, and she was arrested, *but she remembered that I looked nervous?*

I was at the door trying to see if the keys we had confiscated at Azzam Ahmed's house would fit the Dublin Street house door. If they did, they would be used in evidence to further connect Ahmed to the drug house. I had said as much in my statement.

But please, decide for yourself. Could a woman who was a self-admitted regular ice user, who had just been arrested, spent the night being interviewed by cops, and had police in droves combing her drug house for evidence, really remember one cop who was there for a couple of minutes to check keys?

And that I looked 'nervous'?

Hmm.

CHAPTER 29

Nicola Gobbo and the Office of Police Integrity

Tony Fitzgerald, anti-corruption judge, was asked by the Office of Police Integrity (OPI) to question Nicola Gobbo about her involvement with the myriad characters on the periphery of the Hodson murders.

Right from the start, it was clear to investigating officers that Nicola Gobbo was playing both sides of the fence. Indeed, when Murray Gregor gave a statement in the office of the State Ombudsman in February 2005 he detailed his position – unique among Victoria Police – that he saw her as being connected to way too many of the people involved in the Oakleigh drug house break-in and the subsequent murder of the Hodsons.

Gregor said that in the days following the break-in he had a meeting with Nicola Gobbo and Terry Hodson. Terry agreed to wear a covert listening device at all times in case Dave or I contacted him. Afterwards, Terry told Gregor that the best way to prompt contact with me was to use Nicola – because she and I were friends. Terry later told Gregor that Nicola was happy to organise a meeting between Dave and me and Terry. You've got to wonder what game she was playing.

I asked Nicola for legal advice as soon as I suspected things were happening behind my back – never for one minute thinking she would be involved. Murray Gregor said in his statement that the day after the Melbourne Cup in 2003 he had spoken to Inspector Peter De Santo, who told him he had bumped into

Nicola at the Cup and had a drink with her. It was De Santo's opinion that Nicola was fishing for information on whether I was a suspect or not.

Gregor told the OPI investigator interviewing him that Nicola's legal advice to Terry Hodson was for him and Miechel to roll over on me.

•

By July 2007 Carl Williams had made formal complaints against Nicola. In a bout of return fire, Nicola was quoted in *The Weekend Australian* as saying: 'Any suggestion or inference by a pathological lying serial killer as to me having knowledge of any plan to murder anyone is preposterous. It is appalling that police enthusiastically accepted the ravings of a psychopath who was prepared to say anything about anyone for a reduced sentence and financial gain as well as holidays from prison and prostitutes.'

My thoughts exactly.

However.

I would hazard a guess that things weren't looking good for Nicola Gobbo and her respected legal career. She was called to answer questions put to her by Tony Fitzgerald at the OPI.

Years later, when I subpoenaed her transcript for my own legal defence, much of what she said was redacted from her interview on 19 July 2007. Also at the beginning of the interview, there is much said about secrecy and privacy and a 'what happens in fight club stays in fight club' sort of thing.

So I probably can't tell you the line of questioning. Instead, I'm going to pose a hypothetical. Imagine that, when questioned, a lawyer revealed an interconnectedness between clients that when spoken out loud was cause for concern. Then imagine that, after hours of questioning, the lawyer was told to come back the next day at, say, 2 p.m., but there were no further transcripts until over a month later. And then imagine that the first thing the lawyer was told at that visit a month later was that some of the previous testimony was evasive and untrue. Then imagine that lawyer was suddenly advised to seek legal representation on account of this. And then imagine turning over the pages of the transcripts to read the next thrilling round of questions, only to find ... nothing.

No more pages of transcripts.

No further questioning.

Not a whisper.

But away from the hypothetical and back to real Nicola. When she didn't return to the OPI Fitzgerald hearings, I assumed some kind of deal was struck. A theory I had was that maybe Fitzgerald recommended charges against her and she agreed to wear a wire to wrangle herself out of a legal quagmire.

I spent years wondering why she would do it. Of course, the 2019 Royal Commission would expose the extent of Nicola Gobbo's work as an informer for the Victoria Police, so another possibility exists – when Fitzgerald's questions to Nicola became uncomfortable, the police hierarchy might have stepped in and extracted her.

The Royal Commission published hundreds of documents online during the hearings. One of them was from 'Officer Fox' – a lot of the police handlers were given pseudonyms – and detailed what I can only assume was the scrambling going on behind the scenes when Nicola started answering Fitzgerald's questions. Here's the part of Fox's electronic diary that wasn't redacted referring to Senior Sergeant Gavan Ryan, who headed up the Purana task force:

S/t Gavan Ryan,
- He has just found out and had it confirmed by Mr Overland that Mr Fitzgerald does not know 3838 is a registered informer.
- He has been told she has assisted police once and life in danger.
- He confirmed though that there is an agreement re not to delve into finding out who she has spoken to as it may put her life in danger. As known.

- Apparently Mr Brower knows but has not told Fitzgerald.
- Questions tomorrow may be hard and she may not like them.
- Told him I would deal with it and expecting it.
- Confirmed she is bringing her diary tomorrow to refer to. Does not want to hand it over though because of irrelevant and personal matters in it including LPP.

Does that mean the police lied to or misled Tony Fitzgerald? Goodness, I hope not, because wouldn't that mean the OPI got him all the way down from Queensland to get to the bottom of things then didn't tell him what those things were?

Another Royal Commission document shed further light on the subject. In Sol Solomon's statement to the Royal Commission, he wrote: 'I received a phone call from 3838. She advised me that she had just received a phone call from Paul Dale and that he was asking to meet her urgently. She wanted to know if I would like her to meet with him. I asked her if she was comfortable with meeting him and if she was prepared to do so then by all means go ahead. She then asked me if I wanted her to record the meeting. I never contemplated that she would ever agree to do this which is why I didn't ask her, so it came as a surprise to me when she actually asked the questions. I responded with words similar to: "Would you be prepared to do that?" She replied with words similar to, "Yes if you would like me to."'

So for all my wondering *why* Nicola Gobbo would agree when the police asked her to wear a wire, if Sol's recollection is correct, they never did.

She offered.

And so, when we met in December 2008, Nicola Gobbo wore a listening device to secretly record our conversation. I trusted her. She was a friend as well as my legal advisor. So what did I say that day? I had a long and rambling conversation and one of the things I said was that Carl Williams must have kept a diary of our meetings, because in his statement he referred to a number of them. I didn't know then that the police had helped him put his statement together using phone taps and statements from others – which, when you think of it, is like referring to a diary provided by the Victoria Police.

Sitting opposite me, Nicola looked like she always looked. There was nothing to indicate that she was wearing a wire and taping our conversation. She was very attentive – no more or less than normal – and listened sympathetically to me rambling on and on about all the allegations that had been put to me about meetings with Carl Williams. I suppose that I also wanted to suss Nicola out about what she knew about all of this, because some of those people involved were her clients as well.

My wife, Ditty, arrived at the café later. She had left me there to discuss my legal issues with Nicola, then came back to pick me up. Ditty sat with us for a coffee. She and Nicola walked into the café to pay while I waited outside.

Later, Ditty told me that Nicola had said something strange while they were waiting in line. She had asked Nicola how she was going, and the lawyer had replied in a low voice that she soon had to do something that she didn't want to do. Then it was their turn to pay and Ditty didn't get to ask what she meant.

CHAPTER 30

Sam Jennings number 4

On 9 November 2007, Samantha Jennings, my ex-colleague from the MDID, was called in for her fourth statement. It had been over four years since the first three statements. The tone of this new one was quite different. In the first, she had talked about Dave Miechel being a loner and hard to get to know. And she had given her impression of me as a boss – she said I was 'extremely helpful, patient and thorough', and that she had every confidence in my 'abilities and leadership'.

This time, she spoke to Cameron Davey at the Petra task force. After going briefly over the night of the robbery, Sam talked about the Monday afterwards. She said there was a meeting on Monday, 29 September at 8 a.m., run by Sergeant Graham Sayce, to fill people in on what had gone down over the weekend. She said that the meeting didn't go for very long and that when she returned she saw me at my desk.

'When the meeting was over, I walked out to my desk and Detective Sergeant Dale was seated in his chair. I didn't realise until then that he had not been present at the meeting. At this time, I saw him rip out a page/s from his day book. I noticed that he was rewriting his day book at his desk.'

It doesn't take Einstein to figure out what happened in the interview. I'm guessing it would sound something like this:

Think, Sam! Was there anything you ever saw Dale do that looked suspicious?
Um, I think that he ripped out pages from a day book once.

Great!

It was in the open office, so it couldn't have been anything underhand —

Don't worry about that! Put it in your statement anyway.

I'd like to point out here that when she said 'day book' Sam was not talking about my official police diary. She was talking about the Spirex notebooks that we all used to make notes on the fly, to later transcribe properly into our diaries. Sure, if I had a page that I'd messed up or a page that I'd made, say, a shopping list on, I would rip it out. Most cops would do the same thing. I reckon if they did an audit of all the Spirex notebooks used by cops, most of them would have pages missing for the same reason. And, most importantly, there were no rules about not tearing out pages from the notebooks.

The next part of Sam's four-years-later statement was curious, and before I quote her exact words I want to quote from Superintendent Tony Biggin's statement to refresh your memory.

Superintendent Biggin: 'At about 12.15 p.m. that day [Sunday, 28 September – the day after the Oakleigh robbery] I spoke to Acting Superintendent Richard Daly of the Ethical Standards Department. I was requested to remove all items from the desk on issue to Miechel at the MDID. At about 12.20 p.m. with the assistance of Detective Sergeant Martin Duggan, I then removed all items from the desk and placed them into a cardboard box. I also seized a two drawer filing cabinet on issue to Miechel. I then secured these in my office, and retained the key in my possession.'

Now let's look at the next bit of Samantha Jennings's statement made in 2007: 'I don't know what day but it was sometime over the next few days, Detective Sergeant Dale asked me to pack up Miechel's belongings in his desk in a box. I put everything out of his drawers into a box. I noticed a laminated IBR photograph A4 size of a female whom I didn't recognise. I forget the first name of the female, but the surname was Hodson. I commented to Detective Sergeant Dale about the photograph and he told me to pack it away, that Miechel had enough ESD issues and that he didn't need that photo floating around. I packed it away and pushed the box under Miechel's desk as I was asked to do.'

Right.

So we have Superintendent Biggin in a sworn statement saying that he came into work the morning after the break-in, and by lunchtime he had cleared Dave Miechel's desk. Then we have Samantha Jennings's sworn statement saying that a couple of days after the break-in I asked her to clear Dave Miechel's desk, and while she was doing it she found a picture of Mandy Hodson, which I told her to hide.

Okay.

But Sam's new version of desk-clearing made sense when she added the following: 'On 2 October, I was asked to make a statement at ESD in relation to Operation Galop investigation. Prior to making my statement, Commander Purton spoke to us and the ESD members in a conference-type room. During this, he stated that it was known that Miechel was having an affair with informer Terry Hodson's daughter, Mandy Hodson. That was the first I had ever heard of that. I thought of the photo that I had seen when I was packing up Miechel's belongings. I couldn't remember the first name of the female, but did wonder if it had been Terry Hodson's daughter. I have never met Terry Hodson or any members of his family.

'I can't remember whether it was this same day when I returned to the Major Drug Investigation Division or whether it was another day. I looked back in the box under Miechel's desk at his belongings that I had previously packed up, that particular photograph was gone from the box.'

She didn't actually say it – just let the implication hang in the air: Paul Dale clearly must have taken the so-called photo from under the desk because it was there and then it was gone. Or maybe Superintendent Anthony Biggin missed a bit out of his statement that should have read: *Hey, I cleaned out David Miechel's desk but I left a picture of Mandy Hodson lying around for Sam to find a couple of days later.*

And here was I thinking that if Superintendent Anthony Biggin was cleaning out Miechel's desk, a photo of Mandy Hodson would have been hot property since Miechel had been arrested the night before with her father?

CHAPTER 31

Rod Collins and his eye-talking

Rodney Charles Collins was arrested on 6 June 2008 and charged with the murders of Ray and Dorothy Abbey in their West Heidelberg home back in July 1987. The brutal murders had been unsolved all that time. Three men used stolen police uniforms and a fake warrant to gain access to the Abbeys' house, and had locked their three small children in a bedroom.

Rod Collins was one of those men.

Rod Collins and Ray Abbey had planned to do a robbery together, using police uniforms reportedly stolen from a drycleaners, but Abbey had pulled out and refused to return the police uniform. Abbey apparently also owed Collins money over the sale of a second-hand car.

Rod Collins was known to have a short fuse and a long memory.

He believed the Abbeys had cash and drugs hidden in a safe in the house. The truth was that Ray Abbey was broke; he had even tried to borrow money earlier that day. In a shed out the back, Collins shot Ray three times in the head. Just before he died Ray yelled out his killer's name – a last act which marked his wife for the same fate. Collins walked back into the house and shot Dorothy Abbey twice in the head. He cut her throat and left her body on the couch to be found by her young children the following morning.

While there were reasons the killer had targeted Ray Abbey, when detectives asked him why he had killed Dorothy, Collins told them, 'Dead men tell no tales'.

Or a dead woman, as the case may be.

Detective Superintendent Jack Blayney of the crime department said, 'When we talk about execution-style killing, they were both put in a position where they were shot in the head from behind in circumstances where it was an extremely callous and calculating act.'

Sound familiar?

By the time Rod Collins was arrested, police knew of his close family ties to Tony Mokbel. At the time of the events of 2003 and 2004, Collins was in a relationship with Joan McGuire – mother of Mokbel's girlfriend, Danielle McGuire – which made him Tony Mokbel's sort-of father-in-law.

During a search of Rod Collins's house, Petra task force detectives found a police report that was said to have tracked the movements, habits and associates of a major drug dealer. They also found a loaded .45 calibre handgun, cannabis, night-vision equipment, a ballistic vest, ammunition, and surveillance equipment.

On 11 June 2008, Rod Collins's new girlfriend, Kylie, contacted Sol Solomon and told him that Collins was considering cooperating with the Petra task force. Six days later, Solomon met Kylie at Eastland Shopping Centre.

Kylie made it clear that her boyfriend expected something in return for his cooperation, and she was keen to discuss this with the detectives. Solomon told her that it was too early to discuss incentives, which would depend on Collins's level of cooperation and the value of his information. Solomon told Kylie about the million-dollar reward for information leading to a conviction in the Hodson murder case.

•

On 17 June, Sol Solomon went out to Barwon Prison to have a chat with Rod Collins. It was apparently during this visit that Collins lay the groundwork for his eventual statement. The statement would later be contradicted by Carl Williams, but the investigating officers pressed on nonetheless.

Solomon would later put notes of the meeting in a statement:

Approximately 6 to 8 weeks prior to the murders of Terence and Christine Hodson he (Collins) was at a bar nearby a solicitor's office in Little Collins Street when he was approached by Paul Dale. Dale told him that he needed [Terence] Hodson killed and asked him (Collins) if he was prepared to do it.

Dale was in the company of another male person who is unknown to Collins.

There was no money offered by Dale for the hit, only an understanding that if he would do this favour for Dale, then Dale would return the favour in the future.

Dale did not tell him why he wanted Hodson killed and he did not ask. He informed me that he never asks why in situations like this; he is not interested in motivations.

He declined the offer.

The approach by Dale was a one off.

Carl Williams possibly may have sent Dale to see him (Collins) about the hit.

He (Collins) has a long-standing friendship with Carl Williams.

It is worth remembering what Rod Collins said from the get-go. That way, later changes in his story will become obvious.

During the interview, Rod Collins told Sol that he'd met Terry Hodson in prison years ago, but that they weren't close associates. He had been to Hodson's house in Kew once to buy marijuana, and had gone into the TV room out the back – the room where Terry and Christine were later shot. Collins said that while he was there, he met Mandy and Christine. He told Solomon that he didn't trust Terry.

When Sol Solomon asked him what kind of person could have done the hit on the Hodsons, Collins said that the murders were very professional, and that the killer must have been a lateral thinker like him.

Indeed.

Collins mused on the type of person that Terry would let into his house. He said that Terry would only open the door to someone he knew or trusted and let them in.

Solomon agreed.

'But who was the person that was behind that known or trusted person that followed him in?' asked Collins, cryptically.

I wasn't part of the investigation so I don't know if this was the first time anyone had suggested that scenario.

Terry didn't trust many people. Was the killer someone he trusted? Someone he would let into his home?

Or could someone he trusted have let in someone he didn't trust?

At the end of the meeting, Collins made his demands clear: he was prepared to make a statement and testify in court repeating his story alleging that I had approached him to kill the Hodsons, on the condition that all the charges he currently faced and was in custody for were dropped, and any reward about the Hodson murders went to his girlfriend, Kylie.

Reading Sol Solomon's statement, I can only assume that Rod Collins was trying to deal his way out of the Abbey murders as well as not being charged with the Hodson murders.

And, of course, the prize in return for his get-out-of-jail-free card was me. Along with the million-dollar reward. Not a bad return for a day's work.

Solomon promised to take the offer to his superiors.

Kylie rang Sol Solomon on 15 July and he and another detective met her the following day, again at the shopping centre. Kylie was ready to make a bigger offer on behalf of her man. She said that Collins could give information about ten unsolved murders after he was given bail. Solomon told her that Collins would have to give full and frank disclosures about the Hodson murders before any deals would be considered.

Five days later, Kylie told Solomon that Collins was prepared to meet him at a location other than the prison or a police station to discuss the Hodson murders. I guess that is the same as asking for bail first, Hodson talk later.

Solomon told her that he would talk to Collins in prison.

After all the wrangling back and forth, Sol Solomon arrived at the prison to talk to Rod Collins on 13 August. The sixty-three-year-old had been languishing in a cell, away from his girlfriend, for a couple of months, and the racy phone calls between them, recorded and transcribed by police, obviously weren't doing it for him anymore.

After assuring Collins that the room was not bugged – a fact that Collins was correct to disbelieve – Sol Solomon used the same sorts of questioning that De Santo used on Terry Hodson four years earlier: establish a rapport, use a bit of flattery, then ever-so-gently ask him to dob on his mates.

But Rod Collins was not the soft mark that Terry Hodson had been. His language was also a lot more colourful, the f-word his only adjective.

Rod Collins was born in 1945 to Thelma Collins-Earle and was raised around Preston by his mother and stepfather, Lawrence Earle. Rod Collins would use both surnames during his life of crime. When he was fourteen years old he left home and went to live with his grandfather, Thomas Collins. By his own account, Rod Collins's younger years were filled with violence.

The transcript of the interview that I got under subpoena began a couple of hours into the interview, so I can only guess what was said in the beginning. When I subpoenaed documents from the Victoria Police I was used to getting only some of what I asked for. Often, I would get pages and pages of documents that had been totally redacted – even the subject of the document was uncertain. So what was said in the first couple of hours is anybody's guess.

Some of the conversation between the detective and the killer is repeated here because I want people to understand the kinds of people the police met with in relation to my case. Judge for yourself if you would be comfortable offering this multiple killer a million taxpayer dollars for a statement.

A million bucks. Of your money. And a get-out-of-jail-free card for a couple of murders.

The conversation that precedes the transcript has clearly contained a request for Rod Collins to be put in a cell with Carl Williams.

'So why do you need to go in with him for a while?' asked Sol Solomon.

'Well, I don't, but ya know, there's little things here and there that I'd like to know for myself too,' he told Solomon. '... I play my cards my way, you play your cards your way, right. We all play our hands different and that. Um, I'm a good thinker, same as you, I suppose.'

'You're a natural thinker,' agreed Solomon.

'I'm a good thinker.'

'That's right.'

Collins told Solomon that he wanted to get bail, and with the usual prison bravado, said that he was confident he would get it. 'I don't give a fuck what you say about the case, right. I will beat it. I've no doubt about that. I'm very positive in that absolutely simply because I wasn't there, all right. Regardless of what the evidence is, that you people have, I wasn't there and I'm confident.'

Pretty soon, Sol Solomon must have realised that he was dealing with an old-school crook with old-school crook values.

'I do not trust people, okay. I'm one of those people. I do not talk out of fuckin' school, do not talk about people, do not tell people anything at all, whatsoever. You talk to me about something, it stays with me. Do not speak to anybody, do not tell anybody about that. I have a million secrets. I do not tell anybody anything at all whatsoever. That is my religion, that is me. That's why, that's the dye that is cast in me, Solly.'

For a guy who didn't talk, Rod Collins was certainly doing a lot of it.

'I know that, Rod,' Sol Solomon assured him.

'It was the way I was brought up, Solly, and I can't help that, ya know. I'm a product of my environment. I didn't fuckin' ask to be brought up like that, ya know. From the fuckin' time, um, six years old, I had the fuckin' shit kicked out of me by fuckin', um by a man that I thought was my father till I was fuckin' fourteen, ya know. Every fuckin' day of my life and that. No wonder I grew up like this, ya know, fuckin' hell product of my environment.'

'Yeah.'

'But I don't hurt anybody that doesn't try to hurt me; fact.'

Collins then complained that he was a person of fuckin' interest in everything that happens in Melbourne.

Sol Solomon told him that it was because of his reputation for being a gun for hire.

'I'm not that at all,' replied Collins.

'And a very, very good one,' said Sol Solomon, laying it on thick.

'I'm not that at all, see?' Collins doth protest too much, methinks. 'I'm not that at all. I tell you that from my heart.'

'That's the reputation you have.'

'I understand all that,' said Collins. 'That stems from the fact I've been growing up and I don't cop all that shit. You don't fuckin' stand over me. I was stood over when I was a kid all my fuckin' life and I grew up like that and that's the person I am today. You don't fuckin' stand over me. You try to hurt me, yeah, I'll fuckin' hurt you first, you know. But I don't like to travel down that road, Solly.'

Rod Collins then lamented the fact that he was always blamed for everything everyone else fuckin' does. But because of that blame, he and people like Mick Gatto had copped a lot. 'And that builds up a reputation, all right.'

'Well, you have got a reputation,' agreed the detective.

'Oh yeah, I know I have, absolutely.'

'People are scared of you,' said Solomon.

'Because I won't cop their shit, Solly. I won't cop their lies. Oh look, I'd rather talk to somebody, have a sensible, decent fuckin' conversation, right, about life.'

Sol Solomon slowly, slowly brought the interview around to bail negotiations. He told Rod Collins that in order to put in a good word at the bail hearing, Collins would have to give him something concrete. Collins told the detective that he was really good when he was on bail and made sure he fronted up every fuckin' day to sign in.

'Well, you know you have a record for failing to appear ...' said Solomon.

And Collins was off. 'I'm fuckin', which is fuckin' bullshit, which is fuckin' from Broadmeadows fuckin' court over the magistrate's fuckin' hearing when the SOGs fuckin' broke into the fuckin' house, smashed all the fuckin' windows out. And I went up there and I waited there for fuckin' two hours, there's no windows in the fuckin' front of the house, so I went up to the fuckin' Clerk of the Courts and I said, "Listen mate, fuckin' when's my thingo come up?" He said, "Oh, it'll be up soon, Rod," and that. I said, "Well, listen, I've been here for fuckin' two hours. I've got no windows in my house. I'm fuckin' going, all right. Will you let them know I'll be there." I got a Fail to Appear, ya know. Fuckin' shit.'

'Do you want bail?' asked Solomon, perhaps resisting the urge to call the *Guinness Book of World Records* to see what the record number of f-words in one breath was.

'Yeah,' said Collins.

'What have you got to offer?'

Collins told him he had three or four other murders he could talk about. 'Or half a dozen.'

When Sol Solomon pressed him for details, the old crook turned cagey. He looked around the room and told the detective the room was bugged.

'I don't believe it is,' said Solomon. It was.

Collins said that he had to be careful because people in prison talked. 'I've done nearly 28 years in jail,' said Collins. 'I know how these people work ... I'm quite aware of what they do, how they talk and everything else. They'll tell me a different story; they'll tell you a different story. Ha, ha, ha. Now cover the wool over my eyes.'

'You've got information about other murders?'

'I can give you information on Laurie Prendergast [who disappeared in August 1985]. I can give you information on Brian Kane [shot dead in November 1982],' he said.

'What about the Hodsons?'

'I can give you information there also too,' said Collins.

'That we can use?'

'Yes, yes.'

'Not just second- or third-hand street talk?'

'Nah, nah, I don't talk that fuckin', that sort of fuckin' bullshit, ya know. He said, she said – I'm not into that fuckin' shit and that. I don't listen to all that crap.'

'That business you told me before about the cop, Dale?'

'Yeah,' said Collins.

'Is that true?'

'That's true.'

'He came to you?'

'That's true. It's true.'

'You wouldn't tell me something that wasn't true, would ya?' asked Solomon of the man accused of being a brutal hit man, of killing a mother and father while their little kids were home, of bashing the mother before shooting her in the head and cutting her throat, of leaving their bloodied bodies for the children to find.

'I'm not going to sit here and talk fuckin' shit to ya,' said Collins.

'So that did happen?'

'I know that time in my life. That's right, that's right,' replied Collins.

'Is there more to that, then?'

'Yeah, there is, but that's as far as I'm going to go, all right? That's why I want to go over to see Carl to find out more of that.'

'So, am I reading this right that you need to talk to Carl because Carl can tell you a bit more about the Hodson job?'

'Yeah, yeah, yeah, yeah.'

Now, even if I wasn't the person involved in this I'd smell a rat. Rod Collins's initial story was contrary to the later police story (provided by Carl Williams, as we'll address later). But clearly, for all his eloquence, Rod Collins wasn't stupid. He wanted to see Carl to clarify his story. And he was even up-front about it.

Sol Solomon repeatedly asked Rod Collins if Tony Mokbel was involved in the Hodson murders, but Collins expertly dodged the question each time.

'Did Tony have any involvement in the Hodson murders?' asked Sol Solomon.

'I'll say nothing,' replied Collins.

'Yeah?'

'I'll say nothing,' repeated Collins.

'What about the cop?'

'I'll say nothing. I'll say nothing more, Solly.'

'Until you get what you want.'

'Until, and that's not asking much.'

Sol Solomon considered this.

Rod Collins promised to be a model bail citizen: 'That's not asking much, ya know. Look, I'll report every day or twice a day, I really don't give a fuck and that. They'll know where I live and I'll be there every day. I won't be fuckin' moving from there. I've got too much work to do up there with the fuckin' house and everything and that. I'll report every fuckin' day or twice a day. I really don't give a fuck.'

When they got round to talking about Terry Hodson again, Solomon described him as a 'fairly high-level drug dealer' but Collins said that he wasn't streetwise.

'He was reckless in the way he used to do business. He was giving up people left, right and centre. And in the end, he was no secret.'

Solomon asked Rod Collins if he'd ever been in Terry Hodson's house.

'I was in the house, yeah. I'll tell you when I was in the house. I was in the house probably oh fuckin' ten years ago – just after he built that little thingo down the back. It was bugged that fuckin' joint he had and that. I knew as soon as I walked in there.'

'Yeah?'

The problem with that was that the TV room wasn't built ten years earlier, and back then the joint wasn't bugged. Perhaps Rod had indeed been there much more recently. But Sol Solomon didn't press the point and let Collins continue.

'I've got good senses. I was born on the streets. I love the night,' declared Collins.

'Yeah.'

'I'm a shadow chaser.'

Sol Solomon pressed the shadow chaser for more information, and finally Collins promised him the Hodsons and information on as many as ten murders.

'But I'll find out for sure who was responsible, right.' Then Collins brought up the murder of Christine Hodson. 'Her. His missus. See I don't believe in that. Regardless of what people think I am or whatever I may be, all right, I don't believe in that. It's not in my code of conduct.'

Considering that Rod Collins was currently in prison facing charges of murdering a man and his wife – and would later be convicted of it – his words should have rung a little hollow.

But, later, he did clarify his personal code. 'I'm not saying I've never hurt anybody; I've never hurt anybody that has never tried to fuckin' hurt me. I've shot plenty of people.'

After chewing some more criminal fat, the cop and the crook finally start talking about me.

'Well, this business with Dale, the corrupt copper,' began Sol Solomon.

'Yeah,' replied Collins.

'When he came to you, did he make any other approaches to you or just that one?'

'No, he only made that one.'

'Did anybody else approach you on his behalf after that time?'

'No, no.'

'Just that one time? But why did he come to you?'

'Well, because he knew me.'

'Did he?'

'A lot of people know me, Solly.'

'And who was the other guy with him?'

'Some other cop.'

'Another cop?'

'Yeah, another cop.'

'Are you sure he was?'

'Absolutely. I know what pricks look like.'

'... has he got a name?'

'He probably does have a name, but I didn't know his name. But I know what he looks like.' And Collins was off again with his crim sidestepping. 'I understand people's lingo, ya know. Lots of crooks talk in code. A lot of people talk in code. Also too, I talk everyday talk, but when I talk business, I talk in code. All depends where I am and who it is. People I grew up with, we talk our own language. We don't have to speak. We can talk with our eyes. We talk with our hands. We don't have to speak. People speak in different ways, I suppose. It's the same as my kids. I grew my kids to talk with their eyes.'

'Yeah, I think you were talking to me with your eyes before,' said Sol Solomon.

'Absolutely. I can talk to everybody. I talk to a lot of people with my eyes. And I bring my children up to talk with their eyes simply because that one day you could be in danger. So talk with your eyes is silent and easier.'

I can only imagine Sol Solomon getting a little frustrated at this point of the interview.

'All right,' said the detective, 'talk with your eyes; answer me with your eyes. Was Tony Mokbel involved in the Hodson murders?'

Solomon then told Collins he couldn't read his eyes.

And so Collins was off again, telling the detective how he had raised his de facto's daughter's child. The daughter was going out with Tony Mokbel, but Collins didn't elaborate on that; he simply told Sol Solomon how he had taught the girl to talk with her eyes.

Finally, the chat was interrupted by a prison guard who asked them to finish up.

After exchanging farewells, Sol Solomon dangled his final carrot. 'Another thing as well – there's soon going to be announced a million-dollar reward for the Hodsons. Any time now.' Solomon told Collins that even if he wasn't interested, his girlfriend could use the money. If the information came from her, said the detective, 'she'd qualify for it'.

'With all the information that I'm going to give, all right, there's not a one reward, there's probably half a dozen rewards, okay,' said Collins. 'And I will give evidence to that.'

So the talk was done, the offer was dangled, the crook was on the hook. As Sol Solomon went to leave, Rod Collins told him that his only concern was for his girlfriend. 'I don't want anything fuckin' happening to her, understand?'

'Nothing's going to happen to you anyway,' soothed Solomon.

'My spirit will come back and fuckin' wreck you,' warned the hit man.

'I know it fuckin' will,' said the cop.

When I read this exchange, what was interesting was Rod Collins's expansion that it wasn't just me who came to see him, I supposedly had another cop with me as well – someone he didn't know the name of. Again, any clarification was easily sidestepped by the wily old crook. Doesn't everyone bring a mate/witness when they try to hire a hit man?

Another interesting thing was that a full month *before* the public announcement of a reward, it was being privately discussed and offered to a convicted murderer to get me. Even Blind Freddy could see that if you offer a million bucks to crooks with nothing to lose and everything to gain, they would sell out their own grandmothers.

The next day, Solomon met with Kylie and explained the catch-22 situation: Collins wouldn't provide anything concrete until he got bail, but he would never be considered for bail unless he provided something concrete. Kylie said she would talk to her boyfriend about the situation.

On 29 August, Solomon rang Kylie and told her that he wanted to visit Collins and take a statement from him about the Hodson murders. Kylie warned that her boyfriend's current state of mind might make that difficult.

When Solomon got to Barwon on 2 September, Collins was immediately hostile. He said he would say nothing more until he got bail. And that was that. The meeting lasted only five minutes. By then, Rod Collins had been in jail for three months, and he was clearly sick of talking.

On 10 September, the million-dollar reward was announced publicly. The reward was not just to find out who killed Terry and Christine – it was designed as a big incentive to any crook who put his hand up for it, and to stir the pot.

Of course, the media immediately camped out at my work and at my house. And to catch all this on tape, the police had all my phones tapped. Later I would get transcripts of taped telephone conversations that I had with my wife and friends.

•

The day after the reward was announced, detectives made a beeline for Carl Williams's jail cell, and he sang like a caged canary.

It would take until 17 October and a bit of negotiation between Kylie and Collins's lawyer for the next meeting to occur. But by now Solomon had Carl Williams. The same carrot-dangling he had tried on Collins had been more effective with Carl, who also had nothing to lose but wasn't as cranky and taciturn as Collins.

And let's not forget why Williams was in prison for thirty-five years: he had been convicted of the murders of Jason Moran

(June 2003), Michael Marshall (October 2003), Mark Mallia (August 2003), Lewis Moran (March 2004) and conspiracy to murder Mario Condello (June 2004). Williams was looking at what would effectively be a life sentence. He would be seventy-one years old before being eligible for parole. He'd lost everything. If someone in authority came and offered him a fortune, who was he to say no.

•

Sol Solomon wrote a summary of the information Collins provided.

> Approximately two weeks after Lewis Moran was murdered, he [Collins] went to a location along Sydney Road, Brunswick near the Brunswick Club to meet an associate to do some wheeling and dealing (would not name his associate).
>
> He (Collins) by chance met Noel Faure and had a short conversation with him.
>
> Faure asked him if he knew Terry Hodson.
>
> Collins stated that he knew Hodson from Barwon Prison.
>
> Faure said to him something similar to 'There's money to be made there'.
>
> He (Collins) believed that Faure was telling him that there was a contract out on Hodson's life and that Faure was going to do it and was sounding him (Collins) out to be involved.
>
> He (Collins) did not discuss this any further with Faure because he didn't trust Faure.
>
> He (Collins) believes that Noel Faure and [name withheld] are responsible for the Hodson murders because of Noel Faure's comments and the fact that both these men are known to be contract killers.

And then, according to Solomon's statement, Rod Collins changed his story. He said that I had approached him around the end of February 2004 and asked him if he knew Noel Faure, and if he could approach Faure for me. But then Collins said that I also asked him if he could give him a 'chop out with Hodson'.

Solomon wrote in his statement: 'Collins told Dale to go away. He didn't know Dale and didn't want to talk to him.'

At the next meeting with Sol, Rod Collins again listed his demands, which included: total immunity from prosecution in relation to the charges he was facing, a guarantee that he wouldn't be charged with any further offences and, last but certainly not least, the million-dollar reward for his girlfriend, Kylie.

On 6 November, Sol Solomon contacted Kylie to arrange to talk to Collins again, but Kylie said that Collins was not prepared to talk. On 14 November, Solomon again met Kylie at the shopping centre. He told her that the police had rejected Collins's demands. He told Kylie that there was evidence that linked Collins himself to the Hodson murders.

Because, by now, Carl was talking.

•

On 19 November, I received another summons for a second Australian Crime Commission hearing on 26 November 2008. Again, they came to the service station to serve it. There was a lot of media hype at that stage on the Petra task force and I recognised one of the detectives as a member of Petra. As far as I was concerned, they could piss off. I wasn't interested in talking to them. I had had enough – five years of continued harassment.

The questions were largely the same, but this time there were new allegations and new connections, and of course, by this stage, they had the statements from Carl Williams to say that I had approached him and that he had organised Rod Collins to kill the Hodsons.

The allegations were different from those that Carl Williams eventually signed up to. By this time, they had clearly settled on their final paid-for version of events from Williams. His story was: I asked him, he organised Collins, I paid cash into a wheelie bin.

Some of the questions suggested that I had met with Collins in a café and asked him to kill the Hodsons. I now know why they were asked: it was Rod Collins's version of events after they dangled the million-dollar reward in the direction of him and his girlfriend.

Also, I was asked about who might be a potential source of information and – under the expectation that this information was secret – I named criminals who I thought could be involved or could provide information.

To my horror, when I was eventually arrested in 2009, the transcripts of these so-called secret Australian Crime Commission hearings were contained in the brief. Not only that, all these transcripts were also handed to Rod Collins in Barwon Prison.

If I had known this, I never would have named names. If the federal judge had opened the hearing with: *Hey Mr Dale, all the answers you give today will be provided to a convicted killer who will then circulate them around the prison system so that every dangerous crook will know you're lagging on them, and not only that if you say anything that will incriminate you then we'll just pass it on to the Victoria Police as well and they'll arrest you*, then I would not have participated.

People need to know that this can happen and they need to be horrified.

I thought that by going to the ACC and telling the truth, the judge would get to the bottom of the farce of the allegations against me. And maybe even start looking at the case afresh.

The Victoria Police and the state government were in damage control, and were clearly prepared to try anything to finally get me on something.

Anything.

•

The Office of Police Integrity (OPI) was created after the Hodson murders and I was the first person dragged into their new premises in the city, over the alleged theft of the blue folder. They didn't even have a formal oath to start an interview. I half made up an oath myself at the beginning of the questioning.

I didn't know what happened to the blue folder – if another one in fact existed outside the one we used after the Oakleigh break-in and the one that was given to Dick Daly. The Major Drug Investigation Division offices were full of blue folders. I don't even know if the offices had ever been fully searched, or if the folder was in someone's desk or one of the boxes that the brass used to clear Dave Miechel's desk. All I know is that it was easier to say that I was the obvious suspect – again without any evidence.

The best they could come up with during the Fitzgerald inquiry was that I was 'the obvious suspect'. It is often repeated in the media that I crept into the MDID that night to steal it, and TV footage 'reconstruction' usually shows a shadowy figure with a torch in a dark office. But Acting Superintendent John Shawyer was already there on duty and by the time I arrived the office was in full swing trying to resurrect what we could from Operation Galop. No one ever said they saw me remove anything. But by now I was used to the Victoria Police pointing the finger.

The media never seems to point out that everyone would have known Terry Hodson was an informer the moment he was caught red-handed with the drug squad detective who had arrested most of the people he had informed against. His identity had been confirmed and no blue folder was going to change that.

Another thing that the OPI did was to reveal that my phones were being constantly tapped – their questions about things I'd discussed on the phone confirmed my suspicions.

I want people to understand just how I was feeling by this stage. I had been hounded since the end of 2003. I had tried to cooperate; I had almost lost count of the number of hearings that I had been subjected to. Every time my family and I thought this was finally over, another thing would come up.

By 2008, it had been five years.

And I gotta say, I was over it. Big time.

Five years of having my phone bugged illegally.

Five years of having my friends targeted and even charged with criminal offences just because they supported me and refused to dump a mate.

Five years of having people look at me sideways, whispering, *That's him!*

Five years of regular front-page newspaper stories about how I was a disgraced ex-detective who 'remains a person of interest in the Hodson murders'.

Five long years.

As you can imagine, I had a rather short fuse when it came to this case.

So when a guy who was not connected to the case at all, a guy who I had hired to do some painting and decorating for me, told me that the police had been sniffing around him wanting a statement, you can imagine my response.

'Mate, I would be very disappointed if I ever see a statement with your name on it,' I told him.

My mate was nervous, though. He was a regular guy who'd never had any dealings with the police. 'But what do I say to them?' he wanted to know.

By then I'd had an absolute gutful. 'Tell 'em to go get fucked.'

And, of course, all of this was caught on the wire tap and later suggested – and reported in the media – that it was me interfering with a police investigation. All because I told a mate that he didn't have to join the Paul Dale circus.

But I urge you to think about it for a minute. Imagine the police hounding you and harassing you for *five years*, and imagine what you would tell your friends if they told you detectives had arrived on their doorstep. Friends who had nothing to do with anything.

What would you be caught saying on a wire tap?

Speaking of the five years of continued surveillance, it's worth mentioning the laws in relation to getting a warrant to tap someone's phone. The police can't get an ongoing phone-tap warrant. There are a lot of really strict rules about telephone intercepts. The police can get one for only a short time, then the tap must be removed unless a new warrant is obtained. To get a warrant, you have to go before a judge and show evidence of continued illegal activity.

Are you beginning to get the point? If my phone had been tapped for five years, that meant the police must have continually gone before the judge and said ... and said what?

What evidence did they ever have of my involvement?

I suppose the OPI highlighted conversations like the ones that I had with the painter and twisted them into accusations of obstruction – as opposed to merely long-running, slow-burning frustration – so they could somehow justify a continued tapping of my phones. That's the only way they could ever legally tap my phones for the five years of their investigation.

And, of course, justify the huge expense, because intercepting someone's phones doesn't end with the wire tap. Victoria Police members need to be allocated to listen to and transcribe every word said in every phone conversation. Think about how much that would cost in resources allocation. Hundreds of thousands of dollars? Millions? I have no idea. The only thing I do know is that in the pursuit of me, money was never an object.

And I hope grassroots coppers think about this every time their boss tells them that the budget doesn't allow for some vital piece of equipment, or that there's no money to pay overtime for the extra gruelling hours they do. Perhaps when they are putting their lives on the line, they can take solace in the fact that we all know that Paul Dale told his painter and decorator to 'Tell 'em to go get fucked.'

•

On 22 November 2008, Carl's mother, Barbara Williams, was found dead in her home in Essendon. She had overdosed on sleeping pills. With her older son, Shane, dead from an overdose a decade earlier, Carl in prison and her estranged husband, George, failing an appeal to have his sentence reduced, her Primrose Street house must have seemed lonely. Apparently, the police found an empty medicine bottle near her body. It was reported that she had been unhappy that Carl had pleaded guilty to murder, and she feared that he wouldn't be released until she was long dead.

Carl and George were told in prison of Barbara's death. George was given permission to attend the funeral. Carl wasn't.

In a death notice, Carl wrote: 'Mum, you used to stir me by calling me a mummy's boy, however it was a tag I wore with pride 'cos you were also my best friend. You were always there to support me, no questions asked. You were the best mum I could have wished for.'

Nine days later, a huge daisy floral tribute covered the front of the altar at St Therese's Church in Essendon. A picture of Carl and Barbara was placed on top of the coffin. From prison, Carl sent a message to his mother. In part, it read: 'There's nothing I wouldn't have done for you mum. Those conversations I had with you each morning on the phone were something I looked forward to. I used to visit you with the kids and all our problems would go away, we didn't want those visits to end ... There's nothing in the world I would not have done for you. Losing you is the hardest thing I have ever had to deal with.'

Carl's ex-wife, Roberta Williams, was a little more blunt in her tribute at the church. 'You provided so much love and loyalty against our enemies the Supreme Court judges and the police,' she said. 'You cared about other people more than yourself, which was the problem.'

One can only imagine how the self-confessed mummy's boy must have felt, sitting alone in his cell while his mother's funeral was being held.

Sad?

Bitter?

Angry?

Vengeful?

Out to get what he could from the cops who'd put him behind bars? Within weeks, he'd be spirited away to a secret location with his dad and the cops to put together his statement.

CHAPTER 32

2009

On 19 January, Cameron Davey again made the drive out to Barwon Prison to talk to the man who he obviously saw as his star witness. Star, but secret.

By then, Carl Williams hadn't seen the light of day without bars in between since October 2004 and he wasn't looking to any decade soon. While he maintained that his last statement was accurate, he told Cameron Davey that he had something to add.

'There were a number of reasons I did not tell the police all I know about the Hodson murders in my last statement,' he wrote. 'I did not think police would be able to charge anyone because of the lack of traceable phone calls, Rod Collins was still out of jail and because I did not want to get charged with the murders. I didn't want to be a dog and be a protection prisoner, but my attitude has changed.'

Carl spoke about the meeting he said we had in Hillside to, supposedly, organise the hit on Terry Hodson. According to Carl's story, I pulled up in my blue ute and we drove off to chat about hit men. The fact that I had never owned a ute, blue or otherwise, didn't deter the eager cops from drinking in the killer's every word.

Carl told Cameron Davey that even though I had already organised a hit man, it was taking too long and I asked him to get me another one.

'Dale told me that he had to get Hodson and he had to get Hodson before Dale's committal. Dale said he didn't want to go back to jail. He said he had been in isolation and it was tough. He said he had someone on the job but it was taking too long to get Hodson ... I do believe Dale was still hoping that the job on Hodson would be carried out by whoever else he had put in place, but I think he wanted the job done and was worried the other person was not going to get it done in time ... I told Dale that I would try to help him. I didn't want to commit until I could confirm that someone could do the job for me. I think at the time that Andrew Veniamin was dead, but Rod Collins was always asking for work and I thought he might do it. Rod was in the back of my mind as someone I could use for a job like this.'

And the price?

'I don't know if I asked him or he just told me the figure to do the job was $150000. He never mentioned where he was getting the money from.'

Now, I'm no expert in how these things work, but two hit men? At $150000 a pop? And how was I, a guy working for the minimum wage digging ditches to support my family, supposed to come up with $150000 in cash – or possibly $300000 for two hit men?

Carl continued: 'I told him that if I could arrange for someone to do it for him, then the money was to be dropped off at my mum's place in the bin which is inside the gate. The money was to be paid on completion of the job. My mum's place was at Primrose Street Essendon.' Carl explained that he told me that we could communicate by 'safe phone' so that it would leave no trace.

Convenient for his story.

Also convenient was Carl's claim that the Hodson job meant nothing to him personally – despite the fact that he had been recorded on phone taps talking about how Lewis Moran and Terry Hodson had a hit out on him. Within weeks of that conversation, Moran and Hodson had both been gunned down.

Carl said that I had handed him an envelope with a picture of Terry Hodson in it and his address: 'I'm not sure how long after the meeting I had with Dale it was that I met Rod in person. It would have been quickly, as in within a couple of days, because I had the envelope that Dale had given me. I should also say that I wouldn't have met with Rod just to discuss this, because quite frankly, I didn't run around organising things for Dale and wasting my time. I can't remember now but Rod and I may have been planning to meet and catch up anyway.'

While he was happy to admit organising the hit on Terry, Carl was at pains to distance himself from the murder of Christine Hodson. 'I should add that the contract related to Terry Hodson. There was never any contract on his wife and I never mentioned Terry's wife to Rod. Dale never mentioned Terry's wife to me either.'

Interestingly, Carl insisted that while he had phoned me to let me know about the hit, he didn't say when it would happen because he didn't know. 'If Dale had an alibi, it was not through the information that I gave him,' he declared.

He went even further to declare: 'I didn't know when the Hodsons were going to be murdered. He wasn't my enemy and so I had no reason to know when it was going to happen and I wasn't even sure if Rod could do it ... I wasn't worried about being linked to the Hodson murders because they weren't my enemies.'

Weren't they, Carl?

He then went into great detail about how I had allegedly phoned him to say I'd put the money in his mum's wheelie bin. He happened to be at his mum's at the time and he went outside and collected it.

It might be timely to remember that Carl and his mum's Primrose Street house were under constant surveillance. Funny how none of this surveillance captured me anywhere near Carl's mum's wheelie bin.

He then said that he bundled the money together and arranged to meet with Rod Collins to hand over the entire amount. In his account, Carl unwittingly revealed how casually he could talk about murder with Collins. 'I said to him, "What happened with the sheila [Christine Hodson]?" He said, "That's not for you to worry about." That was the end of the conversation. I asked him about the sheila because I didn't think she needed to die and she wasn't a part of the contract. Having said that, I didn't push it any further. I didn't keep any of the money for myself as I was travelling pretty well at the time.'

Carl Williams said very clearly that he never introduced me to Rod Collins and never told me who had done the hit, nor Collins who had ordered it.

The fact that this was the *exact opposite* of the statement that Rod Collins had offered appears to have gone unnoticed by Cameron Davey when he took it.

Carl covered for his lack of knowledge about the finer details of the Hodson murders by saying that he and Rod Collins had never discussed them afterwards.

'I don't know how Rod got into the Hodsons' house and he has never told me. I never provided any information to Rod about any security systems at the Hodson house because I didn't know about any security at the house and Dale never told me about any security at the house. I think I have heard through the media that security tapes were taken from the Hodson house, but I didn't tell Rod about the tapes because I didn't know about them. Rod never told me what happened to the tapes that were taken from the house.'

Carl signed his statement at 2.36 p.m. Oddly, he signed another six-page statement just nine minutes later – which meant that either he was a fast talker and Cameron Davey was a fast typist, or these statements were made at another time and brought back for his signature.

As a detective, I knew that a confession had to fit the circumstances of the crime scene. I wonder if this case had moved so far away from actual evidence that this no longer mattered.

Terry and Christine were shot, mid-cigarette, watching TV in their back room. They were surrounded by guard dogs who would alert them to any intruder. While Rod Collins admitted going to the Hodsons' home once before to buy drugs, Terry would hardly have let him in, and certainly not to watch TV with him and his wife. With constant visits from the Ethical Standards Department and increased video surveillance around the property, you'd imagine that Terry would have been very reluctant to admit one of the most notorious hit men in Melbourne into his home.

It also doesn't fit that a casual acquaintance would know to remove tapes from both the garage and the back room. That was someone with insider knowledge. And it must have been someone with insider knowledge or a relationship with the Hodsons who would be granted entry not only into the house, but into the back TV room to sit around with the Hodsons watching TV.

•

Despite being convicted of various drug offences and four murders, Carl Williams didn't spend Christmas of 2008 in prison. Instead, he was taken out of Barwon to an 'undisclosed location' to spend time with either his girlfriend, or prostitutes, or possibly both, depending on whose story you believe.

During his little holiday, Carl gave detectives 'unsigned' statements.

Carl began it with: 'This previous statement was accurate to the best of my memory without my memory being refreshed. The police have requested that I make an additional statement. The police have advised me that they will supply me with additional information which may refresh my memory. This statement will contain any further information that I can remember after the police have supplied me with this information.'

It must have taken hours for the police to play him tapes of listening devices and Carl drew tenuous links to support his story. One recording has him talking to Nicola Gobbo about an 'advisor'. Even though Carl can't think of why Nicola Gobbo would refer to me as his advisor, he nonetheless concludes – helpfully – that it must have been me she was talking about.

Long bows.

Carl also helpfully told Cameron Davey that every time either of them mentions the weather in the frequent calls between himself and Rod Collins, they would probably be referring to the Hodson murders.

Right.

At times, it even borders on the ridiculous.

Carl Williams received a text message from Collins that read: *Hello buddy, catch you tomorrow for sure my friend. Just been tired buddy – catches up to all at some stage mate. Take care see you soon RC*. Here is Carl's interpretation: 'This is possibly a coded message in relation to the murder of the Hodsons but I can't be certain.'

Well, the cops *were* offering him several million bucks in cash and prizes.

Carl was rather sanctimonious in his declaration that it wasn't his habit to discuss murders over the phone in 'uncoded' conversations. He seems, however, to have overlooked the taped conversations with his drug king buddy David McCulloch in the days after the Hodson murders in which they both chatted happily about them.

After Carl Williams sat down with police to piece together his story it took the Petra task force four weeks to arrest me.

CHAPTER 33

The Acacia Unit

On Friday, 13 February 2009, I was arrested in a grand affair put on, no doubt, for the benefit of the media, and perhaps so that the Victoria Police could spend yet more money in a bells-and-whistles approach that had been a feature of my case. As usual, the media were alerted beforehand and arrived with their cameras to catch the show.

And it was a show that all of Wangaratta could witness: their service station operator who had worked for years without incident needed seven cops inside the service station and half a dozen surrounding the premises and a police helicopter to be arrested.

Taxpayers must surely groan at the expense.

Sol Solomon had been pursuing me for a while now. He was a cop I'd worked with for over two years at the Lorimer task force, and who I knew very well from our days of carpooling to work. We had been close.

Emphasis on *had been*.

But by now I had lost a lot of respect for him because he was targeting my mates. Any serving police were strongly discouraged from having any contact with me. Some of those who chose to ignore this did so at their own peril. Several mates were pursued, charged and sacked. It didn't matter what their charge sheets read, they might as well have said: *You are charged with being mates with Paul Dale*. In response, I had made sure that I dropped my feelings about Solomon often over the phone, which I knew was being tapped. Petty, I know, but my right of reply in this was so limited that I vented when I could.

On Friday the 13th Solomon was professional to a point as he told me that he was there to arrest me for the murders of Terence and Christine Hodson. 'The time's come for you to answer for their deaths.'

'Yeah sure, Sol.' I was so weary of this. This was the second time that I'd been arrested for the murders – the first being the morning after the bodies were discovered.

Detective Senior Constable Cameron Davey took out a pair of handcuffs. It was just to embarrass me.

I looked at the handcuffs and shook my head. 'There's no need to handcuff me. I'm not going to run. I'm not violent.'

Solomon looked at Davey and shook his head. 'There's no need,' he muttered.

As we walked out to the car – me surrounded by a bunch of detectives – I thought about what was at the bottom of all of this: the fact that Terry and Christine were good people and I felt sorry for the loss of them. I also felt sorry for their kids because they had lost good parents. Terry and Christine were family-minded people and we had all gotten closer to him than we ever had with any other informer.

Making it worse was that I knew I hadn't killed them, which meant that whoever did it had gotten away with murder. They must have been sitting back laughing, knowing that the police could never turn from me and look in their direction.

The arrest didn't surprise me because by now my wife and I had identified a three-month pattern: they would leave us alone for three months, then something else would happen. I usually knew beforehand because I'd be sweeping the servo driveway and there'd be someone from Channel 10 poking a microphone in my face. They would ask me what I thought about the latest development in the Hodson case and, sure enough, that night on the news something would break. The fact that the media knew before I did told me that they were being fed information – probably from the police media or through planned leaks by detectives.

As we were pulling out of the driveway of the petrol station, Ditty screamed up in her car and cut off the police car. She had got word at the hospital where she worked that the police were there and sped to the petrol station. I wound down the window and told her it was okay. I truly meant it. This arrest was what I thought of as a 'show arrest', where they would drag me in yet again, question me, then release me. I knew they didn't have any evidence against me – they couldn't have, because I didn't do it.

We continued to Wangaratta police station.

As we settled into the interview room, Sol Solomon turned to me and said, 'This is not like Lorimer.'

I nodded, knowing exactly what he meant. We all remembered the elation at arresting Bandali Debs and Jason Roberts. We knew that we felt so good back then because it was a good arrest. Rock solid. We had them on forensics, their own covertly recorded conversation, and the case was tight. There was no doubt.

I had always been open in interviews about anything the police wanted to know. When Solomon started at the beginning of how I'd met the Hodsons, I interrupted him.

'What's changed?' I asked. 'I've already been asked these questions thousands of times. What's changed?'

'We'll get to that later,' said Solomon. 'Are you going to answer our questions or do we have to suspend the interview?'

'No! I've answered all these questions before. You know my relationship with the Hodsons. You know my relationship with Carl Williams. Have you got any questions that I haven't answered before?'

There were no new questions, and while I had been arrested quite a number of times by now, what surprised me was when Sol Solomon told me he was charging me with murder. I couldn't believe it.

What did they have now that they hadn't had for the last five years?

What *could* they have?

Other times I was arrested, I was asked questions then released pending further inquiries. And now I was presented with the charges that had already been typed up. So it didn't matter what I said that day: I was going to be locked up no matter what.

They formally charged me and I found myself in a police cell – the same cell that I had put offenders in when I worked at Wangaratta police station. I was dressed in my short-sleeved APCO service station clothes and my shorts, and I felt, first of all, highly embarrassed. I knew all the cops at Wangaratta and knew that they'd all be having a stickybeak at their latest prisoner in the cell via the cameras. This arrest was designed to be as humiliating as possible.

The taxpayer had funded the flying-up from Melbourne of a prosecutor and a magistrate, even though Wangaratta had a perfectly good court system.

By the time I arrived at court we were joined by media, who filled the courtroom.

When you charge someone with something serious like murder, the system has a set time frame for having a brief of evidence ready. In my experience, we always had a brief of evidence ready *before* we arrested anyone. That was the way things were done, although there was a provision for the police to take a couple of weeks to complete the brief.

The prosecutor stood up and told the court that because I had been charged with murder, he was requesting a six-week extension to put together the brief. I couldn't believe what I was hearing. If he wanted six weeks to put together the brief, that meant I would be kept in custody for that six weeks.

About thirty detectives from the Petra task force sat in the court and I understood that they were all there to see my arrest. We had done the same thing after Lorimer. It was the big show. *We got our man.* I understood that; however, what I didn't understand was the need for a six-week extension. If they had a case against me, where was the brief?

I represented myself and stood up in front of the magistrate and said that none of us were surprised by my arrest today. We could all see it coming, so how was it that the police were claiming not to be prepared?

'I understand that I can't make a bail application before you; however, there is absolutely no reason to provide a six-week extension. In my experience, the brief should be prepared well before this. I have no doubt there is a brief already. I am not a flight risk. I have a business in town. I have a wife and family. I have never failed to appear at any hearing, of which there's been over a dozen. I have previously been arrested over the same matter.'

Even though I made my feeble protest, I knew there was no chance that I would walk away from court a free man. I knew that the legislation does not allow a magistrate to grant bail in a murder hearing – that has to come from a Supreme Court judge. Even making the arrest on a Friday was just spiteful – it was a ploy to put me in a cell without the opportunity to get a hearing until at least the following Monday. It was the unwritten rule that detectives worked by – I had done it myself countless times.

As soon as the court case concluded I was remanded into custody by the magistrate, who had also granted the six-week extension.

The last time it had taken me ten days to get bail, so I began to mentally prepare myself for ten days in prison.

It never occurred to me I wouldn't be granted bail.

•

While I hadn't been handcuffed at the petrol station, I didn't get the same consideration on the trip to prison. As soon as I was walked out the back door of the court, I was surrounded by protective service cops with German shepherd guard dogs. A cop wrapped a thick leather belt around my waist and then shackled me into the back of a prison van, hands shackled to feet. The space in the back of the van consisted of a metal seat and a space physically big enough for a person to sit in and not much else. When the door was closed on me the space was pitch black, until the car started and a small light came on. I wasn't told where I was being taken and I assumed that it would be the Melbourne Assessment Prison, where I was taken last time.

But it wasn't.

The trip dragged on and on, and I called out that I needed a toilet stop, but there were no such niceties afforded a guy shackled in the back of a prison van. I pressed the intercom button and told them I needed to go to the toilet. After another half-hour my need to relieve myself became desperate and painful. I manoeuvred myself in my shackles to unbutton myself, and relieved myself onto the stainless steel floor.

'Are you pissing on the floor?' called one of the guards.

'Yep,' I said.

'Well, you'll be cleaning it up when we get there.'

'Yeah, no worries,' I said, because hosing out the floor was less painful that holding on any longer.

I think that it was about four hours by the time we pulled to a stop. When the door was opened I knew we weren't at the Melbourne Assessment Prison and I knew it wasn't Port Phillip. No one told me where I was, but a sign said Barwon Prison. Like most people, I knew little about prisons and I had never heard of the Acacia Unit, so I didn't know what I was facing.

Despite their threats, the van guards didn't make me clean the floor. They probably just hosed it out anyway.

I was processed and given a medical examination and a red tracksuit to replace my work clothes, which were taken and put into a bag. The significance of the colour of the tracksuit didn't dawn on me till later, when I realised that only occupants of the Acacia Unit wore bright-red tracksuits.

Many twists and turns and locked security checkpoints later, I was placed into a cell in Unit 4.

There are two levels of fear for an ex-cop in jail. One is the same fear that anyone would face being forced into a small cell in a prison containing vicious and violent men. The second is that the prison no doubt contains blokes that you've put away. And they would know that their arresting officer is in their midst.

Little did I know that I wasn't going to be in the midst of anyone for six weeks.

One minute I was a husband, a father of two young children, and a businessman working seven days a week, interacting with hundreds of customers every day. The next minute I was sitting alone in a cell about a metre and a half by two metres long, containing a foam mattress on a concrete base, with a plastic chair, little black and white TV, and the ubiquitous stainless steel bowl without a seat – just like on TV prison shows. It came with a stainless steel basin to match. Above that was a reflective metal sheet, which I guessed was there so you could look at your reflection and remind yourself of your misery.

I sat on the bed next to my pile of emergency rations of a towel, soap, toothbrush and toothpaste. There was no access to a shower – which, I found out later, was behind door number two in my cell. There was a slot in the door which food was pushed through. For a guy who was active and fit, this kind of enclosed cage living was torturous. For a gregarious kind of person, the lack of human contact was hell.

My lawyer, Tony Hargreaves, came to the Acacia Unit to visit me before my first bail application. I arrived in my red tracksuit, shackled. A prison officer removed my shackles and I entered the room. Tony and I sat in a little room with a table and chairs.

Hargreaves looked grim. 'You're not going to believe this, Paul. It's unbelievable. It's blown me away. It's blown all my colleagues away, but Nicola Gobbo is going to be a witness against you.'

'What?' My head spun.

'Apparently she taped a conversation she had with you.'

Nicola Gobbo. One of Victoria's most prominent criminal barristers. Had worn a wire to implicate a client.

By now my level of disbelief had been stretched so far that nothing could really surprise me; however, this came close. She was someone I had spoken to in absolute confidence. How could she? Not just as a friend, but as a lawyer? She could have claimed lawyer–client privilege. Why would she have said anything at all?

It would take several years and a close examination of her later statements to try to understand her motives. And several years on from that to understand the full extent of her treachery. But more about that later.

For the time being, I needed to find strength and I knew that the strength would come from my children. Ava was a baby and Baily was fast growing up; just thinking of them made me understand that I had to fight this. While missing them was torturous, missing them also gave me strength.

For a while.

I could sustain the fight mentality for the first week or so in prison, but after the weeks stretched out full of nothingness and boredom and despair, I began to plan to end it all. People who haven't experienced it will never understand what being in solitary does to you. That I could go from being an average bloke to being suicidal so quickly was a testament to this. Days stretched out so long, and while I could be strong one day and fight it, the next day I would wake up with no strength left and it became almost insurmountable thinking how to survive that day, let alone the day after. Then I'd start to think that if I couldn't survive that day or the next, how could I survive the next week?

I began to pick out the tiny razor blades from plastic razors. As a detective at the Homicide Squad I had investigated deaths in prison before, and I knew ways it could be done. Razors, tying sheets to the side of the bed and wrapping them around your neck and simply leaning forward.

Alone in a cell, you are fighting the devil.

It's like half your brain loves your family and wants to live for them and fight the case, while the other half of your brain is bleak and empty and full of the deepest despair. Your energy levels are completely drained and your world turns black. You are suffering and your family is suffering and it is all because of you. The devil inside starts to reason that if you weren't in the middle of this, if you weren't here, everyone could get on with things. Ditty would be set up if she sold the business. The kids would soon forget and grow up and move on ...

And then you shake the thoughts away and there would be a glimmer of hope. The glimmers were mainly in the form of the monthly contact visits and then weekly visits from Ditty and the kids. I could have two box visits a week – these were non-contact visits, with me sitting in a box-like room behind plexiglass, talking to my visitors who sat on the other side.

Close but yet so very far away.

Ditty would make the long drive with the kids for one visit, and Mum and Dad would come for the other visit.

Before every visit I was stripsearched, even though I was in the most secure unit possible: *Strip naked, open your mouth, bend your ears forward, lift your scrotum, bend over, spread your cheeks ...*

At every visit I was shackled and shuffled down the corridors, and even though I had no contact with anyone through the box visits, I was re-shackled and stripsearched all over again. The process was designed to be humiliating and embarrassing.

Why would I need to be searched when I had no access to anything or anyone?

When I later read through Cameron Davey's notes, he wrote that after I was arrested he let Mandy and Andrew Hodson know. Both immediately advised him that they would be making compensation applications.

CHAPTER 34

Bail applications

When my bail application finally came up on 14 March – one month and one day after my arrest – I went before the courts. The most explosive thing, as far as the media was concerned, was that Cameron Davey revealed that Rodney Collins was about to be arrested for murder.

This all came about because of a vigorous line of questioning from my barrister, Ian Hill QC, directed towards Sol Solomon, who had told the court that there was a gangland figure who could only be identified by the letter 'R' who had told police that I had ordered a second hit man after the first hit man I hired was 'taking too long'.

Right from the early days, police were keen to keep Carl Williams's identity from the public and the media. According to Sol Solomon, 'R' had confessed to contacting a hit man to kill the Hodsons. After all, it sounded much better to say there was a secret witness who could testify against Paul Dale, rather than name him and watch his credibility scuttle away like a rat up a drainpipe.

So of course my barrister asked the obvious question: how reliable could the evidence be if 'the person who is said to be the executioner and the person who is said to be the middleman are known yet neither had been charged?' Hill then asked, 'Isn't it because he is incapable of telling the truth that you have decided not to charge Rodney Collins?'

It was these kinds of sticky questions that made the police squirm. On one hand they had Carl singing like a canary with the promise of conjugal visits and cash rewards, as well as police paying for private education for his daughter (a detail that would emerge later), but on the other hand judge after judge had labelled him notoriously unreliable. The cops couldn't have it both ways: they couldn't prosecute him as a lying psychopath and then, months later, present him as a truthful, honest witness – especially if anyone got wind of the huge incentives he was being offered.

In response, Cameron Davey told the court that Rod Collins was likely to be charged the following week.

My barrister told the court that I was being kept in 'appalling and dehumanising conditions, akin to torture' in Barwon Prison.

Chief Justice Marilyn Warren adjourned her decision on my bail.

On Friday, 20 March, Cameron Davey applied to interview Rod Collins. The police spoke to Collins's lawyer, who said that Collins would not be participating in an interview. Davey told the lawyer that in that case Rod Collins would be charged with the murders of Terence and Christine Hodson.

They had Carl as a 'witness' now. They didn't need Rod Collins.

•

The rogues' gallery of interviewing didn't stop with Collins and Williams. Cameron Davey visited Azzam Ahmed in Loddon Prison on 3 April 2009. I suppose that with all the talk of the money that I was supposed to be throwing around to pay for multiple hit men, the fine members of the Victoria Police needed to suggest a source of such wealth.

So, back to Azzam Ahmed's alleged $700 000 that he said went missing on the night of the Oakleigh break-in. Ahmed must have been pleased: finally someone was ready and willing to believe that there had been money at the house and that somehow I had taken it, despite the fact I was nowhere near Dublin Street that night.

That brings us back to the issue of why Tayluh the drug-house babysitter didn't know about the $700 000, despite the fact that she always knew when Ahmed had brought a large amount of cash there in the past. Here's why: apparently Ahmed snuck it into the house in the middle of the night and put it there.

Well, of course he did, folks.

Ahmed: 'The last time I saw that $700 000 was at about 4 a.m. on the morning of the day of the burglary. I was at the house at Dublin Street until 4 a.m. on that Saturday morning. At that time, the money was located in the kitchen. Inside the kitchen there were cabinets located along a wall and on top of the cabinets, was a space about a foot deep. The space couldn't be seen if you stood in the kitchen, so it was a hiding spot that I used to keep drugs and money. The last time I checked on the money was before I left the Dublin Street house at 4 a.m. on the morning of the burglary ... The money was in plastic shopping bags and those bags were located in a carry bag, but I can't remember what the carry bag looked like. The carry bag was a zip-up type bag. I had counted that $700 000 myself.'

And what of Tayluh, who would surely have noticed the counting of $700 000 since it would have taken a while and she rarely left the house?

'To my knowledge, [Tayluh] didn't know about the money being located in the kitchen cabinet hiding space at that time.'

Come on, Azzam. Really?

'I know that on previous occasions, she knew that large amounts of money had been kept in the house, however, I never told her about that particular $700 000 being located in the house prior to the burglary.'

Yeah, sure.

But that's not all.

Ahmed dropped his next bombshell. 'There was also a large quantity of ecstasy tablets at the house prior to the burglary. I believe there were approximately 165 000 pills located at the house prior to the burglary ... I also became aware when I received my hand-up brief that approximately 30 000 ecstasy tablets had been located by police following the burglary. I believe approximately 135 000 ecstasy tablets are missing and have not been accounted for.'

Really?!

After that bombshell, Azzam Ahmed set about denying any knowledge of the Hodson murders. 'I suspected that Terry Hodson would be killed because I knew that he was with Miechel at the time they were arrested for the burglary on the Dublin Street house. It was obvious to me that Terry must have been working with the police because he was arrested with Miechel. I had never heard of Terry before the burglary. Terry wasn't involved in any way in the Dublin Street drug trafficking operation. I also heard rumours through associates that there were police documents getting around which showed that Terry was a police informer. I had no knowledge that Terry was going to be murdered. No one gave me any specific information that he was going to be killed. It was just something that I suspected. I never told anyone that Terry was going to be killed on a particular night. I couldn't because I didn't know about it.'

Well, we can all be glad he cleared that up.

He finished his statement by saying that he had told Cameron Davey and Sol Solomon about the missing money and drugs in 2007 when they had visited him in jail.

The two cops must have forgotten to put that statement into the Brief of Evidence.

•

On 26 March 2009, my bail application was refused. In a nutshell, Chief Justice Marilyn Warren ruled that while my incarceration was arduous on my family and on the family business, that was part and parcel of the criminal justice system. She suggested we get a manager in to run the petrol station. While she admitted that I wasn't a flight risk, since I had hung around for the past five years maintaining my innocence, she said that 'since about December 2008 ... significant, if not dramatic, developments have occurred in the prosecution case, namely the position and statements of Witness R and Witness F.'

Carl Williams and Nicola Gobbo.

Of course, it was a masterstroke on the part of the police to conceal their identities, because it made them sound like secret, protected witnesses. The public could read all about how two witnesses had come forward to say I conspired to kill the Hodsons, and would imagine that they were under police protection because I was such a threat.

Chief Justice Warren conceded that my imprisonment conditions were 'difficult', then concluded '... as matters stand, and whilst difficult, the custodial arrangements do not constitute exceptional circumstances at this time.'

And to sum it all up: 'Even if I was so persuaded there would remain the question of the risk that would attach to the applicant being granted bail. It is not suggested he is a flight risk. However, the circumstances of the killing of the deceased, alleged as they are against the applicant when a serving police officer for the purpose of eliminating a witness against him, create a risk that in my view would need to be taken into account. In view of the gravity of those circumstances I would be persuaded by the Director's assessment that the applicant would pose an unacceptable risk. It follows I refuse the application for bail.'

And the cell door shut behind me once again, its clang echoing in my ears.

•

Just as they were designed to, the conditions in prison nearly sent me mad. I began seeing the prison shrink, who gave me medication for depression. Another shrink I saw had worked at Guantanamo Bay and likened my symptoms to the ones he had seen there.

After an assessment by the prison psychiatrists, they concluded that if my conditions didn't alter I'd have to be moved to a psych hospital. Attached to my cell was a courtyard of about 8 by 10 metres and I was finally allowed to go into it. The bleak, empty space was bordered by a steel-mesh roof and had no natural light, but it was heaven compared to the tiny cell where I had spent weeks. It gave me the chance to walk up and down and stretch my legs, and examine a new set of walls scratched with marks from prisoners who had come before me.

To get letters in the Acacia Unit took five days, as they were checked and approved. Anything that was a little different, like sparkles stuck by my kids onto a Father's Day card, wasn't approved and wasn't passed on.

Imagine my surprise – not to mention horror – when I received a letter though the so-called monitored and restricted prison mail system from Little Tommy Ivanovic, who was a mainstream prisoner in Barwon. Little Tommy was very upset. He wrote that he'd seen my Australian Crime Commission transcript and read part of it – the parts where I had named him as an informer at the ACC hearing. He wasn't just upset that I had suggested he was an informer – he was furious that he had been moved from the general prison population into protective custody because of it. And he blamed me. His letter quoted the pages of my transcript that he'd seen.

My secret transcript, that is. Remember, the one that the Australian Crime Commission said would remain secret?

Yes, that one.

When I finally got a chance to ring my lawyer to tell him what had happened, he couldn't believe it either. I arranged to send him Tommy's letter so that he could see for himself. Meanwhile, he promised to contact the Australian Crime Commission to find out how this had happened.

The ACC denied releasing my transcripts, but since Little Tommy had quoted from them chapter and verse, detectives from the Petra task force arranged a search of Rod Collins's cell.

Surprise, surprise. They located pages of my transcript.

After the detectives produced concrete proof that the Australian Crime Commission had given my transcripts to a hit man who had immediately passed pages of it around the jail system, the ACC called it an 'administrative error' – in my view a sanitary term for what it actually was: a criminal act.

Then they advised my lawyers that the 'non-publication direction in relation to each of your client's examinations were varied ... to be used in connection with any proceedings related to the prosecution of Mr Dale in connection with the alleged murder of Terence and Christine Hodson ...'

Varied?

Changed. Reversed. After the fact.

Read the above reversal and think about the promises made by the lawyers and the judge at my Australian Crime Commission hearings. 'I want to allay any concerns you may have that this will spill over into the public arena because it will not. I will make what's known as non-publication directions which will bind everyone here and you won't read or hear publicly that you came here and you won't read or hear publicly, while those directions remain, what you said in evidence. Does that put your mind at rest?'

Sure, it would have put my mind at rest if what you said was true. Only problem was that you forgot to mention that circumstances might change.

In his letter to the ACC, my lawyer suggested that their assurances of secrecy were a 'complete fallacy'. My words were a little more colourful.

Despite their astonishing backflip, the Australian Crime Commission took their secrecy very seriously: I would later be charged with telling Nicola Gobbo that I had been subpoenaed to appear at one of their hearings.

•

After yet another appeal, the powers-that-be finally realised the inhumane nature of ongoing solitary confinement and found me some cellmates. Muslim terrorists.

I was in with the Muslim blokes for many months. They were okay. They had their prayer schedule, and they left me alone. And they were company.

I soon settled into the dull routine that is prison. I was allowed one twelve-minute phone call each day but each phone call cost $9.20 and I only got $50 a month in my account, so effectively I could only make five calls each month. I requested more money in my account and it was eventually raised to $100 a month.

I had to admire my wife and kids. They made the almost 600-kilometre round trip every week. The highlight of the month was the one contact visit when we would crowd into a tiny little room with a guard to keep us company. They got used to seeing me in my bright-red tracksuit.

When the second bail application was held, around August 2009, I finally had the brief and examined the evidence. The judge heard the application. Everything went our way. A psychiatric nurse gave in-depth evidence about the horrific conditions I was being held in. He talked about how unjust those conditions were. Not only that, the police weren't able to show that I was an unacceptable risk.

But the judge concluded that I was.

I appealed to the Supreme Court appeals court. As soon as the appeal started I was moved into the remand centre. I reckon the police knew I would get bail if I continued to be held in such inhumane conditions. When the appeal was heard I think the three judges were horrified at where I had been kept. At the start, one canny judge asked what had changed since last week so that I could now be held in the less restrictive remand centre. Of course, nothing had changed. They knew it. I knew it. And the police knew it.

Nonetheless, the remand centre was like a holiday camp. I couldn't believe the freedom of having regular contact visits with my family without wearing the tracksuit and shackles.

CHAPTER 35

Nicola's ten months on the taxpayer

To this day, I don't understand why Nicola Gobbo crossed to the side of the prosecution rather than the defence. I don't understand the widespread nature of her working with the police. It would be widely reported that she got sick of dealing with the likes of Tony Mokbel. But she could have crossed over and become a crown prosecutor if she wanted to fight on the other side. I wondered at the time if the police had something on her to make her do it.

The 2019 Royal Commission heard that in 1993, when Nicola was studying law at Melbourne University, the house in Rathdowne Street, Carlton she shared with her then boyfriend, Brian Wilson, was searched by police. Drugs were found and Wilson was convicted of drug trafficking. Nicola pleaded guilty to possession and received no conviction and a good behaviour bond. In 1995 police registered her as a human source when they were again investigating Brian Wilson for drug and firearms trafficking. The following year Nicola introduced an undercover police officer to Wilson.

And thus began her double life that culminated in her wearing a wire to tape me in December 2008, as I sat with her to get legal advice. A couple of months later, she was living the life of Riley on the Victorian taxpayer dollar.

Under subpoena, I obtained a list of Nicola Gobbo's expenses from March till mid-December 2009. She was listed as

Witness F. The expense sheet will leave taxpayers shaking their heads in absolute wonder at the use of their tax dollar.

To begin with, Nicola was given $1000 a week as an allowance by Victoria Police. And then VicPol also paid for everything else. Some of the items are blocked out for her protection, such as the destinations of the thirty-eight flights she took in ten months – but it is clear from the cost of them that wherever she flew, Victoria Police got her business-class tickets. And she wasn't the only one to fly: two extra tickets were purchased for everything so two police members could accompany her. The thirty-eight flights in ten months cost the taxpayer $27 332.

From mid-March 2009 until the end of December 2009, the expenses list I have says that the Victoria Police paid $22 300 for car hire for her – but the kicker is that it also forked out $2157 for cabs and chauffeur-driven limos during this time. So when she didn't drive there were cabs and chauffeurs at her fingertips, and when she did drive Victoria Police paid for all her parking, including a $113 parking fine.

Not a bad lark.

The list itemises all of the costs of Nicola's Victoria Police–funded expenditures. The taxpayer funded everything from her body corporate fees ($2177) to concert tickets ($344) and her Victorian Racing Club membership ($380).

Nicola Gobbo's accommodation charges for this ten-month period were $76 363 – which will give you an idea of the lifestyle she was enjoying courtesy of the Victoria Police.

The taxpayer also paid for a laptop, her mail redirection, her petrol and a spa treatment. And just in case you were worried, Victoria Police didn't forget Nicola's birthday: they bought her a bunch of flowers that cost the taxpayer $89.95.

And let's not forget the weekly allowance. All up, she received $43 000 in weekly allowances during this time. Not only that, a senior police officer would tell the Royal Commission about discussions to pay Nicola a reward as well.

In ten months, she cost the taxpayer and the Victoria Police a grand total of $304 642.39.

All this was for making a statement against me, and in the end never giving evidence anyway, citing reasons of ill health and fear. But even had she given evidence, the public needs to ask how reliable any testimony that she gave against me would be, given the amount of money it cost to get it.

And this is just stuff that I know about. I tried to subpoena other documents too, but Victoria Police fought tooth and nail to stop me getting hold of other information. Many documents they did hand over were completely redacted.

What were they trying to hide? Since the bigger Lawyer X story broke in 2019, I now suspect they were trying to hide the extent of her broader involvement as a police informer.

Despite living the high life, Nicola's health was suffering. Sol Solomon would later detail his contact with Nicola in a statement to the Royal Commission. In August of 2009 he and Cameron Davey performed a welfare check on their star witness. He wrote: 'I was shocked to see the physical and mental state that she was in. Physically she was thin, pale and had lesions over her body. Mentally she was depressed and stressed. We tried to take her for dinner but she wouldn't eat.'

Solomon described how Nicola had become increasingly disillusioned with the entire process. 'The decline in her spirit since we took her statement in January that year was dramatic. It was clear to me that if this situation continued she would be in no state to give evidence in our case and we would surely lose her as a witness, which would have been catastrophic to the prosecution.'

Nicola spent a couple of weeks in hospital for 'trigeminal neuralgia/thalamic pain syndrome', and then was admitted for two days in October for 'surgery on an ulcerated cavity', and again in December 'for surgery on three further ulcerated cavities and treatment of a number of approximately 15 other ulcerated cavities'.

She called Solomon to her hospital bed on New Year's Day. 'I was at home when I received a call from 3838. She was highly distressed and agitated at the time and told me she had been admitted to St Vincent's Hospital. I asked her if she would like me to come in to see her and she said that she would like that. I went to the hospital and spent approximately 3 hours with her. She looked very unwell. She was being treated for a number of open lesions over her body which she advised me that doctors believed to be an extreme nervous reaction. She was agitated and angry with the members she had been dealing with ...'

As Nicola's health deteriorated, the hierarchy tried to keep the cat in the bag and left detectives like Solomon and Davey working with only half the story. At times Nicola hinted at this to Sol and he would later detail it in his statement.

'I attempted to gain a fuller understanding of the problem from her. I recall telling her that I didn't believe that she should give up her career because of the fact that she was going to give evidence against Paul Dale in this case. I reminded her that she had not breached any of her professional ethics because she was not and never acted for Dale. I tried to reassure and convince her that her decision to provide evidence in a case involving murder and corruption by a police officer would not be viewed with disdain by the legal fraternity, that she should be commended. I told her that I can't understand why she has given everything up just because she decided to make a statement and give evidence in our case. I told her that I didn't see why she needed to cease her employment in the profession which she stated to me that she loved. The response I received from her was that I didn't understand the whole situation she was in. She said something like, "If only you knew the truth."'

If only indeed.

Solomon's statement is revealing to me. His certainty that Nicola was doing nothing wrong was based around his certainty that she never acted as my lawyer. I wonder if he would change his mind if he saw all the evidence that she *had* acted as my lawyer.

Considering the toll it took on her health over Christmas and New Year, Nicola's cooperation with the Victoria Police came to a jarring halt. The expenses report stated that her allowance was paid up to early in January – then things turned sour.

On 4 January 2010, Nicola Gobbo's medical condition was explained to representatives from the office of the Victorian Government Solicitor. And, with that, the bottomless well of money suddenly dried up. The last allowance payment to her was dated the same day. The Victoria Police paid her $3000.

Several January meetings and letters later, Nicola Gobbo's lawyers made it perfectly clear that she would not be giving evidence due to ill health and stress brought on by the whole affair. Despite this, on 8 February, Nicola was served a witness summons to attend court to give evidence at my committal hearing slated to begin on 9 March.

In a letter dated 4 February 2010, Nicola's lawyers discussed their intention to issue 'a Writ against the Victoria Police prior to the scheduled commencement of the committal on 9 March 2010. As advised in our conference on 11 January 2010, that claim will also detail the various promises and representations made by Victoria Police to our client which the Director correctly observed would potentially be highly embarrassing to the prosecution of Mr Dale. Our client has been left with no option but to take this course due to the conduct of Victoria Police and its solicitors, VGSO.'

Could they be suggesting that what had gone on behind the scenes between the police and Nicola might make the police look bad? Now fancy that.

I guess this is always going to happen when witnesses are courted with money.

The letters between Nicola Gobbo's lawyers and the Office of Public Prosecutions became increasingly hostile. The more the Office of Public Prosecutions badgered Nicola to testify, the more she said that her health deteriorated.

By 11 March she had made an affidavit asking to be excused from court because she wasn't 'fit to, nor able to, attend court to give evidence'.

Nicola stated that 'the Crown and the Victoria Police are fully aware of my medical state and were aware of my inability, and the reasons for it, to attend court to give evidence in March 2010 prior to serving me the Witness Summons.'

Then things got testy. Nicola wrote that 'the Crown has advised me that if I do not attend Court to give evidence on 23 March 2010 (or at such other time as directed) they will seek a bench warrant for my arrest.'

Nicola went on to say that she had been informed by nine senior police officers that her life was in danger, and the risk was of the highest order. She said that despite this, she was now without any police protection, other than ringing 000 in an emergency.

'The stress of having to engage solicitors to deal with this matter on my behalf together with the anxiety, stress and worry that has been created by the Crown's threats to have me arrested have each severely aggravated my various medical conditions and compromised my ability to recover from numerous surgical procedures and/or rest before and prepare for my impending further procedures. These circumstances introduce uncertainty which precludes my doctors from presently giving a prognosis about when I may be well enough to answer the summons.'

It must have looked to the Victoria Police like they had just wasted $304 642.39.

Reading copies of the back-and-forth letters, it was clear that Nicola's lawyers got snarky with the Crown solicitors. When the Crown told the court they were ready to proceed with the case, Nicola's lawyers reckoned that since she wasn't able to give evidence the Crown wasn't, in fact, ready and had misled the court.

So after the Victoria Police had spent $304 642.39 in ten months on her protection and fancy motels, thirty-eight flights, limo hire and birthday flowers, she went public claiming the police hadn't held up their end of the bargain.

I found an interview that Nicola Gobbo did with Josie Taylor from the ABC on 30 April 2010. It would be easy to feel sorry for her if you didn't know about the huge amounts of money and resources that Victoria Police had put into her protection.

NICOLA GOBBO: Having had the courage and strength to agree to become a witness for Victoria Police, I was required to give up my home, my security, my sense of life as I knew it.

JOSIE TAYLOR: Until March last year, Nicola Gobbo was one of Melbourne's best-known lawyers, representing the biggest names in Melbourne's underworld. But she says police convinced her to become a witness in their case against former detective Paul Dale. He's accused of murdering police informer [Terence] Hodson.

Ms Gobbo claims early this year police backed out of an agreement to compensate her for the loss of her career.

NICOLA GOBBO: I was assured by Mr Overland [Simon Overland, who was by then Chief Commissioner] that I would be compensated and that I would be left no worse off. It was very disappointing to me that Mr Overland didn't even reply to my last correspondence in January this year, when I wrote to him imploring him to intervene and resolve these longstanding issues.

A closer examination of this exchange poses certain questions. When she says that 'police convinced her' to become a witness against me, how did they do that? Or was she happy to inform on me? How could Simon Overland promise a lawyer that she would be 'no worse off'? How much money would that take?

By June 2010, media headlines screamed that Nicola was suing the State Government and the Victoria Police for 'millions of dollars' for backing out of their agreement to compensate her for the loss of her career after she agreed to testify against me.

By 25 September 2010, *Herald Sun* headlines read: 'High-profile barrister Nicola Gobbo has settled her court case against Victoria Police and the State of Victoria.'

Naturally, the case was settled out of court – who knows what would have come out if it had gone to court. She told reporters that she couldn't comment because of a confidentiality agreement ... and because of her health concerns, of course. The sum was later reported as $2.88 million.

Ker-ching!

That's the sound of the police cash register.

CHAPTER 36

The light of day

Finally on 11 September 2009, after two unsuccessful bail applications, three judges from the appeals court decided that I did not pose an unacceptable risk and granted me bail. I had a $500 000 surety and I wasn't allowed to approach prosecution witnesses or approach any serving member of the Victoria Police aside from those in the Police Association handling my legal funding, and the ones at the local police station I had to report to daily.

Eight months of my life in jail. Two hundred and eleven days. Eight months of my young children's lives. Eight months away from my wife.

Committal was set for the following March.

After I was released, a Russian guy from Frankston rang us at the service station every week. He would threaten to rape my wife and cut up my children in front of me.

All this in response to me naming people at the ACC.

The good thing about having my phones tapped was that the Russian was charged with using a phone to menace, because his threats were recorded by the Victoria Police.

On reflection, I would never, ever, ever answer any questions at an Australian Crime Commission hearing again. Even though the summons compels you to attend, I would refuse to answer once I was there. If they can promise me secrecy to speak freely, then rescind the offer and pass my details around to the lowest of the low and potentially put my family in danger, I would stand up and tell them to shove it.

I thought the ACC was an information-gathering tool. I was told afterwards that you get a thousand-dollar fine if you don't go. Or if you simply don't answer the summons. Apparently, bikies regularly pay their thousand bucks and don't appear.

The Australian Crime Commission has damaged their reputation by what they did to me. Anyone hearing my story would have to think twice about trusting them. And if I had have known the bikies' trick, I would have coughed up the thousand bucks and saved myself and my family a world of trouble.

CHAPTER 37

The committal

The committal hearing in March 2010 was over before it even began – such was the weakness of the police case against me. It fell apart at the slightest testing.

Which was what I'd been saying all along.

The things that were made to sound sinister and suggestive about my case on the front page of a newspaper had never stood up to the slightest amount of scrutiny.

Here's how it happened.

First off, Nicola Gobbo refused to testify.

For the uninitiated, a committal hearing happens before a trial so that a magistrate can determine whether there is a case to answer. On the first day of the committal, we made a point of asking for documents that we'd requested which still hadn't been given.

Day after day the Victoria Police hedged and delayed, refusing to give us the documents we wanted – foremost of which were notes and diary entries of the detectives who were dealing with Carl Williams. We were hearing rumours of huge inducements being offered to the convicted killer. We wanted a record of those inducements. Some of the documents we had already received made mention of many visits to Carl in prison and his release for questioning for a week. Subpoena after subpoena slowly revealed a disturbing story.

Inspector Steve Smith was called as one of our witnesses at the committal. Smith was at ESD on the day I was arrested with the drug-house burglary. He had also been at my house during my first arrest. I might have even worked with him at the Homicide Squad offices, but I'm not sure. At any rate, I knew him to say hello to. Next time I saw Smith was at my arrest at Wangaratta. I figured that he must have been part of the task force.

While Smith's name was not part of my brief, his name had been mentioned in one of the subpoenaed documents. Jumping on this single reference, we asked for his diary notes. The court refused.

I didn't believe the prosecution should try to hide anything, and the more they dug their heels in the more suspicious we got. Which was why we called Smith as a witness.

So far, Cameron Davey and Sol Solomon had both given evidence, but when we asked them about inducements made to Nicola Gobbo or Carl Williams, they both denied knowledge of any inducements.

It was at this stage that I suspected Davey and Solomon had been kept out of the loop. Hence our keenness to get Inspector Smith on the stand. Some of the notes we received made references to weekly meetings of the Petra task force Steering Committee.

What was the Petra task force Steering Committee? Were they looking at the murders of the Hodsons? Or was it simply a 'get Paul Dale' committee?

It took a couple of weeks to get Inspector Steve Smith on the stand, looking nervous and uncomfortable. His answers were vague.

Who was at the Petra task force Steering Committee meetings, we asked.

Inspector Smith said he attended the meetings with Assistant Commissioner Simon Overland and Assistant Commissioner Luke Cornelius.

My lawyer asked him for his notes from these committee meetings.

Smith said he took no notes.

What about the notes from the other police members present?

Smith said that no one took notes.

No notes?

If what he said was true, it would have been the first time in the history of the Victoria Police that a meeting was held without copious note-taking by everyone involved. I smelt a big, juicy rat.

Three barristers asked about the notes over and over again, posing the same question in different ways: *Were there notes?*

No, he said over and over again.

No notes. No recordings. No nothing.

The very next morning we arrived at the committal to find a new lawyer from the Victoria Government Solicitor's Office representing Simon Overland, who by this point in time was Chief Commissioner. The court opened for business and the new lawyer stood up and announced that she was there on behalf of Inspector Smith and wanted to clarify some things he had said in the witness box.

She explained that when Inspector Smith had answered questions about notes, he was under the impression that he only had to answer questions on notes mentioned on the subpoena.

The magistrate looked up. So there *were* notes, he asked.

Yes, said the lawyer.

The magistrate raised his eyebrows. How many notes?

Thirty thousand pages of notes, said the lawyer.

Thirty thousand pages.

The magistrate flicked back through his own notes and reminded the lawyer that Smith had testified that there were no notes taken at these meetings. *No notes at all.*

From where I sat, it looked like the magistrate was fuming. Like everybody else in the room, he could see what had happened.

The magistrate seemed disinclined to give the Victoria Police an inch after that. He disallowed the suppression order on the names of Nicola Gobbo and Carl Williams.

A Victorian government solicitor acting on behalf of the Chief Commissioner jumped in with a legal argument that hobbled the magistrate's ruling on identifying Carl Williams. I can't tell you what the legal argument was because of more secrecy. But in the end, Carl's identity was protected and Nicola's wasn't.

Afterwards, I made a formal complaint to ESD about Smith's denial of the existence of the 30 000 pages of notes. ESD found that my allegation was unsubstantiated.

Unsubstantiated. Sure.

In the end, the magistrate instructed the Victoria Police to hand over all the documentation to the court. He would examine the 30 000 pages then make the decision as to whether my legal team could have them.

In that case, said their side, we need an adjournment.

How long do you need? asked the magistrate.

Eight months, they said.

Eight months?

Yes, eight months.

The magistrate agreed, and adjourned the trial.

But it wasn't going to be eight months. Because a couple of weeks later, a leak made front-page news.

You pay Carl Williams's daughter's school fees.

And Matthew Johnson, a tough guy who headed up the standover gang Prisoners of War – a gang dedicated to old-school crim values and the eradication of informers, or 'dogs' – a guy with a reputation for violence who was sharing the cell with the biggest dog of them all, took the metal stem from the seat off the cell's exercise bike and repeatedly bashed Carl Williams over the head.

Over and over.

Till he was dead.

CHAPTER 38

The killing of Carl

On 19 April 2010, the *Herald Sun* made a startling revelation: Victoria Police was paying for Carl Williams's daughter's school fees to the tune of $8000 per year. The provocative heading, clearly designed to outrage the average taxpayer, read: 'You pay for Carl Williams's daughter to attend top private college'. Another heading was more succinct: 'You pay killer's school fees'. The article (by Padraic Murphy) may have sparked his cellmate Matthew Johnson's rage. It read, in part: 'Taxpayers paid the private school fees for the daughter of multiple murderer, drug dealer and underworld figure Carl Williams. The $8000 payment was made by Victoria Police command for Williams' child to attend a top private school. A letter written by the Victorian Government Solicitor's Office ... shows police admit they paid for Williams' daughter to attend the school ... The letter also shows that Victoria Police offered to pay a $750,000 debt owed to the tax office by Carl's father George Williams ...'

To those in the know, there is only one reason that the Victoria Police starts paying your kid's school fees and your dad's $750000 tax bill – they are getting something in return. In other words, you're a dog.

At 12.48 p.m. on the same day as he was publicly outed as a paid police informer, Carl Williams was recorded on the prison surveillance cameras sitting at a table in the Acacia Unit, reading a paper that looked like the very *Herald Sun* that had published a story that for him would prove fatal.

Behind him, the large figure of Matthew Johnson appeared in the video monitoring system. In his right hand, Johnson held a metal stem. He raised it against the unsuspecting Williams.

Johnson felled Carl with a single vicious blow which knocked him unconscious, then he rained seven more upon Williams's head – just to be sure.

Little Tommy Ivanovic looked on.

Johnson knew that the area was under surveillance and assumed that guards would come running once they saw what was happening over the monitors. But no one came. He dragged Williams's body into his cell and closed the door. Nearly half an hour later, after doing some laps of the exercise yard, the two remaining occupants of Unit 1 approached a guard and asked her to ring the alarm because Williams had 'hit his head'.

Johnson would later claim that it was a kill-or-be-killed situation. He killed Carl before Carl could kill him.

•

If Carl Williams's life was lived large, his funeral was befitting the man he thought himself to be. In a gold-plated coffin – reputed to have cost $50 000 – Williams was farewelled at St Therese's Church in Essendon on 30 April, eleven days after his murder in prison.

The funeral was like so many other gangland funerals: menacing folk, men in black, leggy women, bouncers, helicopters buzzing overhead and, of course, a stretch Hummer – the car of choice for Roberta Williams. While the gleaming gold-plated coffin was unexpected, no one was really surprised.

Roberta spoke glowingly of the man she had divorced in March 2007.

CHAPTER 39

Whodunit?

Given the enormity of the police media unit and the way I suspected it worked in the case against me, a cynical person might ask how the information about Carl Williams being an informer was released.

I had been accused of stealing the 'blue folder' to spread the word that Terry Hodson was an informer, yet here was a leak in the rank and file of the Victoria Police saying that Carl Williams was an informer. And the leak got him killed *on the very day the information was released*. Yet no one seemed to question where the leak came from or the timing of its release. Where's Tony Fitzgerald when you need him?

Was it released to ignite the volatile Matthew Johnson? Regardless of the intentions of whoever leaked it to the media, the headline contributed to the death of Carl Williams. The day after the murder, journalist Steve Butcher from *The Age* was quick to suggest just that. 'The *Herald Sun* has defended its publication yesterday, hours before Carl Williams was killed, of a report that police had paid his daughter's school fees. The newspaper's front-page "exclusive" said Victoria Police paid about $8000 for the private school fees of the daughter of Williams and his former wife, Roberta. In an online editorial posted late yesterday afternoon, the *Herald Sun* said the story was in the public interest ... [Williams's solicitor, Rob Stary,] called for an investigation into all the circumstances of Williams's death to be conducted independently of police and corrections authorities, "with the emphasis on all" ... Mr Stary said that when he spoke to Williams by phone yesterday morning Williams ... was "worried about the sort of harassment his daughter would be subjected to and how this [the story] might undermine her education".'

It was more than his daughter's education that Williams had to worry about, but it wasn't until Matthew Johnson's trial in 2011 that it was revealed why Williams had been showered with incentives – he was meant to help convict me. So, of course, newspapers regarded me as a suspect in his death.

But conspiracy theories work both ways: if I could be accused, with no evidence and no actual means, of somehow conspiring to get Carl Williams killed then equally could not the Victoria Police be accused of the same thing?

They had broken the golden rule by paying huge incentives for a couple of statements naming me – *before* any conviction. You will note that the wording on any offer of a reward from police is very specific – a reward is offered for information *leading to the conviction* of someone. That means it is paid *after* the conviction. Breaking this golden rule would come back to bite the Victoria Police long after Carl Williams was cold in his grave.

Matthew Johnson boasted at his trial that Williams was never going to testify and was simply stringing the police along. He claimed that Williams was 'pulling the wool over the eyes of police' and was going to 'shaft' them.

Could Victoria Police have orchestrated the 'leak' through their massive media machine that Williams was an informer – then simply waited for the inevitable jailhouse revenge? Matthew Johnson had a reputation to consider. Even if he knew Carl was an informer – and he claims he did know – once it was front-page news that he was sharing a cell with a dog, didn't prison etiquette dictate that he make a public statement of his displeasure?

Williams's death made me look like a suspect – like I was trying to stop him giving evidence against me – but I'd had no contact with anyone in the Acacia Unit since I was in there, and only then was it with the Muslim terrorists I was incarcerated with. Having been an inmate, I know how impossible it was to contact anyone in the unit.

I heard that Carl Williams chose his own cellmates. This decision was allegedly part of the bargain that he struck to make statements against me. So I had no power of choosing who Williams was put with. Did the police have a say? An Ombudsman's report would later suggest that they did.

I wonder if it went against their better judgment to put a prison informer in a cell with the head of a gang of prisoners who hated prison informers.

The State Ombudsman could see that too:

> Mr Johnson was a leader of the notorious 'Prisoners of War' gang, a group of prisoners operating within Victoria's correctional system responsible for a series of violent assaults on prisoners and prison officers, with a hatred for police informers. Mr Johnson was known to Corrections Victoria to have participated in two serious assaults on fellow prisoners in the past, with one assault in retribution for a prisoner's cooperation with police.

But, of course, for every story there is a counter story. It was reported during Matthew Johnson's trial that George Williams, Carl's father, claimed that far from having a problem with Carl being an informer, Johnson in fact wanted a piece of the action himself, and wanted to reap the benefits of being on the police payroll.

Whichever way you look at the whole situation, it stinks.

•

On 21 April, after the murder but before Carl Williams's infamous and garish funeral, then Deputy Commissioner Ken Lay announced the formation of task force Driver to investigate Carl Williams's murder. In a press conference that used lots of words to say very little, Lay said that 'there are a number of identities around Carl Williams and his cohorts from some time back that we will actually be investigating as well'. He acknowledged the enormous public interest but asked the community to give the Victoria Police the time and space to conduct a thorough investigation, and he had instructed task force head Detective Superintendent Doug Fryer to 'leave no stone unturned'.

In his statement for the Royal Commission, Sol Solomon would later write: 'My thoughts that the situation couldn't get any worse were dashed with two further developments. Firstly on 19th April 2010 Carl Williams was murdered while in custody at Barwon Prison. Effectively blowing a huge hole in the prosecution case as his evidence was the cornerstone of the case. Secondly, 3838 [Nicola Gobbo] issued a civil writ against Victoria Police for damages allegedly caused to her by Victoria Police from her management in this case.'

The house of cards was falling.

•

On 5 June 2010, I walked from court a free man. The prosecution had notified my lawyers and I was called before the magistrate, who told me the Victoria Police had withdrawn the charges against me.

My co-accused was unnamed for 'legal reasons' in articles reporting the dismissal of charges. Funny how they protected the identity of hit man Rod Collins but were happy to name me. One article mentioned the difference between the smiling faces from my side of the court juxtaposed with the glum faces on the Victoria Police side.

Journalist Steve Butcher, covering the case for *The Age*, alluded to the so-called mystery surrounding my case. 'But why one of Victoria Police's biggest investigations collapsed and, more importantly, what shut it down, cannot, and may never, be told – for "legal reasons".'

Simple.

Piece by piece, the testimony that the Victoria Police had paid good money for was proving its true worth. Nothing.

Of course, I was happy to be free, but it was naturally frustrating. While this case remained unresolved, I would never really be free. Every article mentioned me as remaining a person of interest.

On 19 August 2010, Superintendent Fryer led a press conference announcing that the Petra task force was to be wound up, and the investigation into the Hodsons' murders would be taken over by task force Driver.

In media reports clearly designed to keep my name linked with the death of the Hodsons and the death of Carl Williams, articles the following day rehashed the same old story – how the charges against me had been dropped after the Hodsons and Carl Williams had been killed, making it sound like I killed whoever made statements against me.

People believe what they read in the papers.

•

On 9 September 2010, three judges in the Supreme Court dismissed Dave Miechel's appeal against his conviction and sentence.

His fifteen-year sentence was upheld.

•

So how did this all play out for Sol Solomon? He would detail this in his statement for the Royal Commission:

> The death of Carl Williams was a significant setback to the prosecution of Dale and Collins. However the [task force] was still committed to the task and determined to keep working. Deputy Commissioner Sir Ken Jones attended at the [task force] office and addressed us shortly after the death of

Williams. He complimented us on the exceptional work we had performed during this long investigation. He also stated that he remained committed to this investigation and asked us to be the same. He said that he expected us all to take this set back on the chin and get back on the job and get this prosecution back on track again. He pledged his support and expressed his confidence in us. There was no suggestion of winding up the investigation as far as he was concerned. This motivated us a great deal and we commenced the work of searching for further evidence to resurrect the prosecution. We were buoyed by the encouragement and positive attitude expressed by the Deputy Commissioner.

But despite the pep talk and some 'promising leads', Sol was again blindsided by the sudden writ lodged by Nicola Gobbo against the Victoria Police. Three months later, it was settled.

'This seemed remarkable to me,' wrote Sol, 'as I expected this matter to take much longer to resolve. A writ of this nature being resolved in 3 months seemed very unusually rapid particularly as I expected Victoria Police to put forward a defence to the writ as in my view the writ was unfounded and easily defendable. However the decision was made to settle and this wasn't any of my business. My concern was to keep up the momentum on our investigation.'

Sol detailed plans to pursue Nicola Gobbo now she wasn't helping them. Apparently, Nicola and I had met two days before some informer documents were faxed from Tony Mokbel's fax machine, so the task force had concluded that I must have passed documents to Nicola, who passed them to Mokbel.

Sol: 'Then the situation suddenly changed again. Shortly after the news that 3838's writ was settled instruction came down from above that we (the task force) were no longer to have any contact with 3838 in any form whatsoever. Cease all contact with her was the direction. This was despite the fact that we had advised the steering committee of our plans to investigate her possible role in leaking the information reports, which if determined to be the case made her an accessory. Despite our plans to engage with the ACC to coercively examine her.'

Ha! Good luck with that, fellas. Of course, Solomon and Davey had no idea of the true nature of what Victoria Police was trying to hide in the settlement of their writ. But they were about to find out.

Sol: 'On the 18th August 2010 an Assistant Commissioner attended at the Petra [task force] office and advised us all that of this day the Petra [task force] is to shut down and all personnel will be assigned to other duties within Crime Command ... I recall this day vividly as the decision to shut us down was completely unexpected and a shock. Most of us sat in silence as we tried to process this news. I don't think I have ever felt more demoralised in my career. I recall asking the Assistant Commissioner why. He didn't explain other than to say words similar to "that's the decision" "for fresh eyes." There was no mention of formal handover of the job to the new [task force] despite it being a 6 year long investigation. It was just you people are now out and the new [task force] is in.'

•

After a long legal battle in 2016 to get hold of Carl's prison computer, the Williams family finally got it and published his prison letters in a book called *Life Sentence: My Last Eighteen Months*.

In a letter dated 11 November 2008 to a mate, Carl wrote about his deals with the Victoria Police. 'The police recently came out here to see me again, I seen them because if I didn't, and they really wanted to see me they'd just 464 [interrogate] me, plus I have no problems listening to what they have to say. Anyway, they said if I would be prepared to jump on board with them, they'd give me virtually anything I asked for – anything within reason – unbelievable isn't it.'

Yes, Carl. It is unbelievable.

CHAPTER 40

The new charges ...

In January 2011, the improbably named Detective Senior Sergeant Boris Buick came up to Wangaratta and served me with a set of the most unlikely charges conceivable. These charges stemmed from my appearance at the Australian Crime Commission – remember the one that promised no charges could stem from my appearance? Yes, that one. Here are Judge Hannaford's exact words at the ACC:

> Mr Dale, you having sought the general protection from self-incrimination, can I now advise you that you do have the benefit of a general protection from self-incrimination in respect to all of the evidence that you're required to give me during the course of this Examination. Now just to reassure you as to what that now means. It now means that absolutely nothing that you say to me during the course of this hearing can now ever be taken from this room and produced in a court as some evidence against you in any criminal prosecution proceedings against you, nor will it ever be able to be taken from this room and produced as some evidence in any other proceedings for the imposition of some penalty against you and that protection will also extend to every document or thing that I might require you to produce during the course of this hearing. Do you understand? Do you have any questions of me about that?

Yes, Judge Hannaford, I had a question. After seven years, how much longer was I was going to be hounded by these people who had never been able to make a case against me?

So, here are the charges that were brought against me.

Charge 1: The accused on the 7th of March, 2007, being a person summonsed to give evidence at the examination before an Examiner of the Australian Crime Commission, did give false evidence namely that he recorded all meetings that he attended with Carl Williams.

I believe that I did record all meetings that I had with Carl Williams. I was never given the opportunity to refer to my diaries and day books, and they never suggested that I had a meeting with him that I didn't record.

Charge 2: The accused on the 7th of March, 2007 ... did give false evidence namely stating that he was always 'on duty' when he met with Carl Williams and was not aware of any occasion when he met with Carl Williams when he was 'off duty'.

So they say that I was not aware of a meeting, so that's why they were charging me.

Charge 3: The accused on the 26th of November, 2008 ... did give misleading evidence namely stating that he was uncertain if he had ever met Carl Williams at a time he was not on duty.

Huh? Isn't that the same as Charge 2?

Charge 4: The accused on the 26th of November, 2008 ... did give misleading evidence namely stating that he could not recall any reason why Carl Williams would have contacted him while he (accused) was suspended from duty by Victoria Police.

Was I being charged because I couldn't read Carl Williams's mind?

Charge 5: The accused on the 26th of November, 2008 ... did give misleading evidence namely, evasive answers to questions relating to the frequency of meetings that he had with Carl Williams.

Huh? What constitutes 'evasive'? Who makes that decision? Did they think they were reading my mind? If you say you can't remember something from years earlier, is that evasive?

Charge 6: The accused on the 26th of November, 2008 ... did give false evidence namely, stating that all the meetings that he had with Carl Williams were in his (accused) professional capacity.

How many different ways could they charge me with meeting with Carl Williams? Six, apparently.

Charge 7: The accused on the 26th of November, 2008 ... did give false evidence namely, stating he did give false evidence stating that he never met Carl Williams at the Brunswick Club.

I never met Carl Williams at the Brunswick Club. And they never brought any evidence – aside from Carl's paid statement – to say that I did meet with him there. So how could they charge me with lying about it with no evidence other than the word of someone like Carl Williams, who Justice Betty King had described as 'a most unsatisfactory witness virtually incapable of telling the truth'?

Charge 8: The accused on the 26th of November, 2008 ... did give false evidence namely, stating that he did not ever meet Carl Williams at Noodle Box or Noodle Bar in Centreway in Keilor.

A charge that has the word 'noodle' in it twice. Did anyone see us near noodles? There was certainly a pattern to these allegations. No corroboration, just the word of a man 'virtually incapable of telling the truth'. Who of course, by now, was deceased and unable to tell anything at all.

And it went on and on.

Charge 9: The accused on the 26th of November, 2008 ... did give false evidence namely, stating that he did not ever purposely provide Carl Williams with information in relation to police operations.

Charge 10: The accused on the 26th of November, 2008 ... did give false evidence namely, stating that he could not recall ever meeting Carl Williams at the Centreway shops in Keilor.

Charge 11: The accused on the 26th of November, 2008 ... did give misleading evidence namely, stating that he was not sure that he'd ever met Carl Williams at the Keilor Baths.

Charge 12: The accused on the 26th of November, 2008 ... did give misleading evidence namely, stating that he could not recall entering the water at a pool with Carl Williams in order to have a discussion with Carl Williams, however, he may have entered the water at the Brunswick Baths with Tommy Ivanovic.

Was I being charged as well with possibly entering the pool with Tommy?

Charge 13: The accused on the 26th of November, 2008 ... did give misleading evidence namely, stating that he could not recall ever meeting Carl Williams on his (accused) own.

Charge 14: The accused on the 26th of November, 2008 ... did give misleading evidence namely, stating that he was using a throw-away line when he said to Carl Williams during a phone conversation between himself and Carl Williams on 27th February 2004 that he (accused) wanted to catch up with him.

I was being charged because they were judging the difference between the 'let's catch up, mate' that most men finish phone conversations with and 'let's catch up, mate' meaning *let's catch up.*

Charge 15: The accused on the 26th of November, 2008 ... did give misleading evidence namely, evasive answers about his familiarity with Carl Williams.

Charge 16: The accused on the 26th of November, 2008 ... did give misleading evidence namely, stating he could not recall meeting with Carl Williams after the 27th February 2004 because he had so many allegations put to him over the years that his mind was 'mash'.

So I was charged with saying my mind was mash.

Charge 17: The accused on the 26th of November, 2008 ... did give misleading evidence namely, stating that he could not recall asking Nicola Gobbo to pass on a message from him (accused) to Carl Williams.

Charge 18: The accused on the 26th of November, 2008 ... did give misleading evidence namely, stating that he (accused) did not know if he had asked Nicola Gobbo to pass on a message to Carl Williams.

Is it just me, or are these all starting to sound the same?

Charge 19: The accused on the 26th of November, 2008 ... did give misleading evidence stating that he could not recall asking Nicola Gobbo to have Carl Williams contact him (accused).

Huh?

Charge 20: The accused on the 26th of November, 2008 ... did give misleading evidence namely, stating that he could not recall ever having a discussion with Nicola Gobbo about mobile telephone numbers in use by both he (accused) and Nicola Gobbo in order that they contact each other without being detected.

Charge 21: The accused on the 26th of November, 2008 ... did give misleading evidence namely, stating that he did not know where Hillside was, or Goulay Road, and could not remember doing that, in response to a proposition put to him that he met Carl Williams along Goulay Road in Hillside on 6th May 2004.

I was being charged with not knowing where a street was?

Charge 22: The accused on the 26th of November, 2008 ... did give false evidence namely, stating that Mr Williams never paid him (accused) money for information.

And finally ...

Charge 23: ... that on the 7th day of December, 2008, being a person who was served with, or otherwise given, a summons containing a notation made under section 29A, disclosed the existence of a summons or any information about it namely by discussing the examination with Nicola Gobbo.

But you *are allowed to* discuss your appearance at the Australian Crime Commission with your lawyer. Right from the start, Nicola Gobbo had offered to be my lawyer and act pro bono for me. While I had gone with the Police Association option of legal assistance, I had always gone to her for legal advice and interpretation. I regarded her, therefore, as my legal advisor. And not only that, she even encouraged me on the taped conversation to say anything I wanted because I was speaking to her as a lawyer.

In the police force, we call charges like this a 'hamburger with the lot'. While they brought the twenty-three charges against me, they never brought up any evidence to say any of my answers were false. This is especially relevant to my *can't-recall* responses. Some of the questions were dealing with things five years earlier. If you can't remember, you can't remember – and if they can't prove otherwise it shouldn't be a charge.

Think about this for a moment: if they charge you with saying you can't recall something, who can they call as a witness to prove otherwise?

You?

How crazy is that?

•

These charges are Commonwealth offences under the *Australian Crime Commission Act*, but the ACC itself wasn't going to pursue them. Like a Labrador with a slipper, the Victoria Police wouldn't let it go. Task force Driver, under Simon Overland, decided to proceed with the charges.

When I first got the brief I couldn't understand how I could be charged with allegations that Carl Williams had made with no other evidence. Then again, that has always been a pattern with the charges against me: induce a crook to say whatever the police wanted to hear then lay any charges they want.

At the next court appearance, they dropped twelve of the twenty-three – which to the average person might suggest that those twelve were made without the evidence to back them up. A lot of the charges about Carl Williams were withdrawn because there was no evidence.

Well, *der.*

They finally conceded that they couldn't use Carl Williams's statements against me. But once there had been a proper review, they were informed that every charge relating to Carl Williams, unless otherwise corroborated, would be withdrawn.

And because Nicola Gobbo had refused to give evidence, their case pretty much fell away. But the fact that the case was crumbling around their ears didn't daunt the fine detectives determined to put me in the frame.

When the prosecution withdrew so many of the charges, I claimed three-quarters of my costs because much of the preparation with my legal team was for charges that had then been withdrawn. The court agreed.

The charges that still stood were the ones to do with the tape recording made by Nicola Gobbo, even though her lawsuit against the Victoria Police made it clear that she wouldn't testify.

The only other witnesses were George Williams and another old crook, Witness B, whose identity the police wanted to hide – both gave evidence at my committal and both gave conflicting evidence. I think I walked past George Williams at a café once, and I think I arrested Witness B once, years ago, so I knew the only evidence they could give was jailhouse gossip.

What was George Williams getting now? I didn't know. First time around, the Police Association paid for my legal team and I could afford to look into this and spend weeks going back and forth to get information. But these latest charges were dated after my time on the force and I had to finance the defence myself, so I didn't have the luxury of digging deeper.

A tape recording without context and the word of George Williams, perjurer and drug dealer, was what it all hinged on. George Williams had a conviction for lying to the ACC and he got a $3000 fine. And now they would rely on his statement about me. When they'd already convicted him of being a liar. Not to forget Witness B, triple murderer and drug dealer.

The pattern continued.

CHAPTER 41

The Moti precedent

Around the time the Victoria Police was offering inducements like candy, a case was being heard in Queensland that was about to change everything.

In 1997, lawyer Julian Moti was charged with raping the thirteen-year-old daughter of his business partner in Vanuatu. The charges were dismissed, and a subsequent out-of-court settlement was reached, which marked the end of the matter. A decade later, when there was talk Julian Moti might be appointed Attorney-General of the Solomon Islands, it was known that Moti was opposed to the continued presence of peacekeepers. In a move that had a strong whiff of political interference, the Australian High Commissioner resurrected the case under the *Child Sex Tourism Act*.

Between February 2008 and November 2009, the girl and her family had received around $150 000 in subsistence witness payments from the Australian Federal Police. The girl's father later said he didn't realise the political implications of the investigation, which dug up allegations that hadn't seen the light of day for a decade. The family ended up being so disillusioned with the Australian police and the Australian government that they refused to testify. The girl's father called the police 'superficial' and 'artificial'.

There were several unsuccessful attempts to extradite Julian Moti to Australia to face charges. Meanwhile, in December 2009, Justice Debbie Mullins of the Queensland Supreme Court ruled that there had been an abuse of process and stayed the indictment against Moti. She questioned the integrity of the investigation 'when witnesses who live in a foreign country, expected to be fully supported by the Australian Government until they gave evidence at the trial in Australia'. The payments to the girl's family were judged to be 'a sum far in excess of regular subsistence witness payments'.

While it might have been 'far in excess' of what people were paid in Queensland, it seemed a little on the low side compared to what people were offered in Victoria to testify against me.

What the Moti judgment effectively meant was that if large inducements were offered to witnesses, there could be a fair assumption that their evidence was tarnished. After the Moti judgment, the Victoria Police shit itself and quickly withdrew the $750 000 payment they had made for George Williams's tax bill. In what must have been a red-faced moment, on 22 February 2010, Assistant Commissioner Luke Cornelius of the Ethical Standards Department wrote to the Australian Tax Office and said in part:

> Victoria Police has reviewed the provision of assistance to Mr George Williams following the recent decision of Justice Mullins in the Supreme Court of Queensland *R v Moti* (2009) ...
>
> It is now clear that the proposed arrangements relating to the taxation affairs of Mr Williams are no longer an option for Victoria Police as it is unlikely to be considered by the courts appropriate for a witness in a criminal prosecution to have the benefit of such an arrangement.
>
> I can advise that any arrangements of undertakings for the Victoria Police to provide monies on behalf of George Williams in regard to any tax debt owing to the ATO have been withdrawn ...

I love the bit about withdrawing the money – not because paying George Williams's $750000 tax bill was just plain wrong, but because it was 'unlikely to be considered by the courts appropriate for a witness in a criminal prosecution'.

I don't know what you reckon, but shouldn't the Ethical Standards Department have higher ... er ... ethical standards?

CHAPTER 42

2011

In September 2011, as the inquiry into Carl Williams's death continued, a lot of journalists took the opportunity to repeat the same old story: *Terry was arrested. Terry blamed Paul. Terry died. Paul was released. Ergo ...*

But over at *The Australian*, journalist Pia Akerman looked beyond the worn narrative and started to question the dangers of the police courting people like Carl Williams and paying for their testimony. Finally someone was stating the bleeding obvious in a case where the obvious was so deeply buried. Here's an excerpt from Akerman's article:

> The case has raised questions about how far police were willing to go to cut a deal with Williams and how much weight could be placed on his evidence, given that it was provided in exchange for substantial benefits. More important, questions are being asked about increasing use generally by Victoria Police of jailhouse informers to build and substantiate cases, and what risks this creates for successful prosecutions.
>
> Among Melbourne's legal fraternity, there is clear concern. Defence barrister Peter Morrissey SC believes Victoria Police is relying on the evidence of informers to 'fill up gaps' in prosecution cases. 'I find that among offenders and people in prison, there is a much greater awareness of the benefits of being an informer,' Morrissey tells *The Australian*. 'If the police aren't careful, they will end up with a professional class of informers.

'It's good policing to encourage witnesses to come forward, and they have to be presented fairly and openly by the police and prosecutors, but the worrying reality is that these informers, the honest ones just tell their story and the dishonest ones workshop their story and go through numerous changes in order to accommodate the known facts.'

... Criminal lawyer Bill Doogue agrees there is a trend of increased reliance on criminal informers, saying the incentives offered for crooks to turn are 'outrageous'.

... Doogue says, 'If you can't get traditional evidence to get over the line against somebody and you're resorting to getting a Carl Williams-type character to give evidence, then you know that you are just trying to win at all costs.

'There are a number of things about the rule of law that have been lost in that process.'

As Williams bragged in prison, it seemed that whatever he wanted from the cops, he could get. 'They wanted to close the Paul Dale case for the Hodsons and they were offering him the world to help,' [Matthew] Johnson, in his defence, told the jury. 'He was told that [former Victoria Police Chief Commissioner Simon] Overland would give him whatever he wants to have charges laid on this case.'

The court heard that in return for his co-operation, police helped move Williams's father, George, from another prison into the same unit and agreed to pay his daughter's school fees and George Williams's $750 000 tax debt.

Carl Williams was even let out of jail for a week, under police supervision, so that he could be questioned at length. Police allowed his girlfriend to join him and turned a blind eye when his conjugal rights were exercised.

Of most concern, police agreed to support Williams's bid for a reduced sentence. Williams allegedly boasted in jail that he could get up to 15 years off his 35-year sentence with his information.

He also demanded indemnity from prosecution for his alleged role in the Hodsons' murder and received an assurance from then director of public prosecutions Jeremy Rapke that this would happen if the case against Dale and the hit man went forward.

James Dowsley, co-chair of the Law Institute of Victoria's criminal law section, says transparency must remain paramount for the system to work ...

Williams's statements against Dale also were never fully tested in court. Their veracity was not the subject of Johnson's trial but enough evidence was given to raise questions about their content and the source's credibility.

Johnson, founder of a jail gang called the Prisoners of War, which hated 'dogs', told the court Williams had boasted of 'spinning a yarn' to police about Dale, helping them with their case so he could get preferential treatment.

'The yarn was that he was going to say Paul Dale paid for the murder and that a friend of Carl's ... was the shooter,' Johnson said. 'He said that they knew he had had dealings with Dale and he could just fill in the spots for the rest of it and they'd gobble it up.'

Williams's police handler, Steve Smith, meanwhile, told the court: 'Carl knew what he wanted to get out of his relationship and his association with us.'

From Johnson's perspective, the former gangland boss was playing one last game with the cops, planning to end his co-operation before the case against Dale went to trial.

'He told them what they wanted,' Johnson says. 'He was pulling the wool over their eyes ... then he was going to shaft 'em.'

The statement in which Williams named Dale as the plotter behind the Hodsons' murders was not the first he gave to police. It came nearly two years after information he gave in April 2007, while he was awaiting sentencing for the murders of Jason and Lewis Moran, and was given on the understanding that it could not be used against him.

In that original statement, Williams alleged Dale had approached him and asked if he knew anyone who could kill Terence Hodson, but claimed he had promised to help only if a pre-existing plot failed and Dale still needed a hit man. Williams's original statement didn't help him win any time off his sentence as police withdrew support for leniency based on inconsistencies in his evidence. But they kept pushing him.

In July 2008, Detective Inspector Steve Smith was assigned to the Petra [task force] investigating the Hodson murders.

He eventually formed a rapport with Williams, who called him 'the coach' and ended up calling Smith five or six times a week in the months leading up to his death in prison. In late 2008, while on the week-long break from jail with his father and Smith, Williams made two more statements to police, which he signed three weeks later.

'There were a number of reasons I did not tell the police all I know about the Hodson murders in my last statement,' he said. 'I did not think police would be able to charge anyone because of the lack of traceable phone calls. [The assassin] was still out of jail and because I did not want to get charged with the murders. I didn't want to be a dog and be a protection prisoner, but my attitude has changed.' According to the jury, it was that changed attitude, and Johnson's response to it, that cost Williams his life.

Rare articles like this proved some journalists were prepared to look beyond the repeated misinformation and seek a greater truth about what was happening to me.

And, finally, someone was questioning the police tactics of paying for testimony.

Journalist Adam Shand, who has since written a book on Carl Williams, echoed the thoughts of *The Australian* when he wrote an article highlighting career criminals who dealt their way into both wealth and indemnity, entitled 'Worst criminals are now "untouchable"'. And he quoted an unnamed source at commissioner level who agreed with him.

'... it has been said that cops must be prepared to deal with crooks to catch other crooks. That's essentially true, but the extent of those deals must be limited and must meet community standards. A career policeman of commissioner rank tells *Inquirer* the tactics adopted by Victoria's Purana [task force] to end the gangland war went well beyond deals offered to crooks by Victoria Police in the past.

'Once you get into conjugal visits, all sorts of perks and lurks, promises of education for children, all sorts of gifts and gratuity to purchase their evidence, you know that you can expect, at some point, some man in a horsehair wig in a court representing the other parties to savage your witness and your methodology,' he says. 'Just what (is) the community prepared to accept as legitimate tactics by their law enforcement agencies?'

This is the question Victoria is asking itself, now that the gavel has fallen on all the major gangland cases. Yet it is a difficult judgment to make because we haven't been told the full details of deals with a string of villains.

In early November 2011, I pleaded not guilty to the whittled-down twelve charges of giving false evidence or misleading the Australian Crime Commission and one charge of disclosing to a person that I had been summonsed to appear before the ACC.

Late November, Supreme Court Justice Terry Forrest lifted the suppression order on Nicola Gobbo's name. Nicola's lawyers said that her life was in danger because a sympathy card had been sent to their office. The inscription on it was: 'Tell your client she is dead. Dogs die dead.'

Explaining his decision to lift the suppression order, the judge said that it had been widely reported that Nicola Gobbo had worn a wire, and that she was probably already at risk, so the disclosure of her name wouldn't make things any worse.

One minute, Nicola's statement was a key part of the evidence against me, and then she refused to testify.

•

In early December 2011, 38-year-old Matthew Johnson was sentenced to life in prison for killing his cellmate, Carl Williams. The judge, Lex Lasry, was unequivocal in his condemnation of the bald-headed killer.

'This was an appalling murder. It was a killing which appears to demonstrate your belief that you have some special entitlement to kill when you think it is appropriate, or your ego demands it according to some meaningless underworld prison code.'

Justice Lex Lasry said that he was left with no choice but to punish Johnson with an 'appropriately heavy sentence' before ordering him to serve a minimum sentence of thirty-two years.

While Johnson had pleaded not guilty, he had admitted killing Williams with the metal stem of the seat of an exercise bike. He said that he had acted in self-defence because Tommy Ivanovic, the other cellmate in Unit 1, had told him that Williams was going to kill Johnson.

Video surveillance footage of the murder, however, showed Carl Williams sitting at a table reading, and Matthew Johnson approaching him from behind to strike him over the head with the metal stem.

CHAPTER 43

Lies, damned lies, and the media

It's an open secret that the Victoria Police leaks like a sieve when it comes to dealing with the media. This is how it works officially: there is a media director who is directly responsible to the Chief Commissioner. He or she leads a bunch of people whose job it is to deal with media releases and inquiries. Some will compile accident statistics, or organise access to divisions or squads, and basically wrangle the huge machine that is the media. It has been like that for years as a way of controlling the flow of information.

Sounds good in theory, but the model doesn't take into account the personalities involved – both the ones wearing the blue uniform and the ones madly rushing for a deadline.

In the same way cops court informers, the bigwig journos court the cops. At one time there was a lot of kudos in getting a call from John Silvester or Andrew Rule or Geoff Wilkinson or Keith Moor. And so, instead of using the official channels of applying to Police Media to get information, some journos would go have a coffee at the Homicide Squad, or hang out with the Armed Robbery Squad detectives. Lines have always been blurred between the cops and journos with this fraternisation, just as it was when the cops dealt with the likes of Terry Hodson.

In the olden days, if leaks were too big and too significant, the police Ethical Standards Department would make a real effort to identify the source. These days, I'm not sure what happens.

From where we stood as regular coppers, when Christine Nixon became Chief Commissioner she was very good at using the media. The media department changed from a half-dozen people to, I think, over one hundred.

Now, I'm not pointing the finger at anyone, but think about this question for a minute: *Why do most members of the public think I'm guilty of something?*

Because of the media.

The half-stories, the photo angles, the 'leaks' that counter my story.

Coincidence?

Don't ask me – I'm jaded and cynical.

CHAPTER 44

The usual suspects

When Terry and Christine Hodson were murdered, detectives investigating the case put together a long list of suspects. I obtained this under subpoena. Terry had informed on so many people that the list of crooks who might bear a grudge was almost endless.

There was also an incredibly twisted inter-connectedness about so many.

Detective Sol Solomon spoke to Detective Superintendent Biggin on 25 May 2004. He added the superintendent's information to an official information report. This is what he wrote:

[Terence] Hodson first became involved with MDID as an informer in 2001 during Operation Kayak. During Kayak, Terry Hodson was arrested and charged with drug trafficking. After his arrest, he was recruited as an informer by S/Sgt Wayne Strawhorn. David Miechel became his handler and has been so ever since. Hodson's value as an informer during Kayak was minimal and he was eventually speared off into other directions of which he was far more useful. It was during Operation Kayak that Terry Hodson informed on his son Andrew and daughter Mandy which resulted in their arrest on drug trafficking charges. These charges have still not been finalised at court yet. Superintendent Biggin is of the opinion that at some stage after Andrew and Mandy's arrest over these matters, they would have found out that Terry Hodson had given them up. Most likely time for the revelation would have been after Hodson's arrest with Miechel over the Oakleigh job and Hodson's subsequent outing by the media as a police informer.

In the early days of the murder investigation, detectives focused on who Terry and Christine would let into their house, and every suspect was considered against this criterion.

From my copies of subpoenaed documents, it is clear that Dave Miechel was helping the investigators find out who had killed his friends. A lot of the information reports (IRs) included his opinion on the likelihood of each suspect.

One possible suspect was a guy called Mark Smith. In the IRs, Dave commented that when there was suspicion that Terry was an informer, Mark Smith had stood by Terry. But then, after the Oakleigh break-in, when Terry was publicly outed, Smith would have looked suss himself because of his loyalty to Terry. Not only was Smith a possible suspect, he was also a buddy of Peter Reed, Terry's notorious son-in-law. Terry had never informed on Mark Smith and a number of people who knew Terry believed he would have let Smith into his home.

Another lead came when detectives found a business card for a female homicide cop in the Hodson house. When they questioned the detective, she added a bit more to the story. She had been a member of the Tactical Response Group when Peter Reed was a target. She said that Dave Miechel had approached her with information from a Major Drug Investigation Division informer that Reed was in possession of a handgun. After his place was raided Reed made formal complaints that items of his property were damaged and some were stolen during the search.

The police put covert surveillance at the Hodsons' double funeral, which was held at Le Pine Funerals in East Kew on 25 May 2004. They also contacted Terry's solicitor, who agreed to hand over the brief of evidence to the Ceja task force investigators. He didn't have much to add, but he did tell detectives that George Williams had turned up at Terry's last court appearance. While the solicitor was also acting for Carl, he didn't know what interest Carl's dad would have had in Terry Hodson.

As well as the more obvious suspects, there was also every drug dealer Terry had ever informed on.

CHAPTER 45

What's in a name?

On 28 May 2011, I read an article in *The Age* by John Silvester elaborately entitled 'Hey, fellas, did it moniker to you that a nickname can be a bit crook?' Silvester waxed lyrical on the names and euphemisms of gangland figures. He wrote about how Andrew 'Benji' Veniamin killed Nik 'the Bulgarian' Radev and the driver of his getaway car was the crim and 'star informer' known as 'the Runner'. Silvester wrote: '... we invented the name "the Runner" as it relates to his career-long habit of running from an armed robbery to his stolen getaway car. It also relates to the time he escaped from an armed robbery squad car when it stopped at lights on the way to court while the detective next to him nodded off for a quick power nap.'

To my disbelief, in this article Silvester named me as a detective who had let the Runner escape, even though eight years earlier he had written an article on the Runner which clearly said: 'In March, 1990, he escaped from the Northfield Jail in South Australia where he was serving a long sentence for armed robberies. The following month he was arrested in Melbourne and questioned over four armed robberies. As he was being driven to the city watchhouse he jumped from an unmarked police car and escaped again.'

While I know more than anyone the propensity of the media to lump as many disgraces on the chosen ones as they can, if Silvester had access to a calculator he would have realised that in 1990 I was twenty years old – a junior constable wearing down shoe leather on the streets of Brunswick, not a detective at the Armed Robbery Squad. Indeed, I was never in the Armed Robbery Squad.

While most of the articles about me contained a seed of truth spun and twisted every which way, this one was blatantly wrong and I could prove it.

On my next visit to my solicitor, I showed him the article and asked for advice. I told him that I could prove that Silvester was wrong and I'd even found out the name of the detective who had been in the car at the time the Runner escaped. My solicitor arranged for me to meet a barrister who dealt with civil cases. I went in there full of righteous indignation until the barrister looked at me and told me that while Silvester wasn't allowed to do what he had done, I would have to *prove* that my reputation had been damaged.

'And let's face it,' the barrister said, 'your reputation is damaged anyway.'

Irony?

Catch-22?

In what sort of world can the media say whatever they like to turn you into a villain, then be allowed to lie about you and get away with it because the public think you're a villain?

Sometimes this stuff makes my head spin so much, I reckon one day it'll twist right off my shoulders.

And speaking of head-spinning, have a look at the lead paragraph of a news article published by the ABC on 11 November 2011 under the banner headline: 'Secret transcripts of ex-cop's testimony revealed'. Keep in mind the Australian Crime Commission promises of secrecy and protection.

The Melbourne Magistrates' Court has released details of previously secret conversations between former drug squad detective Paul Dale and the Australian Crime Commission (ACC). In the transcripts, Dale denies asking slain gangland boss Carl Williams to kill anyone. Dale has been committed to stand trial in the County Court on 13 charges of misleading the commission. The court has released transcripts of those conversations.

Secrecy and protection, my backside.

And on the same day, counsel for the Australian Crime Commission Garry Livermore made his famous comment in court: 'People who assist authorities in endeavouring to prosecute Paul Dale have got a pretty poor life expectancy. Two of them have been murdered.'

Good one, Gazza.

CHAPTER 46

Finally, someone's asking the right questions

Reading *The Age* on 20 February 2012, I saw an article that finally began asking the right questions. In 'Overhaul begins as ombudsman slams handling of Williams', journalists Nick McKenzie and Richard Baker discussed just who was responsible for the death of Carl Williams in the Acacia Unit and the fact that the Victorian justice department was overhauling its management of high-security prisoners before the ombudsman's report into systemic failures following Williams's murder was handed down. Not only was the ombudsman expected to criticise the decision to move Williams to the Acacia unit, it was anticipated that 'the poor security measures that enabled Johnson to arm himself with gym equipment and attack Williams without being interrupted by guards, who were slow to arrive at the scene of the killing' would also be criticised.

After media suggestions that I had played a role in his death, it was refreshing to see the media begin to cast blame where blame was due. Reading the article made me feel, for the first time in a long time, the beginnings of vindication.

The article went on to say, '... police are investigating whether Williams' death was a hit ordered by underworld figures outside prison, who seized upon Williams' move to the Acacia Unit to have him killed.

'The decision to move Williams to Acacia was approved by senior police and justice department officials.'

Of course, my feelings about Carl Williams's move from isolation to the Acacia Unit lean towards the more suspicious, but at least the article acknowledged publicly that the decision by the Victoria Police to move Williams into the Acacia Unit contributed to his death.

It was also refreshing to see Victoria Police and decisions made by its officers put under the microscope – just like I have been. I think the public has a right to ask if these decisions were deliberate. Can they keep making the same mistakes over and over and never face the consequences – or at least bring about policy changes? Is it just me, or does anyone else see a familiar theme here? Rod Collins was given copies of my confidential documents in prison and the result was that my family and I received death threats. And, still, Carl Williams was given copies of similar documents, which his violent cellmate had access to.

What did the police expect would happen?

And as for the leaking to the media of information that Williams was a paid police informer, and then him being murdered *on the very same day* by a killer well known for his hatred of informers ...

Accident or design?

CHAPTER 47

Being declared innocent ... by the media

Something unexpected but quite incredible happened on 21 May 2012: I got a bunch of texts and messages from wellwishers. For the first time in about eight years, I hurried to get copies of the newspapers instead of dreading what was in them.

In a backflip of gymnastic proportions, John Silvester in *The Age* declared 'Dale cleared of jail killing' in an article that released the finding of the investigation into the killing of Carl Williams in prison.

I think that for the first time ever I was referred to as 'Paul Dale, former policeman' rather than 'disgraced ex-detective' or worse. Another really interesting difference was that a lot of the papers dumped their sinister photographs of me and replaced them with pictures of me looking like a normal bloke. In one picture, I was almost smiling.

The change in pictures and descriptions reinforced what I'd come to know. Using words and pictures, the media can make you into whoever they want. Jowly and threatening disgraced ex-detective. Innocent and smiling former policeman.

The upshot of the story that made headlines was that after a long investigation, task force Driver – the task force set up to get to the bottom of the prison murder of Carl Williams – had concluded that while I was an 'unwitting beneficiary' of the murder of Williams, I had nothing to do with it.

Silvester quoted Acting Assistant Commissioner Doug Fryer as saying, 'We have found no evidence to support the theory that he was involved at all.'

The 25-month-long investigation also found no evidence that any prison officer or prison staff had a hand in setting up the attack. That leaves two alternatives: either Matthew Johnson murdered Carl for his own reasons, or things were put into place to ensure a naturally occurring response.

Think about it for a minute. Carl Williams was placed in a cell with Matthew Johnson – a self-confessed hater of 'dogs' or prison informers. Add a police leak that Williams is getting a lucrative deal from the police ... sometimes all you have to do is put two people in a powder keg then light the fuse.

Matthew Johnson later admitted knowing that Carl was a dog – but it was one thing a cellmate *knowing*, and quite a different thing entirely having it splashed across the front page of the *Herald Sun*. I was in prison for eight months and gained some insight into how things worked. A guy like Johnson is only as good as his jailhouse reputation. And with the public declaration that he was cellmates with a paid police informer – a dog – he'd be forced to ignore it and lose his rep, or walk the talk.

Whichever way it was, it was a sure-fire guaranteed recipe for disaster.

A couple of journalists who have detoured from the usual path of quoting each other posed some serious questions. After Matthew Johnson's conviction, Steve Butcher wrote an article in *The Age* published on 30 September 2011 that began to touch on the danger that the police possibly exposed Williams to. He questioned why police would risk placing Williams, who was 'crucial' to police investigations of myself and the 'alleged hitman' over the Hodson murders, with Johnson, and quoted the evidence of Peter Hutchinson, a senior manager with Corrections Victoria, that 'close consideration had been given whether Williams and Johnson should share a cell and that a senior policeman who was briefed on the situation had expressed no concerns. Yet that officer told the court that "we weren't involved in the decision to place them there".'

Even if Matthew Johnson did know that Carl was helping the police, it might not have bothered him much. He later said in court that Carl was shafting the cops. However, what wouldn't have made him laugh was the fact that Carl's statement had not only implicated me as an ex-cop but had implicated another crook, Rod Collins.

And that was breaking the code.

A big no-no.

A big, front-page no-no.

•

So, exactly *who* was involved in the decision to match the police informer with the violent psychopathic killer who hated police informers?

The prison said the police and the police said the prison.

The truth would later come out.

It was Carl Williams himself.

He had asked to be put with Matthew Johnson. In fact, Carl had not only asked, he had actually threatened to stop cooperating with the police if his request wasn't granted. So, of course, the police agreed.

Here's where it gets interesting. If Matthew Johnson was telling the truth about Carl Williams 'shafting' the police, then the police were about to look really stupid. Of course, there were some of us who thought they were about to look really stupid anyway because the minute Carl Williams was brought forward in court to declare his statement against me – made only after lengthy negotiations for his father's tax bill of $750 000, a possible sentence reduction, his daughter's private school fees and, naturally, the same million-dollar reward that they had offered to Rod Collins before him – the defence would have pointed out the bleeding obvious: it sounded nuts.

A sensible person might also wonder why detectives from Victoria Police flattened a path to the cell door of this witness that the court had deemed 'virtually incapable of telling the truth' to *pay him* to 'tell the truth' against me. And which truth would they use? The *truth* when Williams denied any knowledge of the Hodson killings? Or the *truth* they obtained after their offer of cash and prizes?

And if my theory of putting Carl Williams in a powder keg then lighting the fuse sounds like a conspiracy theory, a report in *The Age* on 26 June 2012 lent support to it. While the task force was finding me innocent of any involvement in Williams's murder, some heads had to roll and the Secretary of the Department of Justice, Penny Armytage, was one of them.

The Ombudsman found Ms Armytage and Corrections Victoria acting commissioner Rod Wise were both aware of the potential threat posed by Williams' fellow inmate Matthew Charles Johnson, but approved their pairing in a cell.

As a result, the department failed in its statutory duty to ensure Williams' safety, the report found.

Johnson fatally bashed Williams at Barwon Prison on April 19, 2010 and was later found guilty of murder.

No adverse recommendations were made against Ms Armytage in the report, however it noted Mr Wise had written to her warning of the threat three months before Williams' murder.

'There is little doubt that Johnson is capable of causing Williams harm if he were to find out the true nature of Williams' co-operation with police,' Mr Wise wrote on January 6, 2009.

Rod Wise was almost clairvoyant in his prediction.

CHAPTER 48

The Victoria Police pursue the ACC charges

The pre-trial arguments for my case went at a snail's pace. We would go to court for a day, present arguments, then the judge would adjourn for a month. The next month, the same thing would happen.

The case was adjourned four times – the last time was my appeal to have the case thrown out on the grounds that the initial investigation was outside the charter of the Australian Crime Commission.

The *Australian Crime Commission Act* dictates that the ACC was formed to investigate national organised crime, predominantly drug trafficking and importation. They can investigate state offences if they have a federally relevant aspect to them. They can also investigate state offences which involve particular crimes listed under the Act. Technically, murder in Victoria is not a state offence but a common-law offence. Common-law offences have arisen from the law over centuries, and often were imported from England. Nowhere in the Act does it say that the ACC can investigate a common-law offence in Victoria.

Not surprisingly, the judge was not prepared to rule on this because it would have huge ramifications for the Australian Crime Commission and the manner in which they investigate their cases – not to mention the impact it might have on their current investigations.

Legal mumbo jumbo, I know, but you are forced to fight fire with fire. When you think about it, the Victoria Police used the Australian Crime Commission and its coercive powers to haul me in yet again for questioning. All my summonses to the ACC were for the murder of the Hodsons. I believe the ACC was used by the Victoria Police because I would be compelled to answer any questions put to me and the strict rules of evidence of the Victorian courts don't apply there. You must attend. You have to answer questions. If you want to take a lawyer, you have to get ACC permission. Your lawyer can't object to a line of questioning. Everything is on their terms and, of course, there is the whole secrecy thing – you can't tell anyone that you're going and you can't tell anyone that you've been there. A clear violation under any other circumstances of your civil rights.

Our appeal against the charter of the ACC was heard by three judges. I had faith in them because the Appeals Court of the Supreme Court was the only place that I'd ever got justice. For me to get any form of justice, I had to go all the way. Remember, it was the three judges from the Appeals Court of the Supreme Court who decided straightaway that I shouldn't be held in the Acacia Unit and I was released immediately.

But it wasn't to be. Rather than being dismissed, the case was put down for the following February 2013 – almost ten years since the whole thing began.

CHAPTER 49

When will the public stop paying?

In April 2012, George Williams was featured in *The Australian* in an article about his legal challenge to his $750000 tax bill. He told journalists that in 2009 Victoria Police had agreed to pay his tax bill when Carl had agreed to help detectives in the Hodson murder investigation. George Williams said he had received a letter in July 2009 from the Australian Tax Office saying that the payment had been made in full, but a couple of days later had received another letter saying that the payment had been withdrawn courtesy of the Moti ruling backflip.

But, of course, it doesn't end there.

As if this whole story wasn't twisted enough, in September 2012 George Williams and Carl's ex-wife, Roberta Williams, decided to sue the state government, claiming damages over his death. They claimed that as a consequence of Carl's murder, they had been deprived of the financial benefits expected in return for him cooperating with police.

Financial benefits, you ask?

For the money he was promised to make a statement against me?

Clearly, in the minds of George and Roberta, I was the cash cow that might still pay off.

Steve Butcher in *The Age* wrote that Roberta was claiming compensation for 'psychiatric or psychological injury, abnormal grief reaction and anxiety and depression'.

The lawsuit claimed the Department was at fault for placing Carl Williams with Matthew Johnson despite the fact that they knew Johnson headed up the Prisoners of War group dedicated to harming those cooperating with the police.

What the article didn't mention – and I'm guessing the writ might not have mentioned it either – was that Carl Williams insisted he be put in with Matthew Johnson. And not only insisted but threatened to withdraw his cooperation with the Victoria Police unless he got his way.

Might be a good time to have a look at two paragraphs from the Ombudsman's Report into Williams's murder:

> In a letter dated 7 January 2009, Mr Williams also wrote to the Sentence Management Unit requesting that Mr Johnson be accommodated with him and his father.
>
> Mr Williams also made several requests to Victoria Police to be placed with Mr Johnson and stated that his cooperation with Victoria Police was dependent on this placement. At [an] interview on 30 June 2011, Detective Inspector Smith said that 'Mr Williams was adamant that he would withdraw his cooperation with Victoria Police unless he was placed with Mr Johnson'.

I get that the Williams family want to sue, because the Department of Corrections has a duty of care towards all of its inmates, but to claim *loss of income*? On the money that he would have got for his statement against me?

Come on.

There was a public backlash against the suit and George and Roberta requested a hearing by a judge alone, rather than a jury. Surely they would never find a jury of their peers that would allow any kind of financial compensation for them by virtue of their relationships to a convicted multiple murderer.

But perhaps the response to this is best left to Herbert Wrout, who was with Lewis Moran at the Brunswick Club when he was gunned down on Carl Williams's orders. Wrout himself was shot in the chest and arm, and survived the murderous assault with ongoing health issues. He was quoted in *The Australian* in response to the Williams family's legal scramble for cash.

'I've got five bullet holes in me because of that animal and his family,' Mr Wrout said, describing the Williams family legal actions as obscene. 'I'm just a shell of my former self. All I could get was $7500 as a victim of crime, and medical expenses. And the family of that rat police informer Williams reckons they can get a $1 million pay cheque on the taxpayer.'

Indeed, Mr Wrout. Indeed.

But despite the ire of Bert Wrout, Roberta and George Williams settled a claim against the state government. A six-figure sum was reportedly put into trust for Carl's daughter, Dhakota, for when she turns eighteen. The terms of the settlement were confidential and no liability was accepted for Williams's death.

In August 2013, journalist Adam Shand wrote an article about Roberta Williams. According to Shand, Roberta said Carl had made up a story that I had paid him $150 000 to organise the 2004 murder of Terry Hodson. She said Carl decided to go along for the ride since the police were so keen to get me and that I was a fall guy to get him a reduced sentence. Shand quoted Roberta as saying, 'I have often felt sorry for Dale. He was set up for something that he didn't do.'

When the Hodson inquest called Roberta as a witness, she denied saying any of this, calling Adam Shand a 'lying snake'.

CHAPTER 50

The Queen v Paul Noel Dale

We did our best to avoid the ridiculous charges going to trial, but it wasn't to be. At the end of February 2013, I walked up the steps of the Supreme Court to begin what I hoped would be the last episode in this whole thing.

As much as I wanted to clear my name, I mostly wanted to avoid going to trial because of the cost. The Victoria Police had funded all my other cases, but this one was going to hit me in the hip pocket big time. How many people can afford $4500 a day to defend themselves against a relentless never-ending attack from a police force that had already flaunted its deep pockets? From a financial point of view, I hoped it would be over in around two weeks, but I grossly underestimated the prosecution's ability to draw it out.

Including trial preparation, pre-trial legal argument, and the actual trial – which would last into its *seventh* week – my legal bill alone would eventually be $310000. Add to that thousands of dollars in seven weeks' worth of lost income, as well as paying for seven weeks of city accommodation and eating out for breakfast, lunch and dinner.

I knew the strategy well: if the cops could drag a trial out and financially bleed a defendant dry, win or lose the cops win.

More importantly for you, the taxpayer, is how much the trial cost *you*. A trial of twelve charges based solely around whether I was closer to Carl Williams than I said I was probably cost you at least $400000 just for the legal team alone.

Four hundred thousand dollars.

Despite the horrendous cost, a part of me wanted to go to trial, wanted to have this ridiculous, flimsy case aired in front of a jury of my peers, wanted a resounding not guilty verdict.

But as much as I went to court with high thoughts of vindication in mind, I reckoned that one of the aims of the opposition was to publicly air any scrap of dirty linen they could – whether or not it had any bearing on the case. And the media lapped it up. Here's an example.

A court revelation from 2008 repeated by a witness cop that I had admitted 'infidelity in my life' became the screaming headline: 'Paul Dale had multiple mobile phones so he could cheat on wife, court told'. Headlines to embarrass and disgrace.

By the end of the trial, it would become clear that the danger was not in what the media *said* but, rather, what it *didn't say*. But more about that later.

A jury pool is normally thirty people. For me, they got a pool of sixty. Potential jurors were asked both if they could be available for a longer trial and if they felt that they could be impartial in a Paul Dale trial. Twenty-five people bowed out – some had preconceived ideas about me. Others would find a longer trial onerous.

The remaining names were put into a hat and each potential juror walked across the front of the court. In the end, we got six men and six women of mixed ages and backgrounds. The foreman sounded like an educated bloke and he looked really switched on.

And then it all began.

It's strange, sitting in the dock looking over at a dozen people in whose hands lie your future. I tried not to catch the eye of any of them. It's an awkward thing – you don't want to look at them and they avoid eye contact. Throughout the trial, I would cast surreptitious glances at them to see how they reacted to things, and I guess they did the same back to me. It's like a huge elephant in the room.

Directly opposite the jury were the media. There were a lot at the opening and there would be a lot at the closing, and not so many in between.

THE QUEEN V PAUL NOEL DALE

Right from the start, it became clear that prosecutor Chris Beale was going to drag the trial out as long as he could. His monotone would put members of the jury to sleep on more than one occasion.

I always knew that the prosecution's case relied for the most part on a couple of sentences from the tape that Nicola Gobbo had recorded – or 'the Gobbo tapes', as they were referred to. When Chris Beale went on and on in his opening address, it became clear I was right: the Crown's case was based on my use of the words 'mate' and 'buddy', which anyone who knows me knows I use all the time to everyone I talk to. I also realised that the Crown was going to rely heavily on 110 seconds of tapes of me drunk at the Casino with Nicola Gobbo, calling George Williams to ask him to call Nicola.

And that was about it.

They had not one credible witness who saw Carl Williams and I meet on any occasion other than those I had documented in information reports when I was a cop.

In my day as a detective, a case this flimsy would never get through to the keeper. And if by some miracle it did, I would have been embarrassed as a cop to rely on a few sentences on tape and the word of a couple of shifty crims. Back in my day, the cops wouldn't even charge anyone on that kind of evidence.

So why did they charge me?

Buggered if I know.

Spite?

If we can't get him on anything else, we'll settle for something pissy.

Who knows.

From where I sat, it seemed like senior police and senior prosecutors wanted me in the dock at any cost. That meant that the only thing between me and the malice of the prosecution was the jury.

•

Sol Solomon had always been keen to get me, so I guess it was only fair that he was first cab off the rank. The main thing that Beale seemed to want from Solomon was the backstory of the Hodson murders. I suppose this was to make it seem like I was connected to something bigger and darker than what I had been charged with.

The main thing that my lawyer, Geoff Steward, wanted from Solomon was the incentives that Carl Williams was offered in return for his statement.

Beale tried in vain to keep the offers from the jury.

'You are aware that on 7 March 2007, Mr Dale appeared at an Australian Crime Commission examination?' asked Beale.

'Yes, I am,' said Solomon.

'Into the circumstances surrounding the deaths of Terry and Christine Hodson?'

'Yes,' said Solomon.

'You were actually an observer there?'

'Yes, I was.'

'After that examination, and I don't want you to go into detail, can you simply confirm this: did Carl Williams provide certain information to police?'

'Yes, he did.'

Of course Beale didn't want to go into any detail. Details like, *Gee, what was he offered for his story? Millions of dollars? Well, I'll be darned.*

Beale quickly skipped over to Nicola Gobbo's involvement, again keeping it short and sweet. And, therefore, lacking in detail.

'Four days after that,' said Beale, 'on 30 November 2008, did you receive a telephone call from anybody?'

'I did,' said Solomon.

'Who?'

'I received a telephone call from Ms Nicola Gobbo.'

'A criminal barrister?'

'Yes.'

'Did she have anything to say in relation to Mr Dale?'

'Yes, she did.'

From the dock, this line of questioning was like pulling teeth.

'What did she indicate?' asked Beale.

'She called to advise me that she had received either a phone call or a text message from Paul Dale, who stated that he was coming to Melbourne that day and wanted to catch up with her.'

'Yes?' said Beale.

'She asked whether I would like her to tape-record the conversation and I said to her, "Are you prepared to do that?" She said she was. So I said, "Well that would be fine if you're okay with that, tape-record the conversation."'

Beale didn't ask Solomon whether he thought it was weird for a top criminal barrister to ring a detective and offer to tape a client. Nor did he mention that the moment she did it, her career would be over. What client would use a lawyer who, on a whim, might tape them for the police? And how would her range of underworld clients take it if they knew that she did something like that?

Beale also didn't explore any reasons or inducements she might have had for taping me. He made it sound casual. Like lawyers did that every day.

On cross-examination, my lawyer, Geoff Steward, was quick to get Sol Solomon to describe the week out of prison that Carl Williams enjoyed with his father and their respective girlfriends. Sol denied that the prisoners would have had any opportunity to fraternise with their girlfriends, even though he admitted that he wasn't with them all the time. Again, Solomon made it sound like murderers were released from prison all the time to have Christmas with their crim dads and girlfriends.

That exposed a kink in Solomon's previous evidence. While the detective had said at the committal hearing that he had been present at the secret location at all times during the week Carl and his dad had been released from prison, now he admitted he hadn't been.

'So to be suggesting at the committal, as you did, on 9 November that you were there the whole time that they were there, is wrong, isn't it?' asked Steward.

'Yes,' admitted Solomon.

'You made a genuine mistake,' coaxed the lawyer.

'Yes,' said Sol.

My lawyer pushed a little more. 'You made a genuine mistake in attempting to recall events from three years earlier, didn't you?'

'Correct,' said Solomon.

I snuck a peek at the jury and hoped that the point wasn't lost on them.

At the committal, Solomon had done what they were accusing me of doing: had difficulty in recalling the particulars of events from years earlier.

Steward quickly switched tack. From Sol Solomon he got a detailed list of all the people Carl Williams had admitted killing as well as those he had been involved in killing. Creating an image of the litany of bodies Carl left in his wake, my lawyer then asked Solomon to confirm exactly what the police had offered this drug-dealing multi-murderer for his statement.

After a bit of a legal stoush, finally it was Beale, in re-examination, who extracted some details. 'Can you just clarify for us, please, the basis on which those negotiations were conducted?' he asked.

'In return for his truthful and accurate statement and sworn evidence in relation to the Hodson murders and some other matters,' said Solomon, 'he wanted the following conditions: he wanted an indemnity from prosecution in all of those matters, he wanted to be entitled to make a claim for the $1 million reward which had been offered by the State government regarding the Hodson murders, he wanted a tax debt in the vicinity of $700 000 which was owed by his father George to the Australian Tax Office to be dealt with, either removed or dealt with or paid by some other organisation, he wanted his father looked after in that regards, and he wanted an undertaking that when the time came for him to appear before the Appeal Court in relation to his sentence for the murders that he'd pleaded guilty to, he wanted an undertaking that the Crown would not oppose his application to request a reduction in sentence. They were the conditions.'

So there you have it, folks. That was the price Victoria Police *agreed to pay* in order to get Paul Dale.

'Was he to receive any of those things prior to giving truthful sworn evidence?' asked Beale.

'No, he wasn't.'

I shook my head in disgust. You have to remember: Carl's daughter *was* in private school and Carl's dad's tax bill *had been* paid (Victoria Police only took the money back after the Moti ruling) and all this despite the very clear wording on all Victoria Police rewards: ... *for information leading to the arrest and conviction of the person or persons responsible for* ... That's right – the arrest *and conviction*.

But I had never been convicted of anything. And Carl had received his cash and prizes.

Again, the Victoria Police rules seemed elastic when it came to their pursuit of me.

•

My wife, Ditty, and Mum came to court every day of the trial. Dad came a couple of days each week, but he still had the butcher shop in Yackandandah to run. We had rented a friend's place in the city for the duration, and had friends back in Wangaratta looking after the kids, who were at school during the week. We drove home each weekend to be with them.

Before the trial, Ditty and I went to the kids' school and spoke to the principal and the teachers to let them know what was happening, and to make sure our kids were supported. Ditty and I were actively involved in the school and every fundraising event it had. I was the main barbecue hand at the school fete each year, and I coached the kids' Auskick. Not only did we get amazing support from the school but we got a lot of support from the community of Wangaratta. It was really heartening to have people give me a wave, or stop me in the street and shake my hand and wish me luck. If Ditty was in the supermarket she would be ushered through the checkout first. Mates offered to mow the lawns at home while we were away. These gestures of support meant so much to us.

It makes a bloke humble.

•

The next witness was George Williams. As an ex-cop I couldn't believe the judge, Justice Elizabeth Curtain, had even allowed witnesses like George Williams. She'd heard the crux of his evidence and inducements at the pre-trial stage but let him through anyway. Early on in the trial I couldn't help but feel that the judge was favouring the prosecution side. After George Williams gave evidence, though, the judge would surprise me and go a small way to restoring my faith in the system.

Here's how it happened.

Led by Chris Beale, George Williams began his story. He said that he and Carl and some others had run into me one day at Albert Park. This was the day I received my commendation at Government House and I had been out celebrating with my family.

As Beale asked George Williams about the accidental meeting (which I had documented, as per protocol, in an information report), a clear picture flashed into my head – a vision of me back then, a cop, getting an award for service before all this started. Back when life was simple and easy. I suddenly got quite emotional. I bowed my head a little so that no one could see my anguish.

Back to George Williams. He told the court he'd driven Carl to the Keilor Baths to meet me. He said when he got to the baths, Carl had asked if he had any money. George said that he had $6000 in cash, which he handed over to his son without question.

'Did he indicate what it was for?' asked Beale. The implication, of course, was that Carl would give the money to me.

'I'm not sure if he indicated who it was for, no,' said George Williams.

Beale didn't ask him if it was odd that if Carl was indeed paying a crooked cop for information, he didn't actually bring money with him but relied on whatever his dad might have in his pocket when he got to the location of the meeting.

No sense warping these questions with actual logic, I figured.

Next, Beale played a series of drunken calls I made to George Williams that night at the casino – the crux of which were 'Tell Carl to call Nicola'. Nothing about catching up or meeting or anything.

Next came the odd evidence of the Hillside meeting accusation. One of the questions I was asked at the Australian Crime Commission was if I had ever met with Carl Williams at Hillside. I didn't even know where Hillside was and I certainly had never met Carl Williams there. But the prosecution put up a lame case otherwise.

Their evidence? A tracking device on George Williams's car which put him in Hillside, and a listening device which recorded Carl saying something like, 'Here comes a blue ute.'

In the witness box George Williams said that one day he drove Carl to Hillside, which was apparently near where Carl lived, dropped him off to meet me, then picked him up later. According to George, I was driving a blue four-wheel drive vehicle, and he could see my profile at a distance and knew it was me. He said he left us, then returned. There were no phone records, he said, of Carl asking him to come and collect him because Carl had left his phone in George's car. The whole meeting, he estimated, was around an hour and a half.

My lawyer asked if he was sure if it was a four-wheel drive.

George said he was positive.

When my lawyer asked for the actual tape to be played, Carl was clearly heard saying the words 'blue ute' in reference to whoever it was they were meeting. Now, here was George in court saying blue four-wheel drive. Even to people who don't know much about cars, there's no mistaking the difference between a ute and a four-wheel drive. The cynic in me wondered if this subversion in George's testimony was because the detectives had searched the records and found out that I owned a blue four-wheel drive at the time. Not a ute.

This was so typical of testimony in my case. Squeeze it and squash it till the square peg fits into the round hole.

When Beale's examination finished, the judge interrupted him.

'Mr Williams hasn't been asked about when it was that this meeting at Hillside was said to have occurred.'

Beale told her that the date would be revealed in later testimony.

'Shouldn't he be asked in any event, he was there?' asked the judge.

Beale turned from the judge to George. 'Do you know the actual date on which you took him to Hillside for this meeting with Paul Dale?'

'No,' said George.

The fact that George Williams's car had a tracking device that put him in the vague vicinity of where I was working at the time was pushed and pummelled to become evidence that we met. The fact that I was working construction with a team was not mentioned. The fact that the meeting allegedly took place during my working hours didn't enter into things. The fact that anyone working on a construction team can't just disappear for an hour and a half without being noticed also didn't seem to bother the prosecution.

When my lawyer took over on cross-examination, he asked George Williams how much his Mercedes had cost.

'Thirty-five thousand dollars.'

'Where did you get the money from?'

'Out of the bank,' said George.

'The money that was in the bank,' persisted my lawyer, 'did that come about as a result of proceeds of trafficking in drugs?'

'No.'

'You know that for sure, do you?'

'I know that for sure,' insisted George. 'I was on WorkCover payments getting $840 a week.'

My lawyer let that one hang in the air, certain that the jury could put two and two together and it wouldn't add up to $35 000 cash for a Mercedes.

Next, Geoff Steward led George Williams into a discussion about his Christmas out of jail. George conceded that he and Carl both spent time with their respective partners in different rooms. He also said that after the Christmas break from jail with his son, they both were taken to Barwon Prison together. George had been granted a change of jail so that he could be with his son. Another benefit of their cooperation with the police.

Steward questioned George about the tax bill and how it had been paid. George also admitted that Dhakota Williams's school fees were paid by the Victoria Police.

Then Steward asked George about his past convictions for lying under oath. We needed the jury to hear what kind of person this witness was.

'[Y]ou've previously gone before a hearing and taken an oath to tell the truth, haven't you?' asked Steward.

'That's right, yes.'

'And lied on your oath?' pressed Steward.

'What do you mean I lied on my oath?' asked George belligerently.

'Picked up a Bible, swore to tell the truth and then proceeded to lie. You've done that, haven't you?'

'I think everyone's done it, you know ...' shrugged George.

The judge reminded him that he was being asked about what he'd done.

'I was found guilty by one person of lying.'

'Who was the one person?' pressed Steward.

'A magistrate,' muttered George.

George then repeated his details of the so-called Hillside meeting, and repeated the blue four-wheel drive story. George said that a blue four-wheel drive seemed to loom out of nowhere and Carl immediately identified it as being me.

Again, the glaring discrepancy between George's 'recollection' about a four-wheel drive and Carl's clear words on the tape about a blue ute.

Geoff Steward laboured the point about the blue vehicle, then asked if George Williams was currently suing the Victoria Police to retrieve the money they paid then took back from his tax bill.

'Yes,' he said.

George Williams also admitted that after he and Carl were put in Barwon Prison together they had daily contact for six months before he made his statement to the police after he was released.

'Did you discuss with him what you were going to put in your statements?' asked Steward.

'No,' said George.

'Are you sure about that?'

'Sure about that, yes,' said George.

I hoped it sounded as unlikely to the jury as it sounded to me. Carl was in prison drawing up a wish list of goodies to wrangle out of the Victoria Police, some of them were for his dad – and they didn't talk about it on those long, boring days together?

Hmm.

Before the jury was sent home for the weekend, the judge addressed them. 'You will appreciate that your task is to, as I said to you, to listen and to observe and to comprehend what the witnesses say to you because ultimately you are required to assess the truthfulness and accuracy and reliability of the evidence that's placed before you, and come to a decision as to what evidence you accept and what weight you attach to that evidence in order to determine your verdict.'

The jury listened intently.

'So, you've heard George Williams give evidence about what he says Carl Williams said to him on occasion when he drove Carl Williams to the Keilor Baths and when ... Carl Williams left the car and then at a later time returned to him.' The judge then read the jury the answers that George had given earlier to questions about the Keilor Baths.

'You will appreciate,' she instructed, 'that what's relied upon here is therefore an out-of-court statement of Carl Williams's that is something George Williams says Carl Williams said to him. Do you follow? It is relied upon, if you accept that those statements were made, as proof of that which it asserts, that is that Carl Williams was going to meet Paul Dale and that there was such a meeting between Paul Dale and Carl Williams where they put on trunks, got in the pool and walked up and down. So the evidence is put before you as truth of that which it asserts, because otherwise it would be hearsay ...

'Now, what Carl Williams said to George Williams is hearsay, what we call an out-of-court statement, and as such, the law regards such evidence as potentially unreliable because the maker of it, here Carl Williams, is not here to be questioned about it.'

The judge went on to say that the jury couldn't see Carl Williams tell the story and judge his truthfulness. She said that Carl could have had a reason to lie to his father, or that George could have remembered the events inaccurately. She cautioned them that the law said that they needed to consider the potential unreliability of the evidence.

Yep, that restored my faith a little.

•

As they did with Carl Williams in the early days, the next witness had his name suppressed. If the public knew who he was, they would be sure to question his motives. If they weren't too busy shaking their heads in disbelief, that is.

'Witness B' appeared via a video link from a secret location wearing prison greens. Naturally, one of Beale's first questions had to be about him being in prison, because the jury weren't silly.

'You are currently serving a jail sentence?' asked Beale.

'Yes,' said Witness B, who oozed criminality in his look, his manner, his attitude.

I couldn't help myself: I looked over towards the jury to try to gauge their reaction to the calibre of yet another 'star' witness against me. I might be wrong, but they looked gobsmacked.

Witness B said he had known Carl Williams since the late 1990s. He and Carl met regularly to discuss drug dealing.

'Were you present when Carl got married?' asked Beale.

'Yes, I was on the bridal party,' he said.

I hoped he meant 'in' the bridal party ...

Witness B said he and Carl spoke every day about the amphetamine business they set up together.

He said that Carl had referred to a 'bloke by the name of Paul in the police force, if we ... were under surveillance or something that he could let Carl know. He was Carl's contact inside the police force.'

Oddly enough, Witness B then told the court that they knew they were under constant surveillance. I just hoped that the jury could see that they didn't need to pay any cop to tell them what they already knew.

Witness B added more detail to the meeting at Albert Park that had already been covered by George Williams. Funnily enough, Witness B's story was different from George Williams's story. George said that Carl and I disappeared for half an hour to chat that day in Albert Park. Witness B said we chatted for five or ten minutes. George's story had the rogues' gallery standing further up the road waiting for Carl, Witness B had them all doing coffee at Laurent's. And then Witness B dropped a bombshell. He said that George Williams wasn't even at the meeting in Albert Park.

'I can't remember George Williams being there,' he insisted.

Witness B said that Carl told him after that meeting that I gave Carl information.

On cross-examination Geoff Steward jumped up and laid right into Witness B, who quickly admitted that Carl Williams had lied to him before. Carl told him that he wasn't sleeping with Roberta when in fact he was. (She was married to someone else at the time.) Witness B said that Carl would never lie to him because he would end their friendship and close 'other doors' – whatever that meant.

But Witness B had already admitted that Carl had lied to him and he hadn't ended the friendship.

'You found out that he lied to you?'

'That's right.'

'So rather than cut him off as a friend, what you do is you become a member of his bridal party when he marries the woman he'd been lying to you about sleeping with?'

'Well ... Carl and Roberta Williams know, I opposed the wedding from the start. Even on the day, I said to Carl, "You can change your mind, mate. Let's get out of here."'

Steward jumped from groomsmen to guns.

'Did you forget a rather important part of your business partnership?'

'Supplying guns and murder,' said Witness B matter-of-factly.

Again, the jury looked gobsmacked while they listened to him talk about his role in the shooting of Jason Moran in a van full of kids. They looked gobsmacked when he described his drug dealing. They looked gobsmacked when he told the jury about how he was good mates with 'gentleman' Mark Moran but that didn't stop him supplying the gun used in Mark's killing.

'You live by the sword, you die by the sword,' he shrugged. 'It ain't Mary Poppins school.'

I suppose it ain't – unless Mary Poppins suddenly started trafficking huge quantities of drugs and popping her enemies like flies.

'So you told the police of your involvement in at least three murders and an attempted murder, but you were charged with only one count of murder, is that right?' asked Steward.

Gee, I wonder why that was, I thought.

'That's right,' admitted Witness B.

'That was the deal you did with the police, right?'

'That's right.'

'And the deal was that even though you were involved with a number of other crimes, you'd only be put up on one murder, correct?'

'That's right.'

During the break, it turned out that Witness B didn't have indemnity for everything he was telling the court. The judge quickly fixed that after an adjournment. She offered him a certificate of indemnity.

'Your Honour, I've already incriminated meself just before there,' said Witness B. 'Will that indemnity cover that as well, or it covers from now on?'

The judge assured him she would make it retrospective to cover the morning's evidence as well.

'Okay, I'll take that,' said Witness B, like he was shopping.

When the questioning resumed, Geoff Steward pushed for more details on how Witness B had supplied the killer with the location of Jason Moran – at a kids' footy game.

'You told Carl Williams and whoever it was that he hired to kill Jason Moran that you had information that Jason was definitely going to be at a particular Auskick on a certain weekend?'

'That's right.'

'You knew that that Auskick would be attended by children?'

'That's right.'

'And what happened was that Jason Moran was murdered in front of how many children in his car?'

'I think it was six or eight,' conceded Witness B.

After that, it sounded a little lame when he said that even though he had supplied the location of a children's football game, the hit wasn't supposed to happen there.

One thing that Witness B said that was interesting was that Carl had confessed to him that he had been responsible for the murder of gangland figure Graham 'the Munster' Kinniburgh.

Geoff Steward read out a statement that Witness B had made to police in 2006. 'It would have been within a month or two of me arriving in the unit [at Barwon Prison]. I asked him, "Why did you take the Munster out?" He told me that he believed that Lewis Moran was not about to find anyone willing to kill him, but he'd heard that the Munster was getting involved. Carl told me that he believed the Munster was capable of organising to have him killed so Carl took him out to remove the danger.'

Listening to this cemented something in my mind. I had always suspected that Carl Williams had killed both Lewis Moran and Terry Hodson because they had a contract out to kill him. Carl was later convicted of killing Lewis Moran, then he admitted organising a hit man to kill Terry Hodson. Coincidence? The two were killed within weeks of each other. Now here was a self-confessed close friend of Carl's saying that he had the Munster killed for the same reason.

If my theory is true, then Carl really did take the Victoria Police for a ride. All he had to do was invent a story that I orchestrated a murder that he'd done on his own for his own reasons. For reasons he'd used before. And for that he would get full indemnity and close to two million bucks.

Witness B then admitted under Steward's questioning that he'd made tens of millions of dollars dealing drugs.

'They were admissions you made to the police in relation to your drug trafficking before you pleaded guilty in the Supreme Court to the murder of Jason Moran, correct?'

'That's right,' said the old crook, 'I'm not hiding from the fact.'

'You knew, didn't you, that the sort of trafficking to which you had admitted to the police in various sworn statements was trafficking of an ilk that would attract or had as a maximum penalty life imprisonment, didn't you?'

'Yes, that's right.'

'Despite the fact that you made those admissions to the police as part of the deal for you to give evidence against other people or make statements against other people, I should say, including Paul Dale, you were not charged with one offence in relation to drug trafficking, were you?'

'That's right.'

'This is an arrangement you came to with the police, is that right?'

'And the prosecutors,' said Witness B helpfully.

'And the Victorian Office of Public Prosecutions, is that right?'

'That's right.'

After that, Steward got Witness B to admit that he had lied on oath before. Witness B called it being 'vague' when giving his answers.

'At the time ... there was no deals on the table and I wasn't prepared to tell them the truth,' he said.

'So I take it you lied?'

'Yes.'

'On your oath?'

'Yes.'

Witness B got a little hot under the collar when Steward started to call him a liar and a dishonourable man. He denied that was so.

'Did you have to lie to Nik Radev when you drove him to the secret location where he would then meet his death?'

Witness B shrugged. 'Because like I said, we were planning to murder him and that's how we did it.'

'Did you lie to Nik Radev when you drove him to the place at which he would then meet his death?' Steward repeated.

'Yes, we lured him to the place, yes,' Witness B conceded finally.

'I'm suggesting to you that you are a thoroughly dishonourable human being.'

'Like I said,' said Witness B, 'he wasn't a friend of mine.'

Steward then asked Witness B about the time, in prison, when Carl Williams had asked him to make a false statement for him about the murder of Mark Moran.

'At the time I wasn't ... cutting any deals with the police.'

It made my blood boil, sitting in court listening to a guy admit that after dealing enough drugs to warrant a life sentence and killing three people, he would be only prosecuted for one murder and none of the drugs charges – in exchange for his lame statement against me.

Particularly galling was the fact that he admitted to falsifying statements to back up Carl then lying to the police and to the court. But, he said, those were lies he was happy to tell when there was no deal on the table.

Huh?

What was really laughable was that Beale was trying to make Witness B look in any way like a credible witness.

Seriously.

I just hoped the jury could see what I saw.

•

Now to the noodles. Any charge with the word 'noodle' in it, twice, was bound to be ridiculous: *The accused on the 26th of November, 2008 ... did give false evidence namely, stating that he did not ever meet Carl Williams at Noodle Box or Noodle Bar in Centreway in Keilor.*

Turned out I was right.

Also turned out that there wasn't a Noodle Box or Noodle Bar in Centreway in Keilor. A fact that the prosecution only saw fit to check once the trial had started.

So that meant I had been charged with saying I didn't believe I had ever met Carl Williams at a place that didn't exist.

You'd think prosecutor Beale, with a faint blush, would have had the grace to bow out of that one – but, no, he called a witness from the local council and got her to admit that she had found a planning permit for a Yunos restaurant. She said the proprietor, Mr Yip, probably sold noodles as part of their menu, but she couldn't be sure.

Steward asked: 'The fact, however, remains, doesn't it, that until 2010 the name under which this premises was operating, its name was Yunos?'

'Correct.'

'And I take it you're not in a position to say what was on Mr Yip's menu in 2004, are you?'

'No, I'm not in a position to say that,' admitted the council worker.

And that was the point at which Beale could have said, 'Well, Paul Dale has been charged with saying he didn't believe he ever met Carl Williams at a place that didn't actually exist so we might ditch that charge.' But he didn't.

Good one, Beale.

•

I told Geoff Steward that when Cameron Davey gave evidence, he would be totally convinced that I was guilty and, in my opinion, he would pull out all stops to say so. But on the first day of his evidence Davey was uncharacteristically mild mannered and helpful.

'Mate, might have to take back what I said about Cameron Davey,' I told Geoff after the first day.

But boy, on the second day, the Cameron Davey that I'd come to know reared his argumentative head. And off he went. He got stuck on some point or other and refused to back down. Even the judge took him to task, but Davey refused to budge. From the dock, I watched it all and hoped that the jury could see what was going on.

Witness after witness followed. My old boss said that on the day of the alleged Hillside meeting, his records showed that I either worked from 7.30 a.m. to 4 p.m. or, at the earliest, 3.30 p.m. Which put me at work during the so-called hour and a half meeting with Carl Williams. He also said that every work ute on the site had been white. That was the standard. There were no blue utes at all.

So I didn't have one, and there were none on site.

Then they got Joanne Smith – the woman who questioned me at the ACC hearings – to say she expected that without the aid of diaries I would recall every detail of every meeting because they were with Carl Williams and therefore memorable.

Was she kidding? Even the cops who had so far appeared at my trial had got things wrong, and they had recent access to all their diaries.

•

In his long, long summing up Chris Beale went on and on about how what I'd said to Nicola Gobbo about Carl Williams being 'accurate' in his recall of the times we met was clear proof of my guilt.

Beale was left with the impossible task of trying to make the jury see that the Australian Crime Commission were good guys and what they did to me was okay. He opened with telling the jury that I could have told the ACC that I was a member of Al-Qa'ida if I had wanted to, and made the distinction that while you couldn't be prosecuted for what you said to the ACC, it was clear that they could use your answers in the 'investigative stage'.

Beale: 'The answers before the ACC may, however, be used in the investigative process as verification for investigators that they are on the right track and, depending on how much detail a person provides, the answers may provide leads to the investigators so that they can go away and they can find other evidence which is then admissible evidence in the trial process ...'

Ah, so that's the prosecutor admitting the Australian Crime Commission gets people in, questions them under what the witness believes is immunity, but then uses their answers against them – in my case in aggressive, costly and prolonged prosecution. Remember that ACC witnesses are summonsed, have to give up their right to remain silent, are compelled to appear, and then, according to Beale, the police take notes on how to get them.

Glad he cleared that up for you, folks.

However, just in case the jury started to think this a tad unfair, Beale quickly told them: 'Now, some of you might think, well, that's a bit harsh, that's a bit unfair that a person can be compelled to attend at one of these examinations, compelled to answer questions, the protection they have in relation to the answers is a protection limited to the trial stage, namely, the answers can't be led as evidence at the trial. You may think it's a bit tough because the investigators can still make use of it in the ways I've described. Whatever you think about the powers that the ACC have and the limited nature of the protections that a person has in relation to the answers that they give, protected in relation to being led as evidence at a trial, not protected in relation to helping investigators confirm whether they're on the right track or not, it's not the issue. It's not the task that is entrusted to you. If you get caught up in an argument about that issue, you need to think about the focus that you have to bring to your deliberations.'

Call it a bit harsh, Beale? I call it deception. ACC deception. It was galling to hear Beale talk about the ACC to the jury as if what they did was fair and reasonable. And not only that, the fact that the Victoria Police could then jump in and use testimony to lay charges ... well, you all know what I think of that.

Beale talked a lot about fairness in his closing argument. I just hoped that the jury had a better understanding of fairness than Beale appeared to.

In his closing address, my lawyer pulled no punches. He tore strips off the prosecution's case, piece by piece.

'Here, in this case, you've witnessed a person being forced to answer questions and then being charged as a result of having done so. You've heard of grubby deals being done. You've heard of reliance being placed on scoundrels, murderers, drug traffickers, perjurers, and reliance being placed upon a woman, Nicola Gobbo, who you might regard as a disgrace to what ought be an honourable profession. You've been told about incentives and immunities being given to despicable people. You've witnessed the way in which an opportunistic State Office of Public Prosecutions deals with such people.'

Paul Dale never owned a blue ute. Paul Dale had a shocking memory – couldn't even remember the mailbox number of the house he grew up in. Steward pointed out that without the aid of my diaries, there were 250 occasions in the ACC testimony that I couldn't recall things. While a couple of seconds on the Gobbo tape might have sounded suspicious, the rest of the tape was me declaring my innocence.

And after Steward wrapped it up, the judge gave her summing up, which I thought was really fair and balanced.

All things considered, when the jury finally left the courtroom, I felt confident that any reasonable person would see the case for what it was. I estimated it would take the jury a couple of hours to sort through it all and come back with a verdict.

Despite my confidence, waiting for a jury is like a journey into the depths of hell. Confidence turns to nervousness pretty quickly and then your mind starts swirling with possibilities. If I was found guilty, they would throw the book at me. The maximum sentence for lying to the ACC was five years in prison – on each charge. I was facing twelve charges. A conviction would automatically warrant a jail sentence because the prosecution had applied to have my charges heard in the Supreme Court. When drug dealer George Williams was convicted of lying to the ACC, his case was heard in the Magistrates' Court and he was fined $3000. It wouldn't be like that for me.

Mum, Ditty and I waited on a couch outside my lawyer's office. Sometimes a defendant can be held in custody while a jury is out, but the judge decided that I could be held in the custody of my lawyer. Hence us all sitting on his couch.

I'm a pacer.

In the courtyard-sized corridor, I did a lot of it the first day. The second day, I took my computer with me and caught up on some stuff for my drilling business. Mum brought a couple of books with her. Ditty got hooked on a card game on her iPhone. In between games, she would Google my name and then tell me what the latest media reports were saying.

As soon as a verdict came in, Geoff would get a phone call. So the first day was spent waiting for the phone to ring. Even though the door to his office was closed, every time Geoff's phone rang, Ditty, Mum and I almost stopped breathing. We would then eavesdrop for his faint, 'Yeah, g'day mate,' and know it wasn't the court, then we'd all breathe again.

Time became measured by the ringing of the phone.

Hours dragged like days.

The other pressure was that deliberations began on the Wednesday, and it looked like they might go into the Thursday. Friday was Good Friday, which meant that if there was no verdict soon, deliberations would go into the next week because of the Easter break.

Near 6 p.m. on the Wednesday night we were called back and told that the jury hadn't made a decision yet. We were sent home.

In limbo.

By the Thursday, negative thoughts crept into my head. It was impossible to keep them at bay. The couch outside Geoff's office, the pacing, the Googling – it all closed in and festered, then *bam*, I started to imagine that they would find me guilty and that I would be sent to prison again and everything would be over.

I began to pray for no decision. At least that way the court would be adjourned over Easter and I could go home and be with my kids. Do normal stuff like Easter egg hunts and a long lunch with the family. But that might not happen if I was thrown into prison over Easter to wait out the verdict ...

Bleak stuff.

And then a call.

A jury question. Five-thirty p.m.

Walking over to the Supreme Court, I noticed the media swarming. Cameras flashed.

Was this just a jury question?

Did the journalists know something we didn't?

The media seats in the court were suddenly full. Detectives arrived.

I looked at my wife. There was more to this.

Trying to look strong on the outside. Heart pounding inside.

The judge called the jury in. When the jury walked in, not one of them looked at me. What did that mean?

The judge asked if they had a verdict and if not, were they close?

My future hung on this.

'We want one more hour,' said the foreman. 'We're very close.'

The judge gave them until 7 p.m.

One hour.

Major stress.

'Did they look at you?' Ditty demanded.

'No,' I said, miserably.

It only took a moment to work ourselves into a frenzy. I was sure to be going to jail. We had to plan how Mum and Ditty would get home, assuming that I would be taken away.

It was the toughest hour of my life. Of our lives.

I've never admired my wife more. To see her stand by me. To watch her in this hour that would decide our future. She had lost friends over this. Over her support for me. Friends who started conversations with: *If my husband had affairs, I'd* ... Ditty and I had dealt with this ten years ago, when it all happened. To see my wife looked down upon because she had stood by me was really hard. What was also paradoxical was that friends who could cope with the fact that I've had the shadow of murder and drug theft hanging over me drew the line at affairs.

'I can deal with going to prison,' I told Ditty, 'as long as I know that you're going to be strong and look after our kids. It's not like I'm dying. It will only be for a while. Then I'll be back. We will need to be strong.'

Ditty assured me that everything would be okay. She would stick by me no matter what.

At 6.45 p.m. we all left the waiting room with the couch and headed over to the court. I was shaking like a leaf.

The jury came in. This time I didn't look to see if they looked at me. I stared straight ahead, hands behind my back. Fingers crossed. Rigid. Hardly daring to breathe.

The judge asked, 'Have you reached a verdict?'

'Yes,' said the foreman.

The judge's assistant read out the first charge.

'How do you find?'

'Not guilty.'

My rigid pose relaxed a tiny bit.

The judge's assistant read out the second charge.

'How do you find?'

'Not guilty.'

I relaxed more and more with each not guilty verdict. And then I realised they had got to the end of reading out the charges and each time the foreman had responded with two of the sweetest words I was ever likely to hear: *Not guilty.*

I turned to the jury and said thank you. I hoped they heard me, since my voice cracked in the middle of saying it. Cracked with such a force of emotion and relief.

I stepped down from the dock and scrambled to where Mum and Ditty were sitting and gave them a hug. I vaguely heard the judge thanking the jury and dismissing them, but Ditty, Mum and I were locked in a very emotional embrace. Then I hugged Geoff.

All the hugging lasted till the court cleared.

Standing on the steps of the court, a free man at last, Ditty told me not to say a word to the media.

'Once you start, Paul, you won't be able to shut up,' she warned.

'Aren't you at least going to tell them what a great lawyer I am?' joked Geoff.

In the end, I said nothing.

We started to walk down the street when one of the TV cameramen filming me, walking backwards, tripped over. Other cameramen stepped over him, but I stopped.

'Are you okay, buddy?' I asked. I reached down and pulled

him to his feet. 'I'm not meant to be talking to anyone, but are you okay, mate?'

The guy dusted himself off and kept filming.

Back at Geoff's office, he insisted that we all go out for a drink.

At the pub I rang Tony Hargreaves, who had flown out for an Easter holiday in New Zealand, and told him the good news. Tony was characteristically dispassionate.

'Well done,' he said.

Ten years.

In all the drinking and celebrating and pats on the back, it began to sink in that after ten years of police pursuit, it was all over. For the first time in a decade, I didn't have charges hanging over my head. It felt euphoric.

●

A wildly coincidental event occurred on the night of my verdict. A little after midnight, after my family and I finished our celebratory drinks, we had to drop into a hotel in Little Collins Street to get Mum's bag, which she had stored in the concierge locker. We were all staying the night at a friend's place a little further up Little Collins Street.

As we were retrieving the bag, two people I'd just seen at the courthouse – who shall remain nameless – arrived. One of them was in the process of booking a room and was being handed one of those little cartons of milk you get from the reception. Meanwhile, out the front, the other person stood, looking very sheepish.

The one outside said, 'You caught us! We're sprung!' then incongruously hugged me. The other came out and shook my hand.

I was fairly certain they weren't married. At least, not to each other.

Who were they? Well, I'm not telling and here's why: infidelity is not a weapon. At the end of this, I have to be the better man.

If I stoop to do what they did to me, then I am no different from them. And I want to be different from them.

Very different.

•

As news of my verdict broke in the media, the ABC program *7.30* began their story on my acquittal with the words: 'For much of this time, the media has been unable to tell the full story. Tonight, Senior Sergeant [sic] Paul Dale has been acquitted of the final charges against him, so his story can now be told ...'

What a load of codswallop.

In my opinion, the media has always been able to tell the full story but has been absolutely unwilling to do so. A glance at the headlines during my trial will give you a glimpse of exactly what the media *chose* to report on.

The *7.30* program repeated the same old scenario: David Miechel and Terry Hodson were caught at the Oakleigh drug robbery, Terry said I did it, Terry was murdered before he could testify against me, Carl Williams came forward and said I asked him to kill Terry, then he was murdered before he could testify against me. One story even called me the Teflon cop – nothing stuck.

What none of them *chose* to report was that Terry only offered my name after he was threatened with a life sentence unless he could give ESD another cop – in which case he would get no sentence at all.

Dale did it, he said.

And they didn't report that Carl Williams only named me after he was offered a reduced sentence, indemnity from further prosecution, the ability to claim the million-dollar reward, his father's $750000 tax bill paid, and his daughter's private education paid for courtesy of the Victoria Police, and God knows what else.

Dale did it, said Carl.

Nope, the media *chose* to keep to the script. The Victoria Police script. *Dale did it.* End of story. And not only did he do it, but *he was unfaithful to his wife.*

The media *could have* reported on the Witness B/George Williams court debacle.

But they didn't.

Witness B – a triple murderer and major drug dealer getting offered a twelve-year minimum – all to get Dale on a lying charge. Fair trade-off? Do you really want that guy out on the streets in twelve years? Maybe living next door to you?

You'd think there'd be a media storm.

But not a whisper.

Yet when the real story was aired in the courtroom, the media – the ones who should be serving the public with the truth – were suspiciously silent. Except to splash my decade-old affair across the front pages of papers around the country. It begs the question: *Why did the media leave out all mention of inducements when telling the story?* Surely million-dollar inducements or swapping a life sentence for no sentence should be part of the narrative. So why wasn't it?

For the prosecution, it was important to them to try to humiliate me.

For the media, murder, affairs, and disgraced detectives sell papers.

On bad days I'd think: *What bloody hope do I have?*

But on good days I hoped the system would work and the truth would come out.

And just when it seemed like it would never happen, as 2018 drew to a close, a bombshell dropped.

CHAPTER 51

The Royal Commission

In the months leading up to the bombshell, the Victoria Police had spent millions in a legal bid to block the Victorian Director of Public Prosecutions from revealing that VicPol had used a defence barrister as a police informer. Over five years, journalists from the *Herald Sun* had been dragged into court twenty-eight times in an attempt to stop them, but journalist Anthony Dowsley finally got the chance to break the story.

The story flooded like a bursting dam. Suppression orders were lifted and the public were given an outline of the legal stoush that had been running between the Victoria Police, the Director of Public Prosecutions, and Lawyer X.

On 3 December 2018, newspapers everywhere headlined with the High Court ruling that blasted the Victoria Police for 'reprehensible conduct'. The High Court judgment read: 'EF's [Nicola Gobbo's] actions in purporting to act as counsel for the Convicted Persons while covertly informing against them were fundamental and appalling breaches of EF's obligations as counsel to her clients and of EF's duties to the court. Likewise, Victoria Police were guilty of reprehensible conduct in knowingly encouraging EF to do as she did and were involved in sanctioning atrocious breaches of the sworn duty of every police officer to discharge all duties imposed on them faithfully and according to law without favour or affection, malice or ill-will. As a result, the prosecution of each Convicted Person was corrupted in a manner which debased fundamental premises of the criminal justice system.'

Not ones to mince words, the High Court.

At this stage, Lawyer X wasn't named but of course it was Nicola Gobbo, my former lawyer. My former friend. For me, it was the day the world heard that the Lawyer X/VicPol travesty didn't just affect me: it was more far reaching than anyone could have imagined. Finally, I thought, everyone will see the truth.

Victorian Premier Daniel Andrews immediately announced a Royal Commission. Chief Commissioner of Police Graham Ashton told a press conference, 'I acknowledge the decision of the High Court which has determined that our use of a lawyer as an informer between 2005 and 2009 was not appropriate.'

Ya think, Graham Ashton?

Reports in the media suggested Lawyer X helped police in as many as 386 cases, including those of Tony Mokbel. Of immediate concern to the public was the suggestion that Lawyer X's actions had compromised the trials of her clients, and that criminals might appeal their sentences or walk free.

As soon as I heard about the High Court's decision, I jumped online and read everything I could find. I wanted a chance to explain what had happened to me, so I started putting together a submission for the Royal Commission. Since the revelations of just how widely the police and Nicola collaborated, I had begun to wonder if I had been royally set up by the lot of them. That time at the casino when Nicola rang Carl then put me on the phone when I was drunk – was that a set-up to record me talking to Carl? In the media coverage of my appearance, I was still written about as 'disgraced ex-detective Paul Dale' – but disgraced or otherwise, I got to have my say. I wanted to tell the public Victoria Police had perverted the course of justice by using Nicola Gobbo against me. I also offered access to all the documentation I had – dozens of boxes of documents I'd received over the years under the discovery obligations. The Commission accepted my many boxes and made arrangements to get them all scanned into a searchable database.

The Royal Commission was essentially tasked with the question I'd been trying to figure out for a decade: *Who knew about Nicola and how did they use her?* I knew those at the top were involved, but how far down the chain did it go? Think about it: if detectives were charging people then recommending they use Nicola Gobbo, knowing she would then work with the police, that's unethical in anybody's language.

•

The Royal Commission began in February and was run by the Honourable Margaret McMurdo AC. In the opening statement, Commissioner McMurdo expressed the crux of the investigation. 'Some members of the public may query the outrage expressed by the courts, professional associations and legal academics at the conduct of EF and the police, arguing that it had a positive effect, namely, the conviction of serious offenders.

'But, as the courts have explained, these are matters of high principle, fundamental to our democracy ... Those charged with criminal offences are usually legally represented. Whether handsomely paid, on Legal Aid rates or acting without fee, the law requires lawyers to keep clients' confidences, act in the clients' best interest, and disclose and avoid any potential or actual conflict of interest ... Clients must be able to speak frankly to the lawyers preparing their court cases, knowing their communications remain confidential ... The police use of lawyers to inform on their own clients has the obvious potential to undermine the criminal justice system and the public's confidence in it.'

Opening statements listed the inquiries to date on the handling of 'EF' as a human source. Former Chief Commissioner Neil Comrie had run an inquiry in 2013 and the Honourable Murray Kellam had looked at human source management for the Independent Broad-based Anti-corruption Commission in 2015. Kellam found 'negligence of a high order' while Comrie found Victoria Police's risk assessment 'grossly inadequate'.

•

Months before the scandal broke in December of 2018, Nicola Gobbo was photographed at Government House receiving a Premier's Volunteers Champion Award, looking fit as a fiddle. Her award was described thus: 'The volunteer-run Brighton Playroom is thriving thanks to Nicki's skilled and selfless leadership. Since saving the not-for-profit centre from closure three years ago, Nicki has introduced transformational changes – from strengthening child safety policies to finding ways to help disadvantaged families. Practical and passionate, Nicki has created a true community hub for successive generations of children and families.'

As the hearings began, the big question was whether or not Nicola would take the stand. I was not surprised when she cited similar health concerns to the ones she cited before my trial to avoid appearing. And in a repeat of 2010, the more the Royal Commission pushed for her to make a statement and appear before them, the more she dug her heels in.

But in a move that surprised and impressed me, Commissioner McMurdo refused to excuse Nicola from giving evidence even after a number of doctors declared her unfit to appear. While the commissioner said she was inclined to accept that Nicola was suffering from post-traumatic stress disorder and associated stress and anxiety, she didn't believe this prevented her from giving evidence. Commissioner McMurdo said Nicola could speak to the Royal Commission in shorter bursts by phone or video link. The hearing could accommodate her needs. A cut-off date was given for Nicola to provide a sworn statement as well.

Failing to comply was a criminal offence.

In addition to Nicola's reluctance to appear, Commissioner McMurdo also experienced the same frustration as I had with the Victoria Police and paperwork. She called on the police to provide documents to the Royal Commission. Just like they had with me, they dragged their feet and missed deadlines. A couple of months in, it looked like she'd had enough.

Speaking to Victoria Police's legal representatives, the commissioner said, 'Can I suggest to you and those instructing you, remind your clients that this notice to produce, and their obligations under it, which are ongoing, that it is an offence not to comply with it and an agency of the Crown, under the *Inquiries Act*, can be charged.'

Watching that play out, I experienced a lot of *déjà vu*.

On 28 March 2019 at the hearings, Assistant Commissioner Neil Paterson took the stand to detail Nicola Gobbo's extensive history of informing for the Victoria Police. He was one of a long line of senior police officers to detail his knowledge of Nicola working with the police.

> Royal Commission: Okay. And thereafter she was registered as a human source, that's correct?
>
> Paterson: That's correct.
>
> Royal Commission: Okay. Do you agree that the intention of the police in registering her as a human source and obtaining information from Ms Gobbo was that her information would bring about the arrests of a number of people which might then bring about the downfall of various members of the Mokbel family?
>
> Paterson: Yes, that's part of it, that's right. I believe that it was looking at broadly the Mokbels and all of the organised crime and a number of murders that were committed at that time ...
>
> Royal Commission: And I take it your information, your understanding of the situation was that Ms Gobbo was in fact acting for as a legal representative of a number of members – well certainly Tony Mokbel?
>
> Paterson: Yes, that's correct.

Then he was questioned about the potential repercussions of using Nicola. 'Was there also a concern about the possibility that it may leave convictions, previous convictions, open to being unsafe because of her involvement and because of the issue of legal professional privilege being breached or confidential obligations being breached?'

'That's my understanding, yes,' said the Assistant Commissioner.

'These were issues that were being raised by relatively junior members of the Police Force in the latter part of 2008?'

'Yes, that's right.'

'Those issues were being raised to police officers who were at the very highest echelon of Victoria Police Force?'

'That's correct.'

'Including people such as Assistant Commissioner of Crime Simon Overland?'

'That's correct.'

Superintendent Mark Porter from the Human Resources Department took the stand at the Royal Commission. Porter described Nicola Gobbo as 'the most intense human source' they had and that 'she was contacting the handlers continuously at all hours of the day and night, seven days a week'.

Finally, it was my turn to appear at the Royal Commission. In the hearing room, it seemed every lawyer had a copy of my book *Disgraced?* from 2013, which was no longer available because the publisher had closed down.

When it was time for me to give evidence I told them how I believed the Victoria Police had perverted the course of justice. I felt like I got to have my say. In their questioning, I was a little surprised at some of the things they focused on. They seemed particularly interested in how Inspector Steve Smith said under oath at my committal hearing about no notes being taken at the weekly meetings with the police hierarchy, before a lawyer admitted there were 30 000 pages of notes. I told the Royal Commission how I considered this to be perjury and how I had made a complaint to ESD, which found my allegation unsubstantiated. I was left with the distinct impression the Royal Commission was going to look into this further.

Little by little, the Royal Commission unfolded. In between working, I tried to catch as much as I could by reading documents and watching the live streaming.

When retired Detective Inspector Gavan Ryan, who had worked on the Petra task force and later headed up the Purana task force, gave evidence, he reinforced what I knew back when I was facing committal – that the weekly strategy meetings were held at the highest level in the Victoria Police.

Ryan: And I would provide once a week, I think from memory on either a Monday afternoon or Tuesday afternoon, a briefing to Mr Overland, Mr Cornelius and Mr Ashton who was then at OPI.

I knew Gavan Ryan back in the day. He was totally devoted to the job of being a police officer. He was a stickler for the rules and his testimony showed he was one of the few who questioned Carl Williams and his statement against me.

Ryan: Yes. There was significant difficulties for me personally in relation to the Williams involvement in Petra.
Royal Commission: Yes?
Ryan: Because ... I'd given evidence at his plea ... And he'd lied and I'd said in the box that I would never call him as a witness ... And then I'm the head of Petra.
Royal Commission: I think the judge might have made some similar comments about his evidence?
Ryan: Yes, she doesn't muck around.
Royal Commission: All right. So that caused you a personal difficulty because that was the opinion that you had formed about him and now this new operation had come out, really spring boarded from the fact that he was prepared to assist?
Ryan: Yes, but severe difficulty with his credibility.

While it was great that there were cops who could see the train wreck before it happened, I just wished more had tried to stop it.

As it turned out, many of the cops who knew about Nicola's role also knew that if it ever came out there'd be hell to pay. A number of police officers at the Royal Commission described a workshop that looked at the use of Nicola Gobbo as a human source. Police participants had brainstormed a worst-case scenario of what would happen if the public ever found out. From the line of questioning, it sounds like the dot points on their butcher paper would have looked something like this:

- There would be a Royal Commission.
- There would be retrials of her clients.
- Police might be prohibited from using lawyers as human sources.
- 3838's life might be in danger or she might be in danger from current health concerns.
- There would be a book or a movie about it.
- The reputation of the Victoria Police would be damaged.

Sounds like they had a crystal ball, doesn't it? There are several books on their way (including this one) and a TV series is in production. Over the course of the Royal Commission there have also been a number of TV documentaries.

On Monday, 21 October 2019, the ABC *Four Corners* program went to air promising an examination of the scandalous Lawyer X investigation. I sat glued to my seat to see what they would make of the case. The program had invited me to be interviewed but I said no. At the time I was inundated and I needed space to process things. So, because I didn't take part, I guess I can't complain about the inaccuracies – my alibi for the Dublin Street break-in was reported as me being in Bendigo for the weekend not at my Grand Final BBQ, and Nicola's actions were interpreted through the lens of our 'affair', which was not accurate as we didn't have one.

Despite this, *Four Corners* captured the turning of the tide against the powers-that-be showing a growing public incredulity at the bosses who knew and the choices they'd made to continue.

Featuring regularly in commentary on the Lawyer X scandal, lawyer Ruth Parker spoke vehemently about the effect Nicola Gobbo had on her client Faruk Orman. Gobbo's tendrils stretched everywhere. Parker said that Gobbo helped a witness create a statement against Orman while acting as his lawyer. Gobbo also contacted her police handlers, giving them inside information on Orman's obsessive compulsiveness for cleanliness and his need to be in the company of others. Using this information, the police put him in solitary confinement for eighteen months, until he cracked under the pressure. Nicola contacted police to tell them their tactics were working.

Ruth Parker told *Four Corners* that she believed senior police officers had committed criminal offences. 'Anybody who thinks that registering a criminal defence barrister as a human source, using them against her clients, facilitating dishonesty in the court system, facilitating perjury, and covering up the fact that it had happened – that is the very definition of corruption.'

Well said, Ruth!

•

To finish my story, I want you to consider something. The underlying message in interviews with senior police officers goes like this: *Yes, we used a barrister as an informer against her clients but we had a gangland war on our hands and we had to do anything we could to rid our streets of these murdering scumbags.*

Or, in short, the end justified the means.

But …

In trying to get me, the police offered murdering scumbag Carl Williams a reduced sentence which would get him *back on the streets* sooner. They offered drug-dealing triple-murdering scumbag Witness B two murders for free and only twelve years for a third murder for giving evidence against me at my ACC charges trial, thus getting him *back on the streets* sooner, even though life sentences would have been more fitting. They offered drug dealer Terry Hodson a get-out-of jail free card after catching him red-handed at the Dublin Street break-in. Murdering scumbag Rod Collins tried to wheedle his way out of murder charges in exchange for a statement against me. And now the jail gates will be clanging open as Nicola's former clients are released from jail.

Which suggests that the highest priority of the police was not to get murderers and drug dealers off the streets. It was to get me.

So if the end justifies the means, what exactly is *the end*? Financially, I wouldn't be surprised if *the end* costs the taxpayer upwards of $50 million. Pre-court wrangling before the Lawyer X scandal broke cost around $4.5 million. The Royal Commission budget is currently at $28 million. There was $2.88 million in compensation for Nicola Gobbo. The compensation payout to Carl Williams's family. And now we are going to see huge payouts for people jailed because their barrister was an agent for the police.

How does that end serve anyone?

And the cost to me? Financially, I've had to pay hundreds of thousands of dollars to defend myself in court, not to mention lost wages for eight months in prison. But money is just the start. The toll this has taken on me and my family has been beyond words. None of us has emerged unscathed.

At the end of all of this, I hope the Victoria Police will be held accountable for what they have done. My case should make people think twice. If the public believes the official police line as well as my subsequent portrayal in the media then there's not much I can do about that. If people are happy to accept what has happened to me and dismiss it with, *Well, he must have done something wrong*, they also need to understand the wider implications.

My case set a dangerous precedent where if the police don't have the evidence they need they can buy it, or stretch the truth so much that it can make anyone look guilty.

The public should also question the charter of the Australian Crime Commission. If they promise anonymity and indemnity in exchange for taking away a citizen's right to remain silent, then they can't take it back. *Er, whoops, we changed our mind* should not be a component of our country's legal system.

When I first wrote about this in my book *Disgraced* in 2013, I felt like I was a lone voice yelling: 'Hey, everyone! What happened to me wasn't fair!' Some people ignored my story. Others clung to the version that surely I must be guilty anyway. Few reporters looked at the wider story of payments to witnesses, and even now leave that element out of their stories because it's much easier to paint me as guilty if the reading public don't know about the inducements witnesses against me were given.

It is my view that Nicola Gobbo perverted the course of justice because she acted as a police agent while representing clients. Since top-ranking police officials knew, agreed to it, and encouraged her to do it, surely they've perverted the course of justice alongside her. The police charged me with whatever they could – remember the noodles? – so now I watch with great interest to see who will be charged.

I can only hope they are pursued with the same rigour they used to pursue me.

But, for now, we watch to see what happens.

Paul Dale was a police officer in Victoria Police, serving in the Homicide Unit and Major Drug Investigative Division. He now lives in country Victoria.

Vikki Petraitis is a bestselling author with twenty-five years' experience. Her book *The Frankston Murders* about serial killer Paul Denyer has become a classic in the true-crime genre. Her other books include: *The Phillip Island Murder*; *Victims, Crimes and Investigators*; *The Great John Coleman*; *Rockspider*; *Cops*; *Forensics*; *Crime Scene Investigations*; *Salvation*; *The Dog Squad*; and *Once a Copper*. She has also had stories published in six anthologies. Vikki is a popular public speaker and podcaster, and is currently working on her PhD in Creative Writing. She lives in Melbourne.

hachette
AUSTRALIA

If you would like to find out more about
Hachette Australia, our authors, upcoming events
and new releases you can visit our website or our
social media channels:

hachette.com.au

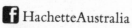 HachetteAustralia

 HachetteAus